Contemporary Psychodynamic
Theory and Practice

Also Available from Lyceum Books, Inc.

Advisory Editors: Thomas M. Meenaghan, *New York University*
Ira C. Colby, *University of Houston*
Wynne Korr, *University of Illinois at Urbana-Champaign*

Straight Talk about Professional Ethics
Kim Strom-Gottfried

Social Work in a Sustainable World
Nancy L. Mary

Cross-Cultural Practice: Social Work with Diverse Populations, 2E
Karen Harper-Dorton and Jim Lantz

Diversity, Oppression, and Change: Culturally Grounded Social Work
Flavio Francisco Marsiglia and Stephen Kulis

Endings in Clinical Practice: Effective Closure in Diverse Settings, 2E
Joseph Walsh

Clinical Assessment for Social Workers, 2E
Catheleen Jordan and Cynthia Franklin

Short-Term Existential Intervention in Clinical Practice
Joseph Walsh and Jim Lantz

*Practical Tips for Publishing Scholarly Articles:
Writing and Publishing in the Helping Professions*
Rich Furman

Contemporary Psychodynamic Theory and Practice

WILLIAM BORDEN
UNIVERSITY OF CHICAGO

LYCEUM
BOOKS, INC.

Chicago, Illinois

© Lyceum Books, Inc., 2009

Published by

LYCEUM BOOKS, INC.
5758 S. Blackstone Ave.
Chicago, Illinois 60637
773+643-1903 (Fax)
773+643-1902 (Phone)
lyceum@lyceumbooks.com
http://www.lyceumbooks.com

6 5 4 3 2 1   09 10 11 12

ISBN 978-0-925065-51-3

Library of Congress Cataloging-in-Publication Data

Borden, William, 1954–
    Contemporary psychodynamic theory and practice : toward a critical pluralism /
William Borden.
        p. ; cm.
    Includes bibliographical references and index.
    ISBN 978-0-925065-51-3
    1. Psychodynamic psychotherapy. 2. Psychoanalysis—Philosophy. I. Title.
    [DNLM: 1. Psychoanalytic Theory. 2. Psychoanalysis. 3. Psychotherapy. WM
460 B728c 2008]
    RC489.P72B67   2008
    616.89'14—dc22
                                                                    2008012804

For Allen

Contents

About the Author

William Borden, PhD, is senior lecturer in the School of Social Service Administration and lecturer in the Department of Psychiatry at the University of Chicago, where he teaches courses on contemporary psychodynamic theory, human development, and comparative psychotherapy. He has published articles, essays, and book chapters on relational perspectives in contemporary psychoanalysis, the developmental theory and clinical contributions of Donald Winnicott, integrative models of psychotherapy, and narrative psychology, and empirical research on stress, coping, and development across the life course. He is editor of *Comparative Approaches in Brief Psychodynamic Psychotherapy*. His forthcoming book, *The Play and Place of Theory in Social Work*, is an edited volume on comparative perspectives in clinical practice.

He is a graduate of Indiana University, where he studied English and psychology, and received his AM and PhD degrees from the University of Chicago, where he was a fellow at the Harris Center for Developmental Studies. He has worked as a psychotherapist, supervisor, and consultant in mental health clinics and community agencies since 1983. Prior to his current position, he was a psychotherapist and supervisor in the University of Chicago student counseling service, where he provided advanced clinical training. He has served on the faculties of the Illinois State Psychiatric Institute, the Michael Reese Medical Center, the Institute for Clinical Social Work, and the Jane Addams College of Social Work at the University of Illinois at Chicago. He is a member of the American Psychological Association, Division of Psychoanalysis; the Chicago Association for Psychoanalytic Psychology; the Society for the Exploration of Psychotherapy Integration; and the National Association of Social Workers. He serves on the editorial board of *Psychoanalytic Social Work*.

Preface

The discipline of psychoanalysis and the profession of social work emerged as radically different endeavors at the turn of the twentieth century, and the course of their relationship has been marked by mutual influence and productive collaboration as well as periods of uncertainty, ambivalence, and contention. Psychoanalysis, rooted in the dynamic psychiatry of late nineteenth-century Europe, looked inward, exploring the hidden depths of human behavior. Thinkers generated new conceptions of self, personal life, and psychotherapy. Social work, shaped by the pragmatic concerns of the charity organization societies and the settlement house movement, looked outward, emphasizing the interdependence of individual well-being, family life, and community. Although psychoanalysis and social work differed in crucial respects, both undertakings engaged essential concerns in the human situation and enlarged ways of seeing vulnerability, need, and problems in living; each project offered ways of understanding what is the matter and what carries the potential to help in efforts to negotiate difficulty and restore health, well-being, and the common good.

Psychodynamic perspectives have shaped fundamental beliefs in the collective wisdom of social work practice over the years, and clinicians have made eclectic and creative use of core concepts in psychosocial intervention. Most practitioners, while professing no affiliation with particular psychoanalytic schools of thought, endorse the importance of basic assumptions and principles of intervention that we can trace to the psychodynamic tradition—the crucial role of the therapeutic relationship in efforts to facilitate change, for example, or the functions of experiential learning in attempts to strengthen coping capacities and negotiate problems in living. As Peter Fonagy (2000) writes, psychoanalysis provides a range of essential descriptions and ideas "without which it would be far harder to talk about ourselves or to understand our own and other people's lives" (p. 2).

Even so, psychoanalytic perspectives remain problematic for many educators, researchers, and clinicians as a result of perceived conflicts with the pragmatic tasks, core values, and humanistic identity of the social work profession. Over the years, trenchant critiques of Sigmund Freud's classical drive psychology have moved successive generations of social workers to reject psychodynamic perspectives altogether and pursue alternative perspectives in efforts to address the social, cultural, political, and economic contexts of vulnerability and suffering; to broaden the scope of psychosocial intervention; and to demonstrate the effectiveness of specific treatment procedures (Borden, 1999, 2000; Brandell, 2002; Reid, 1997). Critics have characterized psychoanalytic paradigms as reductive, deterministic, unscientific, and lacking in empirical support (Frosh, 1999). Practitioners have identified pervasive gender, cultural, and ethnic biases in classical psychoanalytic thought as well (see, e.g., Altman, 1995; Frosh, 1999). One of the harshest commentators, Frederick Crews (1996), argues that there is "literally nothing to be said, scientifically or therapeutically, to the advantage of the entire Freudian system" (p. 63).

Much of Freud's work *is* flawed and out of date, to be sure, but many critics remain behind the times as well, challenging classical perspectives as if they continue to carry currency and inform contemporary thinking and practice (Westen, 1998). Pluralism has been an irrepressible feature of the broader psychodynamic landscape, from the beginning, and very little of what Freud understood as psychoanalysis has remained intact. Psychoanalysis is a human enterprise through and through, an evolving field of understanding and practice.

Fundamental changes in psychodynamic thought, prefigured by a series of original and creative thinkers in the early years of the psychoanalytic movement, have generated divergent points of view, bringing about major shifts in understanding. In departing from classical Freudian views, psychodynamic thinkers have increasingly emphasized concepts of self, relationship, and social life in their theoretical formulations, empirical research, and clinical perspectives. In the domain of practice, clinicians have created realistic, flexible approaches in growing efforts to engage vulnerable, disenfranchised groups and to address a wider range of problems in living. More broadly, thinkers have explored the ways in which psychoanalytic thought deepens our understanding of social problems and has the potential to inform approaches to public policy and political action.

In spite of these developments, however, there is surprisingly little discussion of psychodynamic perspectives in the larger social work literature. Within the field, presentations of psychodynamic theory continue to emphasize classical Freudian perspectives, and most discussions fail to take account of significant developments in the broader psychodynamic tradition that deepen appreciation of crucial concerns in social work practice. Psychodynamic perspectives, largely misread and misunderstood, remain marginal in mainstream social work and psychology.

In view of these gaps, this book seeks to deepen readers' understanding of psychoanalytic thought in contemporary psychotherapy and to demonstrate the relevance of relational perspectives and recent developments in psychodynamic studies for psychosocial intervention. In the following chapters I explore successive shifts in psychodynamic understanding, describe overlapping domains of concern that distinguish the major schools of thought, and trace the emergence of the relational paradigm. I introduce the contributions of seminal thinkers, exploring the historical circumstances, worldviews, and intellectual traditions that have shaped their understanding, and present their core developmental concepts and clinical perspectives. In doing so, I demonstrate the connections between theory and practice through case reports and clinical illustrations. I emphasize the particular themes, concerns, and sensibilities that distinguish their contributions and so prepare students, practitioners, and educators to read original writings with greater facility and deeper appreciation.

As we will see, the divergent perspectives that are encompassed by the broader psychodynamic tradition engage essential concerns in our time, enlarging understandings of personality and self; health, well-being, and the common good; vulnerability and need; and core elements in psychosocial intervention. The ways we come to understand people and formulate our understanding of problems in living have crucial implications for what we say and do in the clinical situation. What counts as theory, as Carlos Strenger (1997) reminds us, is always "an attempt of other therapists to make sense of their attempts to do the best they could" (p. 144). This introduction to clinical theory is an attempt to help us make use of this cumulative experience and insight as we work to understand what is the matter and what carries the potential to help in the course of our day-to-day practice.

Acknowledgments

I have been a clinician for twenty-five years, working as psychotherapist, consultant, and educator, and much of my teaching has focused on the role of theory in practice—how we bring ideas to bear in our efforts to understand what is the matter and what carries the potential to help. This book grew out of my clinical practice and the courses on psychodynamic theory and comparative psychotherapy I have taught at the University of Chicago in the School of Social Service Administration and the Department of Psychiatry over the last two decades. I owe a deep debt of gratitude to the individuals I have worked with as a psychotherapist and the students and supervisees who have shared their experiences and ideas over the years, deepening my appreciation of the place of theory in the complexity and irreducible ambiguity of the clinical situation.

The work of the late Stephen Mitchell has been a central influence in my thinking and practice, not only for his seminal contributions to our understanding of relational thought but because he exemplifies a pluralism and generosity of spirit that sponsor the presence of divergent thinkers in the broader psychoanalytic tradition. The writings of Oliver Sacks and Robert Coles continue to serve as centers of gravity, and their friendship and conversation have deepened my understanding of the thinkers, ideas, and concerns I explore in this book.

Paul Wachtel has enlarged my understanding of the relational paradigm and integrative approaches in clinical practice. Dennis McCaughan and the late Jarl Dyrud, himself supervised by Harry Stack Sullivan, have deepened my appreciation of the interpersonal tradition. Christopher Bollas, Patrick Casement, and Peter Homans have enriched my understanding of the work of Donald Winnicott and other thinkers in the Independent Tradition in Great Britain. Miriam Elson introduced me to the school of self psychology in the early 1980s, and Jill Gardner continues to share her knowledge of contemporary developments in the field. Peter Mudd has enlarged my appreciation of essential concerns in analytical psychology, relational psychoanalysis, and the practice of psychotherapy over the years.

Thanks and more thanks to James Clark, collaborator on many projects, whose ongoing conversation and passion for ideas remain sources of great strength; to Sharon Berlin, who brought a clarity of mind and common sense in her close review of chapters; and to Linda Tartof, who continually reminds me of the limits of theoretical understanding in the concrete particularity of the clinical situation. Bertram Cohler, one of my first teachers at the university, remains a compass in the broader field of psychoanalytic understanding and practice.

Jeanne Marsh, dean of the School of Social Service Administration, remains vigorous in her support of intellectual life, and I thank her and my colleagues for their ongoing conversation and support, especially Beth Angell, Irene Elkin, Malitta Engstrom, Sydney Hans, Janet Kohrman, Stanley McCracken, Dolores Norton, Harold Pollack, William Pollak, Tina Rzepnicki, Bernece Simon, John Schuerman, and Froma Walsh. My thanks and gratitude to Karen Teigiser for the ongoing opportunities she provided to develop new courses on psychodynamic theory and clinical practice in her role as director of the Professional Development Program at the university.

I have discussed the ideas in this book with many colleagues and friends over the years, and I would like to express my special gratitude to Marcia Adler, Paula Ammerman, Wendy Boxer, Anne Brody, Carol Ganzer, Sigfried Gauggel, Nina Helstein, Robert Hsiung, Sandra Kiersky, Oksana Lyubarsky, Colleen Mahoney, Joel Morris, Joan Palmer, Scott Petersen, Julia Pryce, Scott Harms Rose, Erika Schmidt, and Jason Stell. Maureen Kelly, director of the Cathedral Counseling Center, and her clinical staff have provided ongoing opportunities to explore a range of theoretical perspectives in the give-and-take of day-to-day practice. I thank my publisher, David Follmer, and my editor, Sonia Elizabeth Fulop, for their thought, care, and encouragement over the course of this project.

I dedicate this book to my partner, Allen Heinemann, whose love, spirit, and support remain steadfast after a quarter century together. My loving thanks and deep gratitude to our family and friends.

A Note on Language

Historically, thinkers have used the term "psychoanalytic" to designate theoretical approaches that embrace the basic propositions of Freud's drive psychology; the term "psychodynamic" has referred to a diverse group of thinkers who rejected classic Freudian concepts and set forth alternative theories of personality development, psychopathology, and therapeutic intervention. These distinctions are no longer meaningful in light of the theoretical pluralism that shapes contemporary understanding, and so I use the terms interchangeably in this book.

I also use the terms "patient" and "client" interchangeably throughout the book, reflecting the widespread use of both terms in the fields of social work and psychology. Although many clinicians prefer the term "client" over "patient" because it would appear to convey a more democratic, egalitarian conception of the helping relationship, the Latin root of "client" means "one who depends" or "one who follows." The Latin root of "patient" means "one who suffers." As Paul Wachtel (1993) observes, this meaning more accurately reflects what moves many individuals to seek help and characterizes the nature of the therapeutic relationship (see Wachtel, 1993, for further reflection on these terms and other issues related to language and therapeutic communication).

Chapter 1

Orienting Perspectives in Contemporary Psychodynamic Thought

> The world is full of partial purposes, of partial stories. . . . To sum up, the world is "one" in some respects, and "many" in others.
>
> —William James, "The One and the Many"

The growing emphasis on theoretical pluralism in contemporary psychodynamic thought has generated divergent views of the human condition, problems in living, and the therapeutic endeavor. Clinical scholars have enlarged the boundaries of the field over the years, and recent lines of study have been shaped by work in such varied disciplines as neuroscience, cognitive psychology, experimental psychology, personality and social psychology, philosophy, linguistics, political science, social thought, theology, literature, history, and education. Psychoanalytic thinkers continue to share basic propositions about the nature of personality and relational life, as we will see, but the modes of understanding encompassed in the broader psychodynamic tradition are increasingly varied in focus, purpose, and method.

The moves toward theoretical pluralism have revitalized the field of psychoanalytic studies and deepened interdisciplinary interest in a range of projects. Current lines of inquiry—focused on concepts of self, relationship, and social life—reflect fundamental concerns in contemporary thought and culture. Psychodynamic perspectives continue to shape ways of seeing the human situation and inform conceptions of health, well-being, and the common good; vulnerability, need, and problems in living; and crucial elements in psychosocial intervention.

Although the pluralist context of contemporary psychoanalysis complicates our efforts to distinguish the core propositions and essential concerns of psychodynamic understanding, most thinkers emphasize the following domains of concern in their understanding of the broader tradition: (1) conceptions of unconscious emotional and cognitive processes as well as underlying motivational systems; (2) conceptions of conflict and compromise among opposing tendencies or needs; (3) conceptions of defense, coping, and adaptation; (4) basic assumptions about the role of attachment, caretaking systems, and relational experience in the establishment of personality organization, capacities for relatedness to others, and patterns of interpersonal functioning; and (5) conceptions of self, subjectivity, and personal meaning. In the domain of psychosocial intervention, practitioners have established pragmatic, integrative perspectives that emphasize the role of the practitioner-client relationship, interpersonal interaction, and experiential learning in efforts to address a range of problems in living. Clinicians increasingly draw on cognitive, behavioral, humanistic, and ecological perspectives in their attempts to develop integrative approaches to helping and care.

In light of these developments, now is a good time to examine the broader landscape of psychodynamic thought and to see what foundational theorists and recent thinkers offer the field of social work and the other helping professions—to reconsider the nature of the relationship between psychoanalytic understanding and clinical practice, to clarify mutual interests and potential sources of conflict, and to identify ways in which psychodynamic concepts enlarge and inform ways of working in psychosocial intervention.

The Development of Psychodynamic Thought

Ongoing revisions of psychoanalytic theory, often compared to paradigmatic shifts in science, have changed the course of psychodynamic thought. Most broadly, contemporary thinkers distinguish two fundamental perspectives in the development of psychoanalytic understanding: the drive paradigm, based on Sigmund Freud's classical instinct theory, and the relational paradigm, which takes relational elements, rather than biological drives, as the core constituents of human experience (Greenberg & Mitchell, 1983; Mitchell, 1988; Mitchell & Aron, 1999). In his seminal formulation of the relational perspective, Stephen Mitchell focused on a varied group of thinkers in Great Britain and America who converged in their view of the person as a social being. He writes:

> We are portrayed not as a conglomerate of physically-based urges, but as being shaped by and inevitably embedded within a matrix of relationships with other people, struggling both to maintain our ties to others and to differentiate ourselves from them. In this vision the basic unit of study is not the individual as a separate entity whose desires clash with an external reality, but an interactional field within which the individual arises and struggles to make contact and to articulate himself. Desire is experienced always in the context of relatedness, and it is that context which defines meaning. Mind is composed of relational configurations. The person is comprehensible only within this tapestry of relationships, past and present. (Mitchell, 1988, p. 3)

The growth of relational psychoanalysis, shaped by Mitchell's comparative studies and efforts to establish an integrative point of view, has been paralleled by more general moves toward interpersonal and social perspectives in the broader field of psychotherapy (Wachtel, 2008). Practitioners increasingly emphasize the ways in which interpersonal, family, social, and cultural conditions influence personality development, resilience and vulnerability, and health and illness. In the context of psychotherapy, representatives of the psychodynamic, cognitive, behavioral, and humanistic traditions have come to recognize the powerful role of the therapeutic relationship and interactive experience in efforts to promote change, growth, and health (Borden, 2008a, in press; Wampold, 2007).

In spite of the prominence of relational perspectives, however, Freud continues to provide critical points of reference in contemporary thought. Many writers characterize the development of psychodynamic theory as an ongoing reaction to his drive psychology (see, e.g., Wolitzky & Eagle, 1997), and most thinkers continue to relate their particular domains of study to the broader concerns of the intellectual tradition that he established (Elliott, 1994; Flax, 1990, 1993; Marcus & Rosenberg, 1998). In the field of neuroscience, researchers increasingly acknowledge Freud's early efforts to develop an empirical psychology, linking his attempt to form a neural model of behavior to contemporary lines of inquiry (see, e.g., Edelman, 1992; Kandel, 2005, 2006; Sacks, 1998).

Recent translations of Freud's writings promise to deepen interest in his contributions. In order to place contemporary perspectives in context, I begin the book with a review of Freud's theoretical systems. I trace the development of his thought, describe his models of the mind, and consider his work in light of contemporary neuroscience and emerging lines of inquiry in developmental psychology and relational psychoanalysis.

Emergence of Relational Perspectives

While Freud's drive psychology shaped psychoanalytic understanding through the first part of the century, growing numbers of thinkers challenged his instinctual model of motivation and elaborated alternative perspectives that increasingly emphasized interpersonal and social domains of experience. The work of Alfred Adler, C. G. Jung, Otto Rank, Sándor Ferenczi, and Ian Suttie constituted the earliest efforts to broaden the scope of psychodynamic thought. Suttie rejected Freud's instinct model and theorized that innate needs for love and relationship are primary motivational forces in human development. Although his writings remain largely neglected in the contemporary literature, he prefigures key concepts in relational thought and anticipates fundamental concerns in contemporary culture and social life. In chapters 3, 4, and 5, I explore the contributions of these early revisionists, long neglected in the mainstream literature, and show how their growing emphasis on interpersonal experience and the social environment prefigures major shifts in psychodynamic understanding. They emerge as crucial figures in the transition from drive psychology to relational perspectives.

In the following chapters, I examine the development of relational theories in Great Britain and America, which continue to inform contemporary understanding of personality, psychopathology, and therapeutic practice. The widespread experience of trauma, loss, and mourning after World War I led to the development of new relational perspectives in London during the 1920s. Beginning in the late 1930s, further revisions of psychoanalytic thinking were carried out by a second generation of theorists, which included Melanie Klein, W. R. D. Fairbairn, Donald W. Winnicott, and John Bowlby. As we will see, their contributions have shaped the development of the relational paradigm. Although Klein preserved Freudian notions of instinct and privileged the internal realm of fantasy in her theoretical system, she introduced a series of concepts that provided critical points of departure for Fairbairn, Winnicott, and Bowlby in their efforts to elaborate interactive social perspectives. I review her theoretical system in chapter 6.

Fairbairn introduced theories of development, personality organization, and psychopathology that constituted the most radical break with the classical drive paradigm. I review the core concepts of his object relations perspective in chapter 7. Like Suttie, he proposed that the core tendency in human experience is to establish and preserve connections with others. He conceived of development as a maturational sequence of relations with others, focusing on progressive experiences of dependency and individuation in the mother-child relationship. He theorized that personality or self is constituted and structured through ongoing internalization and representation of interpersonal experience. Fairbairn's theoretical system was influenced by his clinical practice with abused children and impoverished families, and his views have increasingly shaped conceptions of social work intervention with vulnerable groups.

As the leading representative of the Independent Tradition in the British psychoanalytic movement, Winnicott introduced original points of view that have enlarged understandings of personality development, psychopathology, and therapeutic elements in clinical practice. I present his theoretical formulations and clinical perspectives in chapter 8. As we will see, his work has brought about major reorientations in psychoanalytic thinking. More than any other theorist, he emphasized the crucial functions of caretaking figures in the development of the person, linking disorders of the self to impingement and disruption in the "holding environment" of infancy and early childhood.

As he developed his thinking, he increasingly focused on the character and quality of subjective experience in his understandings of self, emphasizing concepts of inner coherence, personal meaning, agency, vitality, authenticity, play, and creativity. In recent years he has been recognized as a seminal figure in contemporary psychoanalysis, and his theories continue to influence work in developmental psychology, the humanities, philosophy, religious studies, and the mental health disciplines.

Bowlby drew on Darwinian thought, ethology, cognitive psychology, systems theory, and psychoanalytic studies of children who had been separated from their mothers in developing his concept of attachment. I review his contributions in chapter 9. In his account of human development, the fundamental need to establish contact and connection has adaptive roots in biological survival. His work has informed a tradition of observational research that documents ways in which infants actively seek stimulation and promote attachment to primary figures who provide support and protection. Bowlby believed that working models of self and others, established in early interactions with caretaking figures, guide information processing about relational experience and shape patterns of behavior across the life course. More than any other thinker, he attempted to bridge internal and external domains of experience and to describe processes that influence psychic structure and modes of interpersonal functioning.

The interpersonal tradition in American psychiatry, originating in the distinctive contributions of Harry Stack Sullivan, Karen Horney, and Erich Fromm, rejected classical Freudian thought and introduced social models of personality development, psychopathology, and therapeutic intervention in the 1930s and 1940s. I present the developmental concepts and clinical formulations of Sullivan and Horney in chapter 10 and relate their views to fundamental concerns in clinical practice.

Sullivan elaborated a psychology of the self that centered on interpersonal domains of human experience. Drawing on American pragmatism and the social thought of Jane Addams, George Herbert Mead, Charles Cooley, Edward Sapir, and William Thomas, he conceptualized personality development as successive stages of interpersonal relationship. He deepened our understanding of the ways in which interactive fields shape varying organizations of self and social behavior and introduced pragmatic approaches to psychosocial intervention, focusing on the concrete particulars of the clinical situation.

While Sullivan's developmental formulations centered on the nature of relational experience in the early caretaking environment, he considered the influence of cultural, political, and economic forces in his understandings of behavior and problems in living. He increasingly addressed social problems in his later work, focusing on poverty, racism, and severe mental illness. Further contributions by Horney enlarged understandings of self and continued to examine the ways in which social, cultural, political, and economic conditions influence conceptions of personality, gender, relational life, and neurosis.

Like Winnicott, Heinz Kohut focused on the phenomenology of selfhood, deepening our conceptions of subjectivity and relational life in psychoanalytic understanding. I trace the emergence of his psychology of the self and present the core concepts of his model in chapter 11. He described the essential connection between the self and others as the "selfobject relationship," regarding this bond as the crucial element in the maturation of a cohesive sense of self. Kohut related problems in functioning to earlier lapses and failings in early interactions with primary caretakers and reformulated notions of psychopathology to include arrests or deficits in the development of the self. He emphasized the restorative functions of relational experience in his models of therapeutic action. His psychology of the self increasingly informs empirical study in neuroscience and developmental psychology.

The Relational Paradigm

The contributions of the foregoing thinkers shaped the development of three schools of thought that have served as the foundation for relational psychoanalysis, most broadly characterized as object relations psychology, interpersonal psychoanalysis, and self psychology. I examine the defining features of these theoretical traditions and describe the basic concepts and deeper concerns that distinguish the broader relational paradigm in chapter 12. In doing so, I lay out overlapping conceptions of personality development; health, well-being, and the common good; and vulnerability, psychopathology, and problems in living. In the closing chapter I review core elements of psychosocial intervention in light of relational understanding and show how comparative perspectives enlarge the scope of clinical practice.

The relational paradigm focuses our attention on fundamental concerns in contemporary psychotherapy, as I show in chapters 12 and 13, and it provides crucial contexts of understanding for development of practice methods within the helping professions. In the domain of psychosocial intervention, relational perspectives center on the interactive contexts of treatment. Concepts of therapeutic action emphasize the role of the professional relationship in the process of change and the functions of empathic attunement, interpersonal interaction, experiential learning, modeling, and reinforcement in efforts to deepen understandings of self, others, and life experience; strengthen coping capacities; and negotiate problems in living.

Relational Perspectives and Evidence-Based Practice

In the field of evidence-based practice, relational perspectives promise to strengthen approaches to assessment, case formulation, and treatment planning. Practitioners from divergent schools of thought in contemporary psychotherapy increasingly recognize the helping relationship as *the* facilitating medium of intervention, and converging lines of study document the ways in which the client and the practitioner influence the course and outcome of the therapeutic process (Borden, 2008b; Norcross, 2002; Roth & Fonagy, 2005; Wachtel, 2008; Wampold, 2001, 2007).

The relational schools of thought focus our attention on the role of interpersonal expertise in the establishment of the therapeutic alliance and deepen our appreciation of underlying vulnerabilities and patterns of behavior that compromise engagement and precipitate strain or rupture in the helping relationship, limiting opportunities for change and growth. Concepts of therapeutic action show how practitioners can make flexible use of the experiential dimensions of the therapeutic process in light of various capacities, the nature and circumstances of specific problems in functioning, and the individual, social, and cultural contexts of the client. Relational perspectives center on the dyadic, reciprocal nature of the helping process and view the practitioner as a participant-observer, emphasizing the importance of subjective elements and mutuality in formulations of therapeutic interaction. From this perspective, the helping process occurs *between* subjects rather than *within* the individual. As we will see, relational lines of understanding provide complex ways of conceptualizing interactive experience that enlarge formulations of interpersonal behavior in existing models of evidence-based practice (see APA Presidential Task Force on Evidence-Based Practice, 2006).

Comparative Theory, Critical Pluralism, and Pragmatism

The seminal thinkers in the history of psychoanalysis have set forth powerful accounts of the human condition, offering divergent conceptions of self, relational life, the social surround, and therapeutic action. They focus our attention on overlapping domains of experience from different points of view and enlarge ways of seeing, understanding, and acting in the clinical situation. The growing range of perspectives in the broader psychodynamic tradition enriches the field of clinical practice, as we will see in the following chapters, but it creates challenges as well.

In the course of our development as clinicians, we must inevitably negotiate fundamental tensions between more pure conceptions of the helping process, more idealized versions of the therapeutic endeavor, and more pragmatic renderings of what we do as we carry out our work (Borden, 1994, 2000, 2008a, in press; Strenger, 1997). Some clinicians search for an all-encompassing point of view that promises to unify conceptions of personality, problems in living, and psychotherapy. As we will see, Freud, Klein, Fairbairn, and Kohut offer moving accounts of the human condition, fashioning grand theories of personality development and psychopathology that serve as the foundation of the therapeutic endeavor.

Other practitioners recognize the limits of any particular thinker or theory, realizing that all renderings of the therapeutic endeavor inevitably fail us as we engage the concrete particulars of our work, preferring to draw on a variety of perspectives in view of the actual demands of the helping process, refusing to embrace any single version of therapeutic action. Winnicott, for example, remains committed to a pluralism and pragmatism in his clinical activities; suspicious of grand theory, refusing to practice "standard psychotherapy"; and steadfast in his efforts to carry out "experiments in adapting to need" and develop individual approaches to care. Sullivan, too, is committed to pragmatist ethics in his practice, focusing on the details of intervention (see Strenger, 1997, for comparative account of "purist" and "pragmatic" perspectives in contemporary psychotherapy).

Most practitioners come to characterize their clinical approach as eclectic. Yet, as I have emphasized in critiques of social work education and clinical training programs, there is surprisingly little consideration of comparative perspectives that help clinicians think critically about the ways in which they integrate different concepts, empirical findings, and technical procedures over the course of intervention. Drawing on the philosophical contributions of William James, I have shown how conceptions of pluralism and pragmatism provide frames of reference for critical thinking in comparative approaches to clinical theory (Borden, 1994, 1998, 2000, 2008a, in press). I briefly review these formulations here in order to provide orienting perspectives as we consider the strengths and limits of divergent thinkers and modes of therapeutic practice in the following chapters.

Notions of pluralism emphasize the limits inherent in human understanding. James (1907/1946) argues that no single theoretical system can in itself fully grasp the complexity of actual experience in the real world, and he urges practitioners to approach concerns from multiple independent lines of understanding. There are equally valid descriptions of phenomena that contradict one another, he observes, and divergent perspectives can potentially lead to insight and understanding.

In this sense James challenges notions of grand theory, which presume to set forth universal truths, arguing that theoretical formulations provide only partial, limited renderings of experience (Borden, in press). He reminds us that the world of concrete personal experiences is full of multiplicities, ambiguities, confusions, and contradictions (James, 1907/1946). As he explains, the pluralist rejects "abstraction," "absolutes," "fixed principles," and "closed systems," searching instead for fact, concreteness, action, and adequacy (James, 1907/1946, pp. 43–81).

In his pragmatic conception of truth, James (1907/1946) explains: "The true is the name of whatever proves itself to be good in the way of belief and good, too, for definite, assignable reasons" (p. 76). If we take an idea to be true, he wants to know, "what concrete difference will its being true make in any one's actual life? What, in short, is the truth's cash value in experiential terms?" (p. 200). For James, truth *happens* to an idea—is made true—through experience (see Borden, in press).

In working from a Jamesian pluralism, then, practitioners regard theories as *tools for thinking*. "Pragmatism unstiffens all our theories, limbers them up and sets each one at work" (James, 1907/1946, p. 53). We recognize that each theoretical system encompasses various domains of concern, purposes, rules, and methods that can potentially enlarge or limit ways of seeing, understanding, and working in the clinical situation.

In the pluralist approach to theory that I have described, the foundational schools of thought provide contexts of understanding for engagement of different ideas, empirical findings, and technical procedures over the course of intervention (Borden, 2008a, in press). The practitioner masters multiple theories and therapeutic languages, drawing on concepts and procedures from a range of perspectives in light of the particular circumstances of the clinical situation. The clinician focuses on the individual case, with its particular complexities, ambiguities, and uncertainties, which grand theoretical schemes inevitably fail to represent. Pluralist orientations attempt to foster dialogue across the divergent perspectives that shape the field, working to broaden ways of seeing and understanding as practitioners explore what is the matter and what carries the potential to help. Clinicians explore various points of view and critically evaluate approaches in light of the possibilities and constraints of the clinical situation.

There is an ongoing tension between unity of approach and awareness of alternatives in pluralist approaches to treatment, and the fundamental challenge for the practitioner is to establish a point of view that allows one to engage divergent perspectives *and* preserve a personal idiom and distinctive ways of working in the clinical situation (Borden, 2008a, in press; Strenger, 1997). Following a Jamesian pragmatism, the clinician does not aim for purity of approach. *What matters is what works*, and the practitioner determines the validity of theoretical formulations on the basis of their *effectiveness* in the particular clinical situation (see Borden, 2008a, in press). In working from a critical pluralism, as Strenger (1997) reminds us, the clinician does not deal with "theory for theory's sake but ultimately with a craft committed to helping people" (p. 123). We explore these concerns further in the final chapter as we consider recent attempts to develop comparative perspectives and integrative approaches in the broader psychodynamic tradition.

Chapter 2

Sigmund Freud and the Classical Psychoanalytic Tradition

True insight survives its first formulation.

—Erik Erikson, *Childhood and Society*

Few figures have had as decisive an impact on the course of modern thought and contemporary culture as Sigmund Freud. When he died in 1939, the poet W. H. Auden (1940/1945) remembered him as a thinker who is "no more a person now but a whole climate of opinion" (p. 166). Freud introduced successive models of the mind, founded a discipline, and established an intellectual tradition. He set forth compelling views of human nature in the course of his writings, and many scholars see psychoanalysis as one of the most significant intellectual achievements of the twentieth century. If many of his formulations are flawed and deeply problematic, some of the propositions he advanced have become so much a part of everyday experience that we fail to notice them—a series of unrecognized, unarticulated assumptions about our habits of mind and ways of being. Freud transformed the ways in which we understand ourselves and one another, and many of his ideas have been woven into the fabric of our culture.

While his views continue to generate controversy and debate, Freud remains the point of origin of contemporary psychodynamic understanding. Thinkers have rejected the fundamental propositions of his drive psychology, but many practitioners continue to acknowledge the strength of his clinical observations and the power of his case studies. In the field of neuroscience, researchers are increasingly acknowledging Freud's early efforts to establish an empirical psychology, showing how his efforts to form a neural model of the mind prefigure contemporary findings. Other theorists have rejected his system of psychology altogether and elaborated alternative conceptions of human nature and therapeutic practice. Yet however flawed Freud's vision may be, psychodynamic thinkers are indebted to him for making their points of contact and their divergences possible. In this chapter I trace the development of his thought, describing the core elements of his drive psychology and his conceptions of the therapeutic endeavor, and review clinical applications of core concepts in psychosocial intervention. As we will see, Freud continues to provide crucial contexts of understanding in contemporary thought.

Life and Work

Freud was born in the small Moravian town of Freiberg on May 6, 1856, and died in London on September 23, 1939. He lived in Vienna for nearly eighty years, however, and left the city in 1938, when he and his family were forced to flee following the Nazi annexation of Austria. He worked as a neuroanatomist and neurologist for the first two decades of his career and established himself as a researcher and clinician in the field of neuropathology before he began to elaborate his psychological formulations in the 1890s. By the turn of the century, he had introduced his first model of the mind, a method of inquiry, and a therapeutic mode of treatment. In time, he was surrounded by an international group of followers that included Alfred Adler, Otto Rank, Sándor Ferenczi, Karl Abraham, and Ernest Jones. He continued to revise and extend his ideas over the course of his career, producing what most scholars regard as the first comprehensive theory of personality.

His psychoanalytic writings fill twenty-three volumes in the standard edition of his work, beginning with *The Interpretation of Dreams* in 1900, and they include the theoretical statements that make up his metapsychology as well as the case reports and technical papers that comprise his clinical theory. Freud was an engaging and forceful essayist, exploring a range of cultural, historical, religious, social, and moral concerns, and he won the Goethe Prize for literature in 1930. In addition to his research reports and psychoanalytic papers, he conducted a vast correspondence and wrote thousands of letters, many of which have become available in recent years.

Freud (1935/1952) tells us in his autobiography that he was drawn to the natural sciences and developed an early passion for Charles Darwin and Goethe; he also came to think of Shakespeare as an intellectual hero. He developed a sense of civic responsibility as a child, in the progressive atmosphere of his family and cosmopolitan Vienna, and briefly considered law school as preparation for a political career that would allow him to advance the Austrian agenda of social reform. Although he chose science over law, he remained deeply interested in social and political life and would later describe himself as "a liberal of the old school" in a letter to Arnold Zweig, the novelist (see Danto, 2005; Gay, 1988).

Freud entered medical school at the University of Vienna in 1873, intending to become a research scientist. He was deeply influenced by Ernst Brücke, a leading representative of the Helmholtz school, and worked in his physiology laboratory for six years. The Helmholtz movement rejected the romantic philosophy of nature—particularly notions of vitalism and the life force—and embraced the physical sciences, seeking to create an evolutionary physiology. Brücke believed that all psychological phenomena originate in physiological processes, and Freud came to view the person as a dynamic system governed by the laws of nature. He wrote that his mentor "carried more weight with me than anyone else in my whole life" (Freud,1926/1959a, p. 253), and we see Brücke's influence in Freud's first if unsuccessful attempt to develop a neuropsychological model of the mind, "The Project for a Scientific Psychology," in 1895 (see Freud 1895/1954).

Although Freud had intended to pursue a research career, he eventually decided to pursue clinical practice in neurology. According to biographical accounts, Freud reasoned that there were no immediate prospects for a research position in Brücke's laboratory, and he worried that that growing anti-Semitism in Vienna would limit his opportunities for advancement in an academic career. He wanted to establish himself financially so that he could marry and begin a family (Gay, 1988).

The Development of Freud's Thought

While historical accounts of Freud's thought make sharp distinctions between the pre-psychoanalytic and psychoanalytic periods of his career, scholars emphasize that his early scientific training shaped his thinking throughout the course of his life. His neuroanatomical research and practice as a neurologist were precursors to his psychoanalytic understanding, as Oliver Sacks (1998) emphasizes in his account of Freud's "other life," and they were crucial influences in the development of his psychological ideas. Freud believed that systematic study of physical processes would deepen understanding of mental processes, and he would return to this idea—with considerable ambivalence, by his own reports—again and again in his study and writing throughout half a century (Freud, 1937/1964a).

Two experiences were particularly significant in forming Freud's understanding of psychopathology and therapeutic treatment: first, a brief period of study with Jean-Martin Charcot, the leading neurologist in Europe, and second, his subsequent collaboration with Josef Breuer. He received a travel grant to go to Paris and study under Charcot, who was experimenting with hypnosis in the treatment of hysteria. In the fall of 1885 and the spring of 1886, Freud worked in Charcot's research laboratory and attended his clinical demonstrations at la Salpêtrière, where he used hypnotic suggestion to induce and alleviate traumatic paralyses. Freud reports that he was captivated by the intellectual vitality that Charcot showed in his efforts to determine the origins of physical ailments, and he came to appreciate the extent to which unconscious mental processes could influence behavior. He described Charcot as a "genius" and regarded him an intellectual father. He returned to Vienna in 1887 to establish his own neurological practice, specializing in treatment of nervous conditions and psychopathology.

Charcot encouraged Freud to carry out a comparative study of organic and hysterical paralyses, and he began seeing a number of patients with hysterical paralyses as well as organic paralyses in his clinical practice (see Sacks, 1998). In his efforts to clarify the etiology and mechanisms of the conditions, Freud found that the organic paralyses showed patterns that correspond to neuroanatomy, consistent with the established distribution of nerves, spinal tracts, and centers in the brain. The hysterical paralyses, in contrast, were not linked to anatomical damage in the nervous system. Problems in functioning associated with hysterical conditions, he realized, operate independently of the nervous system, as if anatomy did not exist (see Freud, 1893/1959b). In time, Freud traced their origins to feelings and thoughts generated by psychic trauma that were defensively dissociated and then repressed.

Freud had come to know Josef Breuer, a cultured Viennese physician and scientist—himself an exponent of the Helmholtz school—during his work at Brücke's Institute of Physiology in the 1870s. Breuer had treated a patient known as Anna O. (now known to be Bertha Pappenheim, who would become a leading figure in the German social work movement), during Freud's last two years at the institute, between 1880 and 1882. According to Breuer's report, the adolescent had developed classic symptoms of hysteria, including paralyses and speech dysfunctions, while nursing her father. Using experimental procedures developed by Charcot and others, Breuer placed her under hypnosis, attempting to alleviate the symptoms through post-hypnotic suggestion. Although this strategy proved unsuccessful, Pappenheim began talking about her symptoms while in the hypnotic trance. Breuer encouraged her to continue processing her experience in this way and found that her symptoms disappeared as she related the circumstances of their origin. Anna O. called this "chimney sweeping," her "talking cure"; Breuer called it "catharsis."

At Freud's urging, Breuer prepared an account of the treatment, reconstructed from memory nearly fourteen years later, and offered it as the prototype of the cathartic method. In their classic work, *Studies in Hysteria,* published in 1893–1895, Breuer and Freud located the origins of psychopathology in traumatic experience. Briefly, they assumed that memories of painful events are dissociated from conscious experience, and that the emotion ("quota of affect") associated with the memory is converted to bodily symptoms. What is left in consciousness, they theorized, is a symbol that is connected with traumatic events by unconscious associative connections. If the person can bring memories of the traumatic experience to awareness and release the "strangulated" emotion associated with events, they theorized, then the affect is discharged and symptoms disappear. The goal of treatment, as Freud conceived it, was to alleviate symptoms through recovery and verbalization of suppressed feelings associated with the problems in functioning, termed "abreaction."

Breuer and Freud (1893–1895/1955) offered different theories as to why memories and emotions associated with traumatic experience could remain unconscious long after the original events had occurred. Breuer argued that if the experience had occurred during an altered state of awareness, or "hypnoid state," one did not have the capacity to process what had happened and therefore could not integrate the events into ordinary consciousness. One could imagine, for example, that Pappenheim was depleted by the demands of caring for her father and did not have the capacity to integrate distressing events because she was in an altered state of mind.

Freud, however, introduced a second hypothesis. Given the nature of traumatic experience, he theorized, it was likely that one did not *want* to remember events; one was motivated to keep the experience and its associated emotion out of awareness because they were incompatible with the rest of consciousness (Mitchell & Black, 1995; Wolitzky, 2003). The pathogenic memories and emotions were dissociated not because of a prior altered state of consciousness, Freud argued, but because the actual content of the recollections and feelings was traumatic, unacceptable, and in conflict with one's conscious sense of self and identity.

Freud came to see repression, or the motivated forgetting of a distressing memory or wish, as a way of repudiating impulses that generate anxiety and threaten self. In this sense, he realized, successful defense depends upon self-deception. While such efforts can potentially help to restore and maintain equilibrium in functioning, he believed, they weaken the integrity of the self and predispose one to symptoms and problems in functioning.

Freud focused largely on symptoms in the first phase of his clinical practice, concentrating on a range of conditions associated with the disturbances in senses and musculature that led many in Victorian society to neurologists: paralyses, blindness, mutism, convulsive-like behavior, anesthesia, and loss of sensation (Gay, 1988; Sacks, 1998; Wolitzky, 2003).

As Freud continued to explore the histories of his patients, he increasingly linked repressed memories of traumatic events to sexual experiences in childhood and adolescence, viewing them as critical events in the etiology of psychopathology. In time, however, he began to question his patients' accounts of sexual abuse, and he abandoned the so-called seduction hypothesis in 1897. Freud explained that he found it hard to believe that sexual abuse could be so widespread in Viennese society; further, he had, through his own self-analysis, come to realize the role of fantasy in childhood. He concluded that many of the accounts he heard were the product of early fantasies of adult seduction rather than descriptions of actual events. In his revised formulations, he related neurotic symptoms not to actual events in the outer world but to wishful fantasies and began to see "psychic reality" as the crucial element in psychopathology.

While it is clear that Freud tragically underestimated the prevalence of sexual abuse, his abandonment of the seduction hypothesis was a radical turn in the development of psychoanalytic understanding. Freud refocused his attention from what he took to be actual events and circumstances in the social environment to intrapsychic domains of experience. In doing so, Freud came to privilege psychic reality over actual experience in the outer world, fantasy process over perception of real events, and instinctual drives over social and environmental influences, thereby establishing the defining features of classical psychoanalysis (for further development of these points, see Mitchell, 1988, pp. 41–62).

Theoretical Perspectives

Freud developed successive models of the mind over the course of his career, but he preserved his commitment to materialist and mechanistic notions of psychic energy and instinct that reflected the scientific Weltanschauung of his time (see Ellenberger, 1970; Gay, 1988; Sulloway, 1979; Westen, 1998). Despite ongoing revision and elaboration of his views, he continued to emphasize two ideas: the conservation of psychic energy and the biological origins of human motivation. Most scholars see his theory of instinctual drive as the foundation of his metapsychology and the central force in the development of psychoanalytic ideas through the first half of the century. In order to place contemporary schools of thought in context, it is important to understand the basic conceptions of personality development, psychopathology, and therapeutic action that distinguish the drive paradigm.

The Drive Paradigm

Following his abandonment of the seduction hypothesis in 1897, Freud proposed instinctual drive as the core constituent of psychic life and represented the person as a closed biological system that seeks to maintain homeostasis through discharge of energy. In doing so, as we have seen, he departed from his focus on the interpersonal and social contexts of psychopathology, most clearly seen in his theory of infantile seduction, and set forth what various thinkers have characterized as "one-person" or monadic models of the mind (see Mitchell, 1988, pp. 42–45).

In Freud's revised theory of mental functioning, the most fundamental human motives are rooted in biology. Mind emerges from endogenous forces and predetermined structures within the organism. Ongoing efforts to regulate libidinal and aggressive energies shape the course of development and the structure of personality. Freud formulated a psychosexual model of development and assumed that the course of maturation in infancy and early childhood shapes adult personality—as the twig is bent, so the tree shall grow. Health, well-being, and the attainment of the good life depend upon rational control of drive forces. In this vision of human nature, the continuous play of universal forces gives rise to "the whole variegation of the phenomena of life" (Freud, 1940/1964c, p. 149). All behavior is seen as an expression of primary drives.

In his topographic model of the mind, introduced in *The Interpretation of Dreams*, Freud distinguished three domains of mental process: the unconscious, containing unacceptable feelings and thoughts; the preconscious, containing acceptable feelings and thoughts that are accessible to awareness through the focusing of attention; and the conscious, containing feelings and ideas in awareness at the moment. He assumed that all mental life is derived from fundamental conflicts between unconscious and conscious forces. Drawing on military metaphors, he imagined one part of mind at war with another part of mind; inaccessible and repressed impulses, wishes, and memories are at odds with conscious domains of experience.

From this perspective, the origins of pathogenic material lie not in memories of external trauma but most deeply in the vicissitudes of drive experience; maladaptive ways of negotiating conflict between instinct and defense precipitate and perpetuate problems in living. Actual events and social experience remain important insofar as they provide opportunities for elaboration of primary drives and are "remodeled in the imagination" (Freud, 1918/1957a, p. 119). In the purest reading of drive theory, then, individuals are fundamentally pleasure seeking and establish connections with others because they serve to relieve instinctual tension and satisfy biological needs. There would be no need to form relationships with others, presumably, if it were possible to independently regulate drives and maintain psychic equilibrium. In this sense, as Jane Flax emphasizes, Freud does not see humans as inherently relational or innately social; there is no primary need for attachment. For Freud, she explains, individuals have "no desire or capacity to seek out or experience another person as an independently existing self. True reciprocity is not possible" (Flax, 1990, p. 54).

Freud increasingly engaged relational concerns in his structural model of the mind, introduced in 1923 in "The Ego and the Id" (see Freud, 1923/1961). He moved beyond the criterion of consciousness that had served as the basis of his topographic model and identified three systems of personality: the id, the ego, and the superego. He categorized mental processes on the basis of their functions and purposes, centering on conflict between desire and the dictates of conscience or reality and the social environment. The id ("it"), a "cauldron full of seething excitations" (Freud, 1933/1964b, p. 73), represents the biological basis of psychological functioning; raw, unstructured, instinctual energies press for expression. The ego ("I") encompasses crucial regulatory functions that mediate id impulses and the demands of the social environment. The superego ("above I") encompasses moral values and social attitudes, which are shaped by internalized parental representations. Following the Zeitgeist of nineteenth-century scientific understanding, however, Freud attempted to reconcile relational concepts with instinct theory and remained committed to what Frank Sulloway (1979) has called a "genetic psychobiology" (for further discussion of these points, see Cushman, 1995; Flax, 1990; Lear, 1990; Mitchell, 1988).

The classical psychoanalytic tradition, accordingly, continued to emphasize two interrelated lines of understanding: first, the primacy of sexual and aggressive drives in motivating thought, feeling, and action; and second, the central role of unconscious process, conflict, and defense in human experience. Continued developments in ego psychology increasingly addressed the role of interpersonal experience and the social surround in formulations of personality development, coping, and adaptation, seen in the seminal contributions of Anna Freud, Heinz Hartmann, Erik Erikson, René Spitz, Margaret Mahler, and Edith Jacobson. Even so, theorists continued to privilege classical notions of drive, conflict, and defense, thereby preserving Freudian views of the person as a self-contained system of instinctual energy. In this sense, Freud's ego psychology remained a mechanistic model of the mind, focused on psychological functions rather than on the concepts of self, relationship, and the social environment that would increasingly engage other thinkers in the broader psychodynamic tradition (see Blank & Blank, 1974; E. Goldstein, 1995; Loevinger, 1976; and Vaillant, 1993, for accounts of ego psychological perspective).

Clinical Perspectives

The core assumptions of Freud's drive psychology shaped the development of classical psychoanalytic practice. The task of the therapeutic endeavor, broadly understood, is to deepen understanding of unconscious conflicts that perpetuate problems in living and to facilitate more adaptive ways of mediating inner experience and outer realities. Freud believed that reduction of inner conflict would bring greater understanding and acceptance of self, deepen capacities for love and for work, and improve psychological and social functioning.

Formulations of problems in living emphasize concepts of impulse, anxiety, defense, and conflict. Freudians view neurosis as a closed system of drives and defenses, and clinicians seek to understand the ways in which underlying conflict precipitates symptoms, constricts ways of being and relating, and exacerbates problems in living. The goals of treatment are to help individuals develop greater control over unconscious conflicts, manage distressing emotion, and establish more effective ways of negotiating inner experience and outer realities. Freud (1905/1953) expressed the broader aim of classical psychoanalysis in his famous epigram, "Where id was, there shall ego be" (p. 266)—a revision of his earlier goal of making the unconscious conscious, based on the topographic model he had introduced at the turn of the century.

In the classical version of psychoanalysis, the therapeutic frame and conditions of treatment serve to help the person suspend defenses and allow derivatives of instinctual forces to emerge through free association and transference reactions to the clinician. Freud introduced the method of free association in an effort to override defensive processes and activate pathological conflicts in the clinical situation. He describes it as follows: "Say whatever goes through your mind. Act as though, for instance, you were a traveler setting next to the window of a railway carriage and describing to someone in the carriage the changing views which you see outside. Finally, never forget that you have promised to be absolutely honest, and never leave anything out because, for some reason or other, it is unpleasant to tell it" (Freud, 1913/1958b, p. 124).

In Freud's conception of transference, the person reexperiences in the relationship with the clinician early infantile wishes and fears originating in instinctual experience. The individual displaces historical wishes onto the practitioner. In this sense, Freud sees transference as an alternative to remembering crucial aspects of earlier experience. In the closed-energy system of the drive conflict model, Mitchell explains, wishes gratified in the transference remain inaccessible, unavailable for processing. Frustration and abstinence foster recollection and memory; "that which is gratified is perpetually enacted, but never remembered and analytically transformed" (Mitchell, 1988, p. 283). Within the classical model, conversion of transferential experience into memory fosters change and growth.

Freud believed that varying forms of resistance are inevitable over the course of analysis, and he stressed that clinicians must move beyond intellectual understandings of such behavior and connect the *experience* of resistance to underlying conflict in efforts to deepen understanding and insight. He writes: "The resistance accompanies the treatment step by step. Every single association, every act of the person under treatment must reckon with the resistance and represents a compromise between the forces that are striving toward recovery and the opposing ones" (Freud, 1912/1958a, p. 102).

The clinician adopts a neutral, accepting, empathic attitude in an effort to establish the therapeutic alliance and preserve the working relationship. The primary method of intervention is interpretation, focused on conflict between repressed instinctual impulses and defenses against them. The task of the clinician is to recognize and uncover infantile wishes and longings, hidden in various forms of resistance. Mitchell (1988) writes: "The ultimate aim of psychoanalysis is to overcome the resistance, to flush out the beast, to 'track down the libido . . . withdrawn into its hiding place' . . . , to tame the infantile wishes by uncovering them through memory" (p. 281).

Interpretations of unconscious experience, resistance, and transference reactions work to deepen understanding of underlying conflicts. Carefully focused observations convey the clinician's understanding of the potential meanings behind the manifest content of words and actions, which may remain out of awareness, providing crucial sources of information that deepen insight and understanding. The practitioner engages elements from the flow of free associations, transference reactions, and varying forms of resistance, lending new meaning to experience (see Etchegoyen, 1991, p. 325; Ford & Urban, 1998).

Through ongoing engagement of long-standing conflicts and interpretation of problems in living, in the context of visceral here-and-now transference reactions, the person processes difficulties and comes to develop more adaptive emotional and behavioral patterns (Wolitzky & Eagle, 1997). Deepened understanding and acceptance of disavowed wishes, conflicts, and fantasies—id or drive derivates, in Freud's language—strengthen the ego and foster behavior change. Individuals increasingly come to understand the origins of unconscious conflicts and the ways in which fundamental dilemmas and defenses have influenced patterns of behavior. Over the course of the therapeutic process, individuals are increasingly able to negotiate and control conflicts and establish more adaptive and fulfilling ways of being and living.

Clinical Applications

Freud's earliest conceptions of psychotherapy outline a range of considerations that we have come to regard as essential concerns and basic tasks in psychosocial intervention. He emphasizes the crucial functions of the therapeutic alliance; a clearly specified focus of intervention; active provisions of support and education; recognition and management of transference phenomena; and interpretation of defensive behaviors, which often take the form of resistance (see Breuer & Freud, 1893–1895/1955). He reminds practitioners of the importance of tact, intelligence, and sound judgment in his writings on technique (Freud, 1913/1958b, 1912/1958c), and he urges clinicians to be flexible and pragmatic in their approach to intervention.

Although Freud came to reject his first theory of neurosis, his earliest formulations anticipate the contemporary understanding of the dynamics of traumatic experience and basic tasks in therapeutic intervention (for review, see Huopainen, 2002). In his earliest conceptions of neurosis, as we have seen, Freud assumes that symptoms originate in repressed memories of traumatic experience. The aim of intervention is to help the individual recover memories, process emotion associated with the experience, and integrate past events into consciousness.

The following account from a treatment in progress illustrates how Freud's early formulations provide one way of understanding the dynamics of traumatic experience and defensive operations in the clinical situation.

Case Illustration: The Dynamics of Trauma

John L., age thirty-eight, initiated psychotherapy after he developed a fear of germs that increasingly constricted his behavior and patterns of activity. The practitioner used cognitive and behavioral procedures to treat the phobic symptoms. As they receded, however, he began to develop anxiety states and signs of depression. He was unable to identify the precipitating conditions for his feelings. At the start of one session, however, he departed from his review of the week's activities and told the clinician that it was time to talk about his father's abuse of him. He described a series of sexual violations and then fell silent. When the practitioner reflected his words, John looked at him, appearing confused and frightened. "I don't know what you are talking about."

According to Freud's early trauma theory, John's memories of abuse had been split off from conscious awareness, becoming encapsulated and assuming the form of symptoms; he had yet to process and integrate the experience. Traumatic content had emerged in the session but became inaccessible as a consequence of defensive operations. A resistant force—Freud used the term "defense"—had worked to keep memories out of awareness. Over time, John was able to render his experience into words, process emotion associated with the trauma, and integrate memories of events into his sense of self and life history.

Freud's subsequent reformulations of theory and practice methods changed the nature of the therapeutic endeavor; as we have seen, the task was not to work through repressed memories of traumatic experience and alleviate symptoms but to analyze and restructure the personality. He introduced technical procedures—free association and analysis of resistance and transference—that facilitated efforts to identify and dissolve pathogenic conflicts. The following account demonstrates how Freud's conceptions of conflict and resistance offer one way of understanding dynamic processes in the clinical situation.

Case Illustration: Conflict, Resistance, and Transference

Daniel P., age thirty-eight, initiated psychotherapy because he found himself unable to decide whether to marry the woman he had lived with for nearly three years. "There is so much good in the relationship," he acknowledged, "but I don't know if this is what I want. . . . I don't know the right thing to do." Although his ambivalence about the relationship served as the initial focus of intervention, the practitioner came to realize that Daniel experienced a pervasive sense of fear and doubt that had perpetuated conflict and provisional ways of being, relating, and living since childhood. It seemed as if every action carried the potential for disappointment, regret, or failure. "I'm afraid I'm going to do something wrong," he explained, "so I don't do anything. . . . I keep my options open, but I end up doing nothing."

As he continued to relate his concerns over the course of treatment, Daniel began to experience himself as an observer in the therapeutic situation, judging his accounts of events and reactions as relevant or irrelevant to his worries, fearing that he would fail to "talk about the things I most need to work on." He found himself unable to discuss themes and concerns that he had previously explored, seemed uncertain of himself, and began to wonder whether he should suspend the therapeutic process.

As we have seen, Freud came to view the individual's difficulties in the therapeutic situation—most often assuming the forms of resistance and transference—as crucial modes of experience and understanding that carry the potential for change and growth. The clinician interpreted Daniel's behavior in the therapeutic situation as a form of resistance consistent with the patterns of ambivalence, doubt, and demoralization that had constricted his life and began to focus on analysis of the defensive operations in the therapeutic situation itself. Over time, the process helped Daniel begin to identify core conflicts originating in his experience of aggression and to process feared elements of inner life that had perpetuated vicious circles of thought, feeling, and behavior. In the course of the therapeutic process, he consolidated his capacities to mediate aggressive experience and strengthened his sense of personal agency, increasingly bringing self to bear as he negotiated his relational world and shaped the course of his life.

Brief Psychotherapy

Although psychoanalysis is often viewed as a long-term, intensive form of psychotherapy, most of the treatments that Freud himself conducted were relatively brief by contemporary standards, often completed within weeks or months (see Borden, 1999). For example, he provides accounts of his single-session analysis of Katharina in 1885 (Breuer & Freud, 1893–1895/1955), his six-session treatment of the conductor Bruno Walter in 1906 (Sterba, 1951), and his four-hour consultation with Gustav Mahler in 1908 (Jones, 1953–1957). His analysis of Sándor Ferenczi took place over two three-week periods in 1914 and 1916 (Jones, 1953–1957).

Although Freud tended to downplay the favorable outcomes of his brief treatments, characterizing them as flights into health or transference cures, the first generation of theorists in the field of short-term psychotherapy based their models on principles of classical psychoanalytic thought (see Borden, 1999). Michael Balint (see Balint, Ornstein, & Balint, 1972), David Malan (1979), Habib Davanloo (1988), and Peter Sifneos (1987) all emphasize concepts of impulse, anxiety, defense, and conflict in their formulations of problems in functioning. In the foregoing conceptions of brief psychotherapy, the clinician challenges defensive operations, analyzes transference phenomena and resistance, and interprets behavior in light of wishes, defenses, and core conflicts. Malan employs two classical constructs in his formulations of the interpretive process: the triangle of conflict (representing core elements of conflictual experience, conceptualized as impulse, defense, and anxiety or symptom) and the triangle of person (representing three relational contexts of conflictual experience, described as history of childhood relationship with parents and other significant figures, current social relationships, and transference to the therapist). The aim of intervention is to help patients identify core conflicts that have perpetuated problems in living, revise maladaptive perceptions and reactions to situations, and establish more adaptive modes of functioning (see Messer & Warren, 1995, for a review of case studies and empirical findings).

This group of thinkers emphasized a series of tasks that continue to shape practice in brief treatment, including identification of circumscribed focal problems and formulation of specific goals; rapid establishment of the therapeutic alliance; active maintenance and monitoring of the central focus; systematic interpretation of transference phenomena, resistance, and other forms of defense; use of emotion and abreaction; and careful management of the termination process.

In the context of contemporary relational thought, these early models of brief psychotherapy, based on classical drive psychology, are limited in scope, presenting a series of conceptual problems and practical difficulties (see Borden, 1999). Even so, their efforts enlarged understanding of essential concerns and basic tasks in briefer forms of intervention.

Contemporary Freudians are increasingly attuned to the subjective character of the therapeutic relationship, recognizing the crucial functions of the patient-therapist match and the role of interactive experience and transference-countertransference enactments over the course of the therapeutic process. Thinkers seek to integrate core elements from a range of perspectives in attempts to construct an internally consistent comprehensive theory of personality, psychopathology, and therapeutic treatment (see Wolitzky, 2003, p. 64). Clinicians emphasize the need to carry out process and outcomes studies in order to determine the relative effectiveness of different analytic approaches.

Freud in Context: Contemporary Perspectives

The secondary literature on Freud's life and work is immense. There are many biographies exploring different periods of his career, but the classic work remains the three-volume account by Ernest Jones, *The Life and Work of Sigmund Freud* (1953–1957). While we know a great deal about Freud, he remains an elusive and perplexing figure. He was controlled and circumspect in what he revealed about himself, even in his autobiographical writings, and he destroyed most of his personal papers on two occasions, once in 1885 and again in 1907. Freud's life, as Peter Gay (1988) observes, offers us "inexhaustible fodder for innuendo, speculation, and mythmaking" (p. xvi). Scholars continue to fill in the gaps in our understanding of his life and work—questions, for example, about the origins of his "creative illness" (see

Ellenberger, 1970) and the period of self-analysis that preceded his abandonment of the seduction theory of hysteria; the role of his Jewish identity in the development of his thought; the roots of his antipathy toward religion; the nature of his differences with Adler, Jung, Rank, and other followers that led to strain and rupture; and the impact of World War I on his revisions of his metapsychology.

Commentators continue to criticize Freud for failing to take account of the historical, political, and economic contexts of human difficulty in his theoretical formulations, seeing him as socially disengaged, removed from the realities of ordinary everyday life, and indifferent to problems of politics and class. Although he represented his project as de facto science—a genetic psychobiology—his clinical work was shaped by a deep appreciation of the vicissitudes of social life, as Elizabeth Ann Danto (2005) shows in her history of social activism in the early psychoanalytic movement.

Freud emphasized themes of social responsibility in his address on the future of psychoanalysis and the conscience of society, delivered at the fifth International Psychoanalytic Congress in Budapest in 1918, and published a year later as "Lines of Advance in Psychoanalytic Psychotherapy." In this talk he embraced the social-democratic political ideology of post–World War I Vienna, appealing for social justice, and emphasizing the need to reduce inequality through universal access to mental health services. He imagined a time when "the conscience of society will awake, and remind it that the poor man should have just as much right to assistance for his mind as he now has to the life-saving help offered by surgery; and that the neuroses threaten public health no less than tuberculosis, and can be left as little as the latter to the impotent care of individual members of the community" (Freud, 1919/1955, p. 167).

Freud urged psychoanalysts to establish free clinics throughout Europe in order to provide mental health services for the poor, the unemployed, and the disenfranchised in his address. He called for free mental health treatment for all, emphasizing access and outreach in his vision of a more democratic psychotherapy. He acknowledged the ways in which social position and economic status perpetuate suffering, locating the therapeutic endeavor in the broader social surround (see Borden, 2006). In time, practitioners would establish cooperative mental health clinics in Vienna, Berlin, Frankfurt, London, Budapest, Paris, and elsewhere through the 1920s and 1930s. Many of the early psychoanalysts in Freud's circle were committed to social activism and social reform, seeing themselves as agents of empowerment, change, and liberation.

A growing number of thinkers have questioned whether Freud was the scientific positivist he claimed to be, suggesting that he was more beholden to the romantic tradition and the humanities than he acknowledged. The foregoing matters are important, as commentators point out, not only because they deepen our understandings of Freud's life and work but because they influence our views of psychoanalysis itself—whether we see it as science seeking to establish general laws about behavior or we approach it as a hermeneutic discipline focused on interpretive understanding of human experience.

Contemporary thinkers have increasingly attempted to distinguish Freud's metapsychology from his clinical theory in their evaluations of his work. Generally speaking, they have viewed his metapsychology as an unsuccessful attempt to extend Brücke's physicalistic physiology to the study of mind and provide a mechanistic description of mental functioning. Here, as we have seen, Freud reduces mental phenomena to the interaction of knowable energies and forces, attempting to determine causal connections among events, and seeking to establish general laws.

In developing his clinical theory of psychoanalysis, however, he departs from this mechanistic conception of mind and emphasizes concepts of motivation and personal meaning in his understandings of human behavior. In so doing, scholars have argued, he focuses on concepts of self and subjectivity and, by extension, establishes a hermeneutic method (see Ricœur, 1970; Spence, 1982). Many practitioners have come to see psychoanalysis not as a scientific endeavor but as a hermeneutic discipline focused on interpretive understanding of human actions.

In spite of the growing emphasis on interpretive or hermeneutic readings of Freud, however, other thinkers have continued in their attempts to establish psychoanalysis as a science, much as Freud had envisioned in his early writings. Recent accounts document ways in which Freud anticipated current lines of inquiry in neuroscience and contemporary psychology.

The realms of natural science and human meaning converge in Freud's thought, and a number of thinkers, notably Eric Kandel (2005, 2006), Gerald Edelman (1992, 2004), Oliver Sacks (1998), and Arnold Modell (2003), emphasize the crucial role of subjectivity in efforts to understand the brain and the mind. The field of neuroscience has increasingly moved toward dynamic, constructional conceptions of the brain, as Sacks (1984, 1985, 1992, 1995, 2004) has emphasized over the course of his writings on neurology, psychoanalysis, and consciousness. More and more, he shows, thinkers and researchers have come to view the person as a "human being first and last," engaging the individual as "a subject, not an object . . . the experiencing, acting, living 'I'" (Sacks, 1984, p. 164).

Empirical study in the behavioral and social sciences increasingly provides support for a series of core propositions that Freud advanced in his theoretical systems, including assumptions about the nature of unconscious motivational, affective, and cognitive processes; conflict and compromise among opposing motivational systems; defensive strategies and self-deception; the origins of personality and social dispositions in childhood; developmental dynamics; and the nature of "psychic reality" and subjectivity (Luborsky &

Barrett, 2006; Westen, 1998; Westen & Gabbard, 2002a, 2002b). As reviews of the research literature show, emerging lines of inquiry in cognitive neuroscience, child development, personality studies, social psychology, and experimental psychology converge with essential concerns in Freud's theorizing (see Schore, 2003a, 2003b; Westen, 1998).

Recent translations of Freud's work promise to bring fresh readings and reconsiderations of his contributions. Michel Foucault viewed Freud as one of the founders of discursivity. Like Homer, Aristotle, the Church fathers, Galileo, and Marx, he proposes, Freud has produced "the possibilities and rules for the formation of other texts . . . an endless possibility of discourse" (Foucault, 1984, p. 114).

Chapter 3

Alfred Adler, Individual Psychology, and the Social Surround

We have to realize our duty to our fellow human beings. We are in the very
midst of a community and must live by the logic of communal existence. . . .
The degree to which social feeling has developed in any individual is the only
universally valid criterion of human values.

—Alfred Adler, *Understanding Human Nature*

Although Freud's drive psychology served as the fundamental paradigm in
psychoanalysis through the first half of the twentieth century, growing numbers of thinkers challenged his vision of human nature and introduced alternative perspectives that increasingly engaged relational, social, and cultural domains of concern. The earliest attempts to establish relational points
of view included the divergent perspectives of Alfred Adler, C. G. Jung, Otto
Rank, Sándor Ferenczi, and Ian Suttie.

While each thinker pursued independent lines of inquiry, they all came
to emphasize the role of relationship and social life in their formulations of
personality development, psychopathology, and therapeutic intervention. In
the following three chapters, I examine the contributions of these revision-
ist thinkers, long neglected in mainstream psychoanalysis, and consider
their perspectives in light of essential concerns in contemporary clinical
practice.

Alfred Adler is increasingly recognized as one of the first psychodynamic
thinkers to view the person as a social being, and scholars are reevaluating
his conceptions of human nature, his philosophy of living, and his therapeutic system. Historians have come to see him as a critical figure in the evolution of contemporary psychology, linking his contributions to developments in cognitive psychology, narrative studies, psychosomatic medicine,
family therapy, group treatment, community psychiatry, and adult education
(Ellenberger, 1970; Stein & Edwards, 1998). The optimistic and progressive
outlook of his thinking shaped the emergence of humanistic psychology,
and a number of early theorists, most notably Abraham Maslow, acknowledge him as a crucial influence in the development of their work.

Adler's contributions anticipate essential concerns in relational psycho-analysis and contemporary clinical practice, and his formulations enlarge understandings of person and social environment, problems in living, and therapeutic action. He traced the origins of neurosis to social problems that undermine the individual's sense of dignity and self-respect, focusing particularly on poverty, sexism, and discrimination. In the following, I trace the development of Adler's work, review core elements of his personality theory, and consider his basic concepts of psychosocial intervention.

Life and Work

Adler was born in Penzing, a northern suburb of Vienna, to a middle-class Jewish family on February 7, 1870. He came from a similar background as Freud, and they attended the same gymnasium. Like Freud, he spent most of his life in the city, leaving only after Austria's fascist government closed the child guidance clinics he had established in the 1920s. He emigrated to the United States in 1935, establishing himself as a practitioner and educator in New York, and died on May 28, 1937, after a heart attack in Aberdeen, Scotland, during a lecture tour. Biographical accounts trace Adler's interest in medicine to early experiences of illness and injury (see Bottome, 1939; Ellenberger, 1970). Although he remained frail through childhood, he compensated for his impairments, by his own accounts, through academic work and independent study of natural history and the classics. His ability to quote the Bible, Shakespeare, Goethe, and the Greek tragedies engaged his peers in the Viennese coffee houses, and his colleagues described him as gregarious, spirited, and playful, noting his enjoyment of music and the theater (see Ellenberger, 1970, p. 593).

He received his medical degree from the University of Vienna in 1895, specializing in ophthalmology before turning to neurology and psychiatry. He pursued interests in social medicine and public health, exploring environmental aspects of physical illness, and joined the social democratic movement. He married Raissa Epstein, a Russian-born socialist, and wrote for Vienna's socialist newspaper. He was particularly moved by the social and economic problems of tailors, and his lectures and writings on the deplorable work conditions of underprivileged laborers informed social reform efforts. He established his practice in the Praterstrasse, a lower-middle-class Jewish neighborhood.

Adler met Freud in 1902 and was one of the four original members of his weekly study group. He began to write psychoanalytically oriented papers for medical and educational journals and published a book on the influence of organ inferiority (frequently congenital defects) on personality development in 1907. Adler theorized that physical impairment inevitably precipitates feelings of inadequacy and weakness. In efforts to compensate for such vulnerabilities, he observed, individuals may engage in a variety of activities that facilitate adaptation, growth, and development. As a representative example, Adlerians cite the case of Demosthenes, who stuttered as a child but, through intensive training, became a great orator.

Freud praised his book as a major contribution to psychoanalytic theory, and Adler enlarged his concepts of inferiority to encompass subjectively felt psychological and social vulnerability. He became a charter member of the Vienna Psychoanalytic Society, serving as its first president in 1910. Although Adler and Freud had shared many ideas, Adler increasingly challenged Freud's theory of the sex instinct as the cardinal motivational drive. He left the psychoanalytic movement in 1911 after Freud and his followers rejected his views, dismissing him as a dissident.

Adler established his own school of thought, which he called individual psychology to emphasize his holistic conception of the person, and introduced theories of personality and psychotherapy that generated widespread interest through Europe and the United States. He remained politically active and continued to relate many problems in living to social, political, and economic conditions. He established the first child guidance clinics in the Viennese public schools, beginning in 1919, and founded an experimental school based on his psychosocial theories.

An advocate of social justice, he continued to initiate reform in the city's public school system and pursued interests in a variety of areas, including child development, adult education, community mental health, and social welfare. He was steadfast in his belief that social institutions could be revitalized for individual betterment and increasingly focused his efforts on learning and education (E. Hoffman, 1994). He believed that solutions to political problems lay not in the struggle for power but in the development of social feelings; his motto was "Only a better individual can make a better system" (Bottome, 1939, p. 62). Following his move to the United States in 1935, Adler established a clinical practice and served as professor of medical psychology at Long Island College of Medicine.

Biographers describe him as an energetic lecturer, and he gave many talks for social workers, educators, and the general public. Though he published many articles in his lifetime, he was an undistinguished writer, and most of the books attributed to his authorship are transcriptions of his talks by colleagues. He provides the most systematic overview of his theoretical concepts and clinical perspectives in *The Practice and Theory of Individual Psychology* (1927) and elaborates his relational and social formulations in *Social Interest* (1939). Heinz and Rowena Ansbacher edited two volumes of representative selections of Adler's writings (see Adler 1956, 1980), and they provide useful introductions to his work. Ellenberger (1970) provides one of the most scholarly accounts of his life and the development of his thought. Edward Hoffman (1994) has written an engaging biography that explores Adler's contributions in light of contemporary psychology and psychotherapy.

Theoretical Perspectives

Although Adler did not codify his theories in a systematic, formal manner, as Freud had, he pursued fundamental concerns over the course of his work, creating an independent school of thought that provided a radical alternative to classical drive psychology. He rejected Freud's view of instinct as the fundamental motive in personality development and increasingly focused on the central role of relationship, community, and social involvement in his conceptions of health, well-being, and the common good. He set forth a humanistic conception of the person that emphasized the unity of body and mind, free will and self-determination, the search for personal meaning, and social responsibility. In the final phase of his career, Adler represented his theoretical system as a "social psychology," and he is arguably the first psychoanalytic thinker to introduce a relational perspective.

Adler viewed the person as a social being, motivated by relational needs: we seek contact and connection with others, establish relationships, pursue social activities, and develop styles of life that reflect our social nature. The notion of *Gemeinschaftsgefuhl* serves as a core construct in his system; though the term has been translated as "social sense," "social interest," "social feeling," and "community feeling," Adler (1956) reportedly preferred the phrase "feeling of community" (p. 134). He argued that the development of social interest—what he defined most broadly as a sense of human fellowship and identity with the whole of humanity—is a critical determinant of mental health. In health, Adler proposes, we come to feel a deep sense of connection with humankind: we empathize with others, recognize our interdependence, and realize that the welfare of any one individual depends on the well-being of the larger community.

Unlike Freud, Adler does not see person and society as opposing forces. In his view, the development of the individual and participation in social life are recursive processes that strengthen one another. The greater the level of personal development, he reasons, the stronger the ability to connect with others; the more developed the capacity to relate to others, the more one can make use of social interaction in the service of continuing growth and development (see Guisinger & Blatt, 1994; H. Stein & Edwards, 1998).

In the realm of personal life, Adler theorizes, we strive for realization of innate potential; in the domain of the social world, we work toward development of society. For Adler (1930), all relational life is an expression of what he called "the great upward drive" (p. 398), an inherent press toward "superiority" or actualization of potentialities. Constructive relationships and ideal communities are characterized by empathy, mutual respect, trust, reciprocity, cooperation, and personal equality. Some writers have seen his notion of social interest as reformulations of such fundamental religious percepts as "Love thy neighbor as thyself" (Mosak, 1987). Adler increasingly engaged moral and ethical concerns in the development of his thinking and, in so doing, set forth a distinctive psychology of values.

Of particular relevance to social work is Adler's conception of person-environment interaction, which prefigured systems views and ecological perspectives. He described the interconnectedness and interdependence of human life in his conceptions of family, community, and society; many thinkers now see him as an early field theorist. He stressed the role of social, cultural, political, and economic conditions in his understandings of human need and difficulty. He rejected deterministic views of the social environment, however, and emphasized the idea that people create meaning, actively shape their surroundings, and direct their lives.

His notion of the creative self, one of his most central concepts, encompassed the concepts of consciousness, free will, and capacity for transcendence of life conditions. In moving toward an existential point of view, he placed increasing importance on self-determination and individual responsibility. By virtue of being human, in his view, every person faces a fundamental question: "What will be your contribution to life? Will it be on the useful or useless side of life?" (H. Stein & Edwards, 1998, p. 69). We make choices and so shape our lives.

In developing his humanistic perspective, Adler saw the person as an individual and emphasized the distinctive configurations of motives, traits, values, and concerns that shape particular ways of being and relating. Whereas Freud emphasizes the role of the unconscious in human behavior, Adler sees consciousness as the center of the personality. We are purposeful and intentional in our ways of being; motivated by particular needs, goals, values, and concerns; and capable of self-determination.

As we would expect, Adler's conceptions of personality development center on relational life and the social environment. Parents, siblings, and other family members, as well as larger social and cultural conditions, influence the development of the individual. The family constitutes the primary social environment, in the early years of life, and the child elaborates ways of being and relating in efforts to negotiate need and mediate an inherent sense of inferiority in a world of stronger adults. Mastery of the environment is crucial, in his view, and the individual elaborates a distinctive lifestyle in ongoing efforts to negotiate tasks, strengthen coping capacities, and pursue goals.

The nature and history of relationships with others are critical determinants of personality development and interpersonal functioning. Adler pays particular attention to the family constellation (characteristics of the family structure as they affect each member) and family atmosphere (the nature of emotional relationships among family members) in his considerations of personality development. Supportive social environments, characterized by empathy, trust, respect, and encouragement of personal initiative, foster constructive styles of life. He links experiences of neglect and rejection to disruptive behavior and subsequent problems in functioning (see Hall, Lindzey & Campbell, 1998). Early perceptions of family experience continue to shape views of self, others, and social interactions through the life course.

Adler focuses on two particular concerns in his formulations of dysfunction and psychopathology: feelings of inferiority originating in physical handicaps, family dynamics, or social conditions, and underdeveloped feelings of community. He theorizes that negative life experiences and disappointments may lead individuals to anticipate failure before attempting tasks and perpetuate feelings of helplessness, hopelessness, and inferiority. Under these conditions, we employ what Adler called "safeguarding devices" in efforts to protect and preserve the self; they include neurotic symptoms, depreciation, aggressive behavior, guilt, and forms of distancing. In so doing, one works to avoid life tasks and transfer responsibility to others (H. Stein & Edwards, 1998).

Adler was particularly attuned to social conditions that perpetuate problems in functioning. He linked social discrimination on the basis of physical disability, gender, ethnicity, religion, or poverty to feelings of inferiority. He observed that American culture devalued women and overvalued men; in an ideal society, he believed, we would recognize the equality of value between men and women and facilitate cooperation among them; some writers characterize him as an early feminist (H. Stein & Edwards, 1998).

Clinical Perspectives

Adler had become a physician for the poor, and he identified with the ordinary person, focusing on the immediate problems of everyday life, and remaining close to the individual's sense of what is the matter. As a clinician, he was pragmatic and flexible in his approach to difficulties, preferring brief and active forms of treatment, frequently employing what we would now call cognitive and behavioral methods and task-centered approaches in social work practice. He was particularly interested in developing services for vulnerable groups that had been neglected by traditional psychoanalytic approaches to treatment, including children, adolescents, low-income families, laborers, and minorities. Over the years his therapeutic perspectives have informed approaches in child guidance, family and group therapy, and community psychiatry. One of Adler's daughters, Alexandra Adler, trained in psychiatry and neurology; her research on the survivors of Boston's Coconut Grove fire in 1942 would shape conceptions of post-traumatic stress disorders. She applied her father's theoretical perspectives to psychosocial care of individuals with severe mental illness.

Adler emphasizes two concerns in his approach to intervention. First, he seeks to address immediate problems in functioning in the context of the unique lifestyle of the individual. Second, he attempts to facilitate the development of social interest, so as to enrich the person's experience of others and social life—what Adler (1956) called "the belated assumption of the maternal function" (p. 341). Social interest strengthens solidarity with others. The task of the clinician, Adler (1956) writes, "is to give the patient the experience of contact with a fellow man, and then to enable him to transfer this awakened social interest to others" (p. 341). He compares psychotherapy to the parenting process: "Since his is a belated assumption of the maternal function, he must work with a corresponding devotion to the patient's needs." The therapeutic relationship is essentially a prototype of social interest.

The task of assessment is to understand the particular dynamics of the individual's neurotic style of life, clarifying the concrete particulars of behavior and conditions in the social surround. Adler sought to develop a general diagnosis or "total picture" of the patient through the individual's descriptions of relationships, dreams, attitudes, interests, and activities. He used a range of discussion topics in order to deepen his understanding of the general configuration of the person's situation. The "individualizing examination" involves assessment of childhood recollections that can potentially share core dynamics of presenting difficulties; childhood disorders; precipitating life circumstances, including past and present conditions (e.g., "organ inferiority," neurotic family environment); position of the child in relation to siblings; and content of dreams and daydreams (see Ford & Urban, 1963, p. 354). Adler also regarded the person's spontaneous ways of being and relating in the therapeutic interview a source of data.

Adler (1956) traced neurotic problems in living to failures in relational life—"a lack of ability to make contact" (p. 328). Although Adler minimized the role of transference phenomena in his clinical writings, he saw it as a crucial element in the therapeutic situation. Adler (1956) explains: "I expect from the patient again and again the same attitude which he has shown in accordance with his life-plan towards the persons of his environment and still earlier toward his family" (p. 356). In the therapeutic situation, the lack of ability to connect is revealed through transference. As Schwartz (1999) observes, Adler saw transference phenomena as an inevitable feature of the treatment process that needs to be understood as an unconscious communication of the individual's failures in relational life.

Adler's holistic and dialectical approach guided his use of technique. He framed symptoms and presenting problems in the context of the individual's lifestyle, taking into account current circumstances and the larger social and cultural surround. He emphasized the role of narrative process and personal meaning in therapeutic work and used interpretation in efforts to help individuals create more constructive views of self, others, and the world.

His educational approach appealed to the cognitive dimensions of personality, and he used active modes of intervention in efforts to generate action and help individuals move toward more related and productive ways of thinking and living. As Ford and Urban (1963) observe, he "advised his patients how to behave, he made suggestions as to what they should do, how they should think and the attitudes that they should retain during the intervals between therapy sessions" (p. 358). Adler believed that it was crucial for clinicians to affirm the individual's special strengths and encourage development of new skills. Over the years, Adlerian clinicians have emphasized the ways in which development of passionate interests and involvement in such activities as music, art, and dance can facilitate personal growth and social life.

Clinical Applications

Unlike classical psychoanalysis, the course of Adlerian psychotherapy is generally brief. Adler and his colleagues were among the first to advocate time-limited treatment, and they emphasized essential concerns and active methods in efforts to accelerate the process and improve outcomes. They stressed the importance of motivation, identification of goals, establishment of the focus, development of a collaborative relationship, and use of tasks and educational approaches in efforts to strengthen coping skills, enhance mastery, and negotiate problems in living.

Case Illustration: Healing by Reeducation

The following account provides an illustration of the ways in which Adlerian approaches to "healing by reeducation" encompass concepts of individualism and community. In her history of social activism in the early psychoanalytic movement, Danto (2005) reviews the treatment of Ernest, the first case of the Child Guidance Clinic of Vienna. Hilde Kramer, a psychologist who had wanted to establish a free clinic for the children and families of postwar Vienna, was the psychotherapist (Kramer, 1942). Adler served as consultant and reviewed the course of treatment.

Following the birth of his brother, Ernest, age nine, developed pervasive anxiety states and began to assault his sibling. His aggressive behavior continued, and he became the family scapegoat. His mother attempted to place him in state custody, but the court refused to manage what it saw as a family problem, referring her to community services for help. The parents brought their child to the clinic in desperation.

"The therapeutic work [Kramer] started then was called 'Individual' psychology," Danto (2005) writes, "but in truth it drew in Ernest's entire social milieu, including his family, his school, and his neighborhood. His mother calmed down once the intensity of her own despair was accepted and treated. Then her skewed attention to her son leveled off, and Ernest's anxious behavior subsided. When the parent's peer council at the school . . . called an evening meeting to discuss whether Ernest's odd unruly behavior had become dangerous to the school's other ninety-nine children, his mother felt more supported than reproached" (p. 36).

Adler reviewed the course of treatment. "Only a child who is an entirely autonomous unit is dangerous, he commented, but Ernest's genuine ability to adapt himself cautiously to the community center and to the security and reliability of his classmates was a sign of health. Adler's reformulation of the child's pathology," Danto (2005) writes, "helped the Child Guidance Clinic staff promote his successful 'reeducation' at school and at home" (p. 36).

Case Illustration: Inferiority, Style of Life, and Social Interest

The following case illustrates the ways in which the Adlerian perspective informs our understanding of dynamic issues and formulation of goals in the brief psychotherapy of an adolescent.

Anthony B., an African American youth of sixteen, was referred for psychotherapy by a social worker at his school after he was suspended for assaulting another student. He had a history of aggressive behavior in the school setting, which included initiating fights with peers and intimidating teachers, and he appeared to use his strength as a means of gaining dominance over others. "It's what you have to do to get by in this world," he told the clinician. "If you don't, people mess with you."

Over the course of the interview, the practitioner explored his recollections of childhood and family life, seeking to identify critical events and adverse conditions that had shaped his ways of being, relating, and living (lifestyle). He described his family as poor and explained that his parents had struggled to provide for him and his three younger sisters. His mother had been diagnosed with breast cancer when he was seven and had recently had a recurrence of the illness. His father, an alcoholic, had physically abused him when he was a child; during one assault his father ruptured his left eardrum, leaving him partially deaf. Shortly after the incident, he had a seizure and was diagnosed with epilepsy.

He struggled with his hearing loss and episodic seizures through childhood and adolescence. He described himself as having no close friends—"I wasn't like other kids. . . . They teased me"—and acknowledged feeling "different" and "alone." His father had left the family as his mother's illness progressed, and Anthony no longer had contact with him. He explained that he wanted to "get my life on track," graduate from high school, and pursue vocational training.

In formulating the case from an Adlerian perspective, the clinician assumed that Anthony's earlier life experience had shaped his views of himself, others, and the larger world. His care had been compromised by the constraints of his mother's illness and his father's abusive behavior. Although his grandparents and extended family had provided intermittent care, the dynamics of the immediate family system appear to have perpetuated strain and rupture in his interactions with his parents and sisters throughout his childhood and adolescence.

As we have seen, Adler links the child's experience of rejection, neglect, and abuse to feelings of inferiority and subsequent problems in functioning. In addition to his experience of neglect and abuse, the practitioner identified a series of conditions that may have perpetuated feelings of inferiority: his parents' limited ability to provide care and support his development and his view of his family as impoverished and hard pressed, his hearing loss and seizure disorder, and his failure to establish relationships with peers. Although he did not describe specific incidents, the clinician also realized that his experience of racism as an African American may have intensified underlying feelings of inferiority.

Adler describes two types of safeguarding tendencies that preserve one's experience of superiority, the first distinguished by aggressive forms of behavior, the second characterized by efforts to seek distance. The clinician understood Anthony's aggressive forms of interaction and his extended absences from school as protective modes of behavior. The meanings that he gave to his experience of the world—"You have to *make* others respect you or they mess with you"—perpetuated vicious circles of behavior, leading to demoralization, isolation, and alienation from others ("underdeveloped feelings of community").

From an Adlerian perspective, the individual's lifestyle or assumptive world guides efforts to process experience, negotiate vulnerability, and bring self to bear in the social surround. In formulating the course of intervention from a classical approach, the clinician would emphasize the following tasks over the course of intervention: (1) establishing a therapeutic alliance in efforts to facilitate the intervention process and strengthen capacities for relationship and social interest; (2) identifying, challenging, and revising maladaptive habits of perception and beliefs that perpetuate aggressive modes of interaction and problems in living; (3) encouraging engagement in new activities that carry the potential to strengthen mastery and self-esteem; and (4) supporting involvement in activities that strengthen social skills and capacities to establish contact and connection with others.

Over the course of psychotherapy, the practitioner would seek to help Anthony reduce the negative feelings associated with his sense of inferiority, alter his lifestyle or assumptive world in order to develop more constructive ways of processing his experience and negotiating his interpersonal life, proceed with his education and engage in meaningful activities that reflected his strengths and interests, and extend the level and radius of his social surround.

What is most crucial in all forms of psychosocial intervention, Adler emphasizes, is the development of "social interest," which is reflected in positive feelings toward others. Once the individual can relate to others on "an equal and co-operative footing," he believed, he or she is "cured" (Adler, 1956, p. 347). His fundamental therapeutic aim, as Ford and Urban (1963) observe, was to "render the patient an adequate and effective social being" (p. 348).

Adler in Context: Contemporary Perspectives

We are hard pressed to find a figure, Ellenberger (1970) observes, from whom "so much has been borrowed from all sides without acknowledgement as Adler" (p. 645). His emphasis on relational concepts; the social contexts of vulnerability and suffering; moral concerns; and pragmatic, flexible approaches to treatment foreshadow essential concerns in contemporary clinical practice. As we have seen, his perspectives encompass essential concerns and core values in the social work tradition. Adlerian psychology remains influential through Europe and in the United States, where practitioners maintain training institutes, family education centers, schools, and study groups.

Like the many Americans who welcomed his ideas, as Eli Zaretsky (2004) observes, Adler saw modernity "as the unfolding of a long-term process of democratization, and he wanted to assimilate psychoanalysis to reformism, social-democratic politics, and a results-oriented psychotherapy" (p. 92). Growing concerns over individualism; the culture of narcissism; and the breakdown of relational life, family, and community have the potential to deepen appreciation of his example and his work.

Chapter 4

C. G. Jung and the Psychology of the Self

A neurosis is more a psychosocial phenomenon than an illness in the strict sense. It forces us to extend the term "illness" beyond the idea of an individual body whose functions are disturbed, and to look upon the neurotic person as a sick system of social relationships.

—C. G. Jung, *The Collected Works*

Carl G. Jung introduced a school of thought known as analytical psychology that has enlarged conceptions of self, relational life, and the therapeutic endeavor. His challenges to Freud's classical perspective prefigure fundamental shifts in contemporary psychoanalysis, including the focus on subjectivity, personal meaning, and identity; the development of the self; the psychology of narcissism; and relational conceptions of the therapeutic process. He believed that the search for wholeness and the integration of personality—what he called the process of individuation—is a cardinal motivation in human experience. His writings have shaped understandings of development across the course of life, the functions of religious and spiritual experience in health and well-being, and ways in which therapeutic work can facilitate realization of potential and deepen the individual's sense of purpose and meaning.

More broadly, Jungian views have informed critical discussion of a range of issues in contemporary social life, including gender, race, ethnicity, politics, and multiculturalism (see, e.g., Young-Eisendrath & Dawson, 1997; Samuels, 2000). In this chapter I trace the development of Jung's work, outlining the defining features of his depth psychology, and describe the concerns and ideas that shaped his conceptions of therapeutic practice. Case examples illustrate use of Jungian methods in psychotherapy.

Life and Work

Jung was born in the small Swiss village of Kesswil, in the canton of Thurgau, on July 26, 1875, and died in Küsnacht on June 6, 1961, at the age of eighty-five. He lived in Switzerland throughout his life, although he traveled widely in Europe, North America, Africa, and India. Toward the end of 1957, at age eighty-two, Jung began his autobiography, *Memories, Dreams, Reflections*. He wrote the opening chapters but narrated the rest to his secretary,

Aniela Jaffé, who prepared the material for publication in 1961. The work has become a classic, and it provides crucial points of entry for efforts to understand the development of his thought. It is a spiritual exploration, as Jung (1961) makes clear at the beginning: "My life is a story of self-realization of the unconscious" (p. 3). He centers on the events of his interior life, relating his anxiety, fantasies, and dreams through childhood.

His father was a minister in the Swiss Reform Church; his mother was the daughter and granddaughter of Protestant clergy. His parents and teachers saw him as a troubled child, anxious and withdrawn, and he found it difficult to relate to his peers. He experienced what he describes as a religious crisis in adolescence and began to elaborate a psychological conception of God, rejecting institutionalized forms of religion.

Jung read deeply in philosophy, developing an intense interest in Schopenhauer, and intended to train as a classical philologist or archaeologist. He found himself increasingly drawn to the natural sciences, however, and enrolled in medical school at the University of Basel. He specialized in psychiatry and went to the psychiatry clinic of the Burghölzli in Zurich to work as an assistant to Eugen Bleuler, a well-known psychiatrist who first conceptualized schizophrenia as a mental illness. He began empirical research on unconscious phenomena, conducting word association experiments, which would serve as the foundation for his theory of the complex.

Jung became interested in the work of Freud following his reading of *The Interpretation of Dreams* in 1900. He reread the work in 1903 and sent Freud a copy of his *Studies in Word-Association*; they began a correspondence in 1906 and met a year later. In 1909 Freud and Jung traveled to the United States, where they gave a series of lectures for the twentieth anniversary celebration of the founding of Clark University in Worcester, Massachusetts. In the course of the visit they met William James, whose writings had been particularly important to Jung. Jung became the first president of the International Psychoanalytic Association in 1910, and Freud came to see him as his successor in the psychoanalytic movement.

Jung had preserved an independence of mind, however, and he believed that Freud placed too much emphasis on sexuality as a motivating force in human life. They had other differences as well. Jung found Freud's approach to human experience reductive and mechanistic. Freud saw the unconscious as a repository of repressed material that threatened social life; Jung viewed it as a potential source of growth and creativity. Jung believed that Freud overemphasized the importance of the Oedipal complex in personality development; Jung focused instead on dynamic features of the mother-child relationship and its role in the emergence of the self.

Although their relationship had been taxed by personal as well as intellectual differences, Freud's sexual interpretation of human motivation was the point over which they parted ways. Jung knew that the views introduced in *Transformations and Symbols of the Libido*, published in 1911 (later issued as *Symbols of Transformation* in 1952), would alienate Freud. In this work he theorized that a large part of the unconscious was objective, or collective, and functioned independently of sexual instincts.

Unable to restore the relationship, Jung broke with Freud in 1913 and experienced an extended period of disorientation marked by intense dreams, fantasies, and visions; fragmentations of self; and fears of psychosis. He initiated a deep exploration of his own unconscious experience and began to develop methods of analysis and interpretation that would transform him and shape the development of his depth psychology. Ellenberger (1970) describes Jung's experience as a creative illness, "an intense preoccupation with the mysteries of the soul," and views it as a crucial event in the development of his distinctive point of view (p. 672). George Hogenson (1994) provides a scholarly account of Jung's complex relationship with Freud.

Jung explored an extraordinary range of concerns over the course of his career, which spanned more than half a century. Unlike Freud, he did not initiate major revisions of his work; instead, he preferred to use earlier writings as points of departure for ongoing formulations. Aniela Jaffé (1971) quotes him as having remarked in a seminar: "I can formulate my thoughts only as they break out of me. . . . Those who come after me will have to put them in order" (p. 8). His writings fill twenty volumes in the English-language edition of the collected works; additional publications include collections of letters, lectures, and interviews with Jung.

Theoretical Perspectives

Like Adler, Jung never attempted to organize his system of thought. He was a pluralist by temperament, and he viewed theories as tools for thinking, taking a pragmatic approach to ideas in the clinical situation. He writes: "I have taken as my guiding principle William James' pragmatic rule: 'You must bring out of each word its practical cash-value, set it at work within the stream of your experience. It appears less as a solution, then, than as a program for more work'" (Jung, *CW* 4, para. 86).

Over the years, personality scholars and analytical psychologists have attempted to provide systematic accounts of the defining features, basic concepts, and clinical implications of Jung's formulations (see, e.g., Hall et al., 1998; Samuels, 1985, 2000; Samuels, Shorter, & Plaut, 1986; M. Stein, 1995, 1996). The following overview is informed by a close review of Jung's core writings and careful reviews of his theoretical formulations by Calvin Hall, Gardner Lindzey, and John Campbell (1998). Although a full presentation of his thought is beyond the scope of this chapter, it is important to introduce his conceptions of personality, psychopathology, and psychotherapy, which remain at the periphery of the field and largely misunderstood in the broader psychoanalytic literature. As we will see, he engages a range of concerns that shape contemporary theory and practice.

Personality Development

Jung's conceptions of the self and his approach to psychotherapy emerged over the course of sixty years. In developing his formulations of personality, he describes what he regards as basic structures of the psyche. These include the ego, the personal unconscious and its complexes, the collective unconscious and its archetypes, the persona, and the shadow. The self is the center of the personality. Additionally, in his work on psychological types, he describes the attitudes of introversion and extraversion and the functions of thinking, feeling, sensing, and intuiting; in time, these formulations would serve as the basis for the Myers-Briggs Type Indicator, which is used widely for psychological assessment in counseling, education, and work settings.

Structures of Personality

The ego is the center of consciousness, comprising perceptions, thoughts, feelings, and memories. Ego functions preserve cohesion and continuity in the individual's ongoing sense of self and identity and help the person negotiate inner experience and outer realities in ordinary everyday life. Jung emphasizes the crucial role of the ego in coping and adaptive functioning. In his model, however, he views the self as the more fundamental organizing principle of psychic life and personality.

The personal unconscious is comprised of experiences that have been repressed, suppressed, forgotten, or ignored; it also includes experiences that failed to make a conscious impression on the individual. The contents of the personal unconscious are potentially accessible to awareness, and Jung imagines much give-and-take between the ego and the personal unconscious (Jung, *CW* 9/2, para. 261; see also Hall et al., 1998). His views anticipate recent conceptions of unconscious experience in cognitive psychology.

Jung links archetypal and personal elements of experience in his formulations of the complex, which were influenced by his empirical research on word association. He defined the complex as an admixture of memories, feelings, thoughts, and images that operates in the personal unconscious and influences behavior when activated in particular circumstances (Jung, *CW* 8, para. 253). The complexes connect networks of associations that originate in core constituents of human experience and in the individual's experience as it is shaped by life events and the social surround. The father complex, for example, encompasses archetypal aspects of father figures in the objective layer of the psyche and cultural images of fatherhood as well as derivative elements of the individual's actual interactions with the parent across the course of development, encompassing his or her ways of being, relating, and life experience.

Jung rejected unitary conceptions of personality structure, introducing pluralistic views of the self. His first major work, *The Psychology of Dementia Praecox* (1907), is a study of the ways in which the psyche can be fragmented into independent forces through repression or trauma. He came to see complexes as autonomous entities within the self, believing that "complexes behave like independent beings" (Jung, *CW* 8, para. 253), shaping ways of relating and living. Complexes are charged with emotion, perpetuating repetitive modes of behavior.

Jung views the collective unconscious as the source of latent memory traces inherited from the ancestral past, encompassing the history of humans as a separate species. We can understand it as the "psychic residue of human evolutionary development, a residue that accumulates as a consequence of many repeated experiences over many generations" (Hall et al., 1998, p. 85). Jung regards the collective unconscious as universal, emphasizing the similarity of brain structure in all races.

He uses the term "archetype" to describe the structural elements of the collective unconscious (Jung, *CW* 6, para. 754; *CW* 8, para. 417; *CW* 9/1). The concept of the archetype connects body and mind; it is an inherited part of the psyche that generates patterns of imagery and modes of behavior. Archetypal patterns are shaped by individual forms of expression as well as by cultural expectations. The tradition of Platonic thought, Immanuel Kant's a priori categories of perception, and Arthur Schopenhauer's prototypes prefigure Jung's formulations of the archetype (Samuels et al., 1986). The concept anticipates evolutionary and behavioral genetic approaches in psychology, as Hall et al. (1998) emphasize. As we will see, notions of innate psychological structure are also found in the drive psychology of Melanie Klein.

The term "persona" originates in the Latin word for the mask worn by actors in ancient Rome. Jung uses it to describe the social functions of the public self shaped by tradition and convention, which facilitate efforts to carry out roles and relationships in the give-and-take of day-to-day life. He describes the persona as the individual's adaptation to the world, "a complicated system of relations between individual consciousness and society" (Jung, *CW* 7, para. 305). There is considerable overlap with the concept of the ego. Although the persona facilitates adaptive functioning in the social surround, one may identify too closely with the outer self, leading to an outward orientation that overrides one's capacity to process inner experience and engage deeper core experiences of the personality.

Jung characterizes the "shadow" as "the thing a person has no wish to be" (*CW* 16, para. 262). As he defines the concept, it encompasses animal instincts inherited in evolution from lower forms of life, giving an embodied experience to personality, as well as personally or socially unacceptable thoughts, feelings, and values that consciousness rejects. It is crucial to appreciate, however, that the shadow has the potential to contain generative elements that potentially foster development of the self. As Humbert (1984) explains, the shadow represents what each personality "might have been but has not had a chance to be" (p. 49).

Jung views the self as the unifying principle within the psyche, a fundamental organizing force or agency outside the conscious "I" that shapes the destiny of the individual. He writes: "The self is not only the center, but also the whole circumference which embraces both conscious and unconscious; it is the center of this totality, just as the ego is the center of the conscious mind" (Jung, *CW* 12, para. 444). The ongoing interaction of ego and self shapes ways of being, relating, and living.

The development of the self across the course of life is purposive or teleological, shaped by emerging concerns, values, and goals. The transcendent function is the force that motivates efforts to mediate opposing elements in the psyche, to integrate unconscious domains of experience, and to work toward wholeness or individuation of self (Jung, *CW* 6; *CW* 11, para. 490).

Psychological Types

Jung describes two major orientations of personality in his formulation of psychological types, the attitudes of introversion and extraversion. The extraverted attitude orients the person to the external, objective world; the introverted attitude orients the person to the internal, subjective realm of experience (Jung, *CW* 6). Each of these attitudes is present in the personality, Jung theorizes, but one is generally more conscious and dominant.

Jung also conceptualizes four types of functions that characterize the ways in which people process information: thinking, feeling, sensing, and intuiting. Thinking encompasses intellectual efforts to comprehend self and the nature of experience, including reason, judgment, abstraction, and generalization. Feeling emphasizes the subjective value of experience. Sensing is the perceptual or reality function, which is focused on concrete particulars. Intuition is a mode of perception mediated by unconscious processes (Jung, *CW* 6). Contemporary thinkers would now characterize the four functions as cognitive styles (Hall et al., 1998).

Jung describes basic tasks and essential concerns in his writings on childhood, adolescence, adulthood, and later life. His descriptions of the midlife transition have informed empirical research on adulthood and personality. As we have seen, he emphasizes the progressive character of personality development, embracing a teleological point of view. The ultimate goal of development, in his humanistic perspective, is the realization of self through the process of individuation—the most complete differentiation, integration, and expression of fundamental elements of the personality (see Hall et al., 1998, p. 101). The crucial functions of meaning and purpose in health, well-being, and the good life are recurring themes throughout Jung's writings.

Psychopathology

Although Jung made fundamental distinctions between psychosis and neurosis in his conceptions of psychopathology, he rejected the formal psychiatric taxonomies that the clinicians of his time used to diagnose specific types of mental illness. Instead, he focused on the person as an individual, seeking to understand the dynamics of the psyche.

He carried out studies of schizophrenia early in his career at the Burghölzli, where Bleuler had introduced the term, and used therapeutic methods in efforts to facilitate coping and improve functioning in severe mental illness. From the start of his work, however, he recognized the probable role of organic factors in the development of psychosis and emphasized the need for study of physiological processes in efforts to deepen understanding of the origins and treatment of conditions (Jung, *CW* 1; *CW* 3, para. 552; *CW* 18).

Jung came to understand neurosis as a dissociation of the personality (*CW* 13, para. 473; *CW* 16, para. 27, 36; *CW* 17, para. 359). Complexes have the potential to splinter the psyche and precipitate splits between conscious and unconscious domains of experience, constricting ways of being, relating, and living. Complexes operate autonomously as independent centers of gravity, seemingly with a consciousness of their own, perpetuating vicious circles of thought, feeling, and action. In his formulations of dysfunction, Jung emphasizes the content of complexes and social contexts of neurotic behavior: "A neurosis is more a psychosocial phenomenon than an illness in the strict sense. It forces us to extend the term 'illness' beyond the idea of an individual body whose functions are disturbed and to look upon the neurotic person as a sick system of social relationships" (*CW* 16, para. 27).

If neurotic symptoms reflect underlying pathology, they also provide points of entry into unconscious domains of experience that carry the potential to foster change and growth. The aim of Jungian analysis, as Murray Stein (1998) explains, is to integrate psychic elements "that have been split and pushed apart, so that the normal psychic equilibrating force can take over and offer its creative and healing potential. This knitting together bits of consciousness is the work of integration" (p. 38).

Clinical Perspectives

Like Adler, Jung took a pragmatic, individualized approach to psychotherapy, and he remained uneasy with efforts to reduce psychoanalysis to basic principles and procedures. He believed that the practitioner should remain flexible and vary ways of working in view of individual temperament and particular needs, capacities, and tasks, emphasizing: "The patient is there to be treated and not to verify a theory. . . . There is no single theory in the whole field of practical psychology that cannot on occasion prove basically wrong" (Jung, *CW* 16, para. 237). Although he addressed a range of problems in living in the course of his clinical practice, he came to see the development or individuation of the self as the fundamental aim of psychotherapy.

Jung conceptualizes four stages of therapeutic intervention, seeing them as overlapping and fluid, each carrying the potential to shape the process at varying points in the treatment (see Jung, *CW* 16, para. 114–174). He describes the first stage as catharsis or confession and relates this stage to age-old forms of healing, as carried out in religious traditions. The second stage, elucidation or interpretation, focuses on exploration of personality features and developmental conditions that influence problematic ways of being and relating; Jung views the therapeutic relationship as a crucial medium in efforts to deepen understanding of self and modes of interaction. He emphasizes analysis of transference experience in this phase. The third stage, education, explores adaptations to outer social demands and development of ego functioning; Jung compares this stage to the social learning outlined in Adler's individual psychology. In the fourth stage, individuation or transformation of self occurs; he calls this stage "analysis proper."

Jung emphasizes the ways in which dreams and inner images deepen understandings of self and life experience, and dream analysis remains a defining feature of Jungian psychotherapy. Jung's method of dream analysis encompasses reductive and synthetic approaches. In the reductive method, the clinician and client explore dream content in light of past experience, focusing, for example, on the dynamics of early development and family life. In taking a synthetic approach, the clinician and client focus on future possibilities, exploring dream content in view of broader symbolic meanings, emerging concerns, and efforts to realize potential in individuation of the self.

Jung attempts to override neurotic patterns of functioning and engage unconscious domains of experience through his method of active imagination. In using this approach, the client engages in dialogue with figures of the unconscious as they have emerged in dream images or in the process of imagination. Dream analysis and active imagination carry the potential to provide access to the deeper healing influences of the psyche (for further discussion of methods, see M. Stein, 1996, pp. 92–93).

Jung locates the dynamic interaction of psychotherapy in the two-person field, and he emphasizes the ways in which conscious and unconscious domains of experience in the client and the clinician influence process in the clinical situation. He recognizes the importance of what we would now call the therapeutic alliance, making a careful distinction between the "real" relationship and transference and countertransference states that emerge in the clinical situation. He anticipates reciprocal interactive conceptions of transference and countertransference and introduces ways of understanding projective experience that prefigure modern views. In his understanding, the personal transference is shaped by the patterns of expectation originating in earlier relational experience; the patient's relationships to essential others are projected onto the clinician. The archetypal transference originates in unconscious process rather than in the interpersonal experience of the individual. Drawing on Jung's formulations, Peter Mudd (1990) shows how conceptions of self-preservation and death shape transference experience in the clinical situation, fostering individuation and development of self.

Jung was one of the pioneers in the therapeutic use of countertransference. Although classical Freudians tended to see the clinician's countertransference as an obstacle to treatment, Jung saw it as "a highly important organ of information" for the psychotherapist (CW 16, para. 163). He wrote: "You can exert no influence if you are not susceptible to influence. . . . The patient influences [the clinician] unconsciously. . . . One of the best known symptoms of this kind is the counter-transference evoked by the transference" (CW 16, para. 163). He believed that the therapeutic process has the potential to transform both patient and clinician. Jung was the first to initiate a compulsory training analysis for psychotherapists and anticipated key concepts in the clinician's use of subjective experiences as sources of understanding in the therapeutic situation.

Clinical Applications

Jung emphasizes the importance of matching therapeutic approaches to the personality and circumstances of the client, as we have seen, and practitioners in analytical psychology use a wide range of methods. The following case report shows how Jungian conceptions of individuation informed the use of life review, analysis of dream content, and active imagination in psychotherapy following diagnosis of a life-threatening illness.

Case Illustration: Life-Threatening Illness and Individuation of Self

David W., thirty-six, was referred for psychotherapy by his physician three months after he was diagnosed with an inoperable brain tumor. He had developed diffuse anxiety states and growing feelings of helplessness and hopelessness following his decision to leave his job, withdrawing from family and friends. In the assessment interview he related that he felt alone, lost, and disoriented following the rapid progression of his illness—"I feel like I've fallen out of my life"—and wanted to "learn how to live the time I have left." In spite of the debilitating effects of the cancer, he had remained active in his professional and personal life until recently. His work had provided a sense of control, competence, and meaning in the midst of the dislocation imposed by his illness. His inability to continue his activities had precipitated a crisis of identity—"I don't know what my purpose is any-more"—and he explained that he wanted to better understand himself—"where I've been, who I am, where I'm going."

The first phase of treatment focused largely on the process of recon-structing personal history and developing a life story. From a Jungian per-spective, reconstruction of life experience is a crucial part of becoming con-scious and creating personal meaning. Reconstruction of earlier events is healing because it helps one restore the experience of one's own history and strengthens one's sense of identity (see M. Stein, 1996). David explored the course of his childhood and adolescence, telling the story of his near death as a premature infant, and describing relationships and critical events that shaped his core values and fundamental beliefs about himself, others, and the larger world. The process of rendering his experience into words and af-firming the life that he had lived appeared to strengthen his sense of self.

The second phase of treatment focused on David's acceptance of the ill-ness and his efforts to fulfill his desire to live in light of his continued decline and anticipated death. He related a dream in which he comes upon a child covered with sores, near death; he realizes that there is no hope and begins to run away, abandoning the boy. Drawing on Jung's method of active imag-ination, the clinician asked David to consider what would happen if he were to remain with the child, caring for him. As he imagined himself holding the child, comforting him, he began to sob. The dream and the imaginative process provided points of entry into his deep experience of pain, sorrow, and grief. Subsequent dreams and interpretation of content in light of his current condition brought about a shift in his attitude toward his own suf-fering. He increasingly came to accept his illness, reengage family and friends, and pursue activities within the range of his capacities, working to-ward individuation and wholeness.

Case Illustration: Spiritual Aspects of Psychotherapy

In the course of intervention, many patients discover what Jung charac-terized as the religious instinct. In her essay on the spiritual aspects of psy-chotherapy, Ann Ulanov provides a series of case reports from her practice as a Jungian analyst. The following vignette is drawn from her account of a woman who "reached something holy that named itself as such" (Ulanov, 1995, p. 55). As in the preceding illustration, the clinician used dream analy-sis and active imagination in efforts to foster change and individuation of self.

The patient, who was experiencing an "inner necessity that felt like a search, and like a threat of insanity," entered analysis in her early twenties. Ulanov (1995) summarizes the course of her treatment as follows: "A dead space existed in her because of an early and deep wound—a feeling that her mother did not love her. 'She loved me in a collective way,' this woman would say, 'as one of her children, but she did not love me.' . . . That dead space in her felt like a yawning abyss, a void that would swallow her up, into which she would fall forever and disintegrate. It was this that threatened her with madness" (p. 55). In time, Ulanov explains, her client learned to "face that abyss and engage it in active imagination. Slowly it changed to limitless pain, to sorrow so great that the image expressing it when it came seemed the only fitting one: the Mater Dolorosa weeping tears of blood. This was the holy reaching out to her by indicating that through her personal pain she was touching everyone's pain, the pain of the world" (pp. 55–56).

Ulanov (1995) reflects: "The limitless tears of blood expressing the pain of this dead space in her turned into limitless human tears, and finally found their limits and stopped. What had been dead space in her now filled with personal human feeling" (p. 56).

Jung in Context: Contemporary Perspectives

Jung anticipates central concerns in contemporary psychoanalysis and the broader field of psychotherapy, as we have seen, and his work has had a powerful and enduring impact on culture and social life. In the context of psychotherapy, contemporary Jungian perspectives emphasize the phenomenology of the self and subjective domains of experience, the interactive field of the clinical situation, and relational conceptions of transference and countertransference. The first period of Jung's clinical work focused largely on severe mental illness, and the orienting perspectives of analytical psychology continue to inform approaches to psychosocial care in community mental health settings. His writings on development in later life have influenced conceptions of psychotherapy in the field of gerontology. Peter Homans offers a trenchant critique of Jung's contributions in *Jung in Context* (1995). Deirdre Bair (2005) and John Kerr (1993) provide scholarly accounts of his life and work in their biographies.

Chapter 5

The Emergence of Relational Perspectives: Otto Rank, Sándor Ferenczi, and Ian Suttie

I fully accept Ferenczi's dictum: . . . The physician's love heals the patient.

—Ian Suttie, *The Origins of Love and Hate*

The views of Otto Rank, Sándor Ferenczi, and Ian Suttie, elaborated a decade after the departures of Adler and Jung from Freud's inner circle, constitute yet another break with the early psychoanalytic movement. Rank's "will therapy" and Ferenczi's emphasis on trauma, empathy, and the functions of the therapeutic relationship challenged central tenets of drive psychology and orthodox analytic methods, and both thinkers enlarged ways of understanding interpersonal experience and methods of intervention in the clinical situation.

Although the writings of Suttie have received little attention in the contemporary psychoanalytic literature, he is a rich and imaginative thinker, deeply attuned to the dynamics of relational life and the social surround. He drew on Ferenczi's conceptions of the therapeutic relationship and introduced what some scholars have come to see as the first object relations perspective. In this chapter I review the core concepts of these thinkers, exploring their theoretical perspectives and the ways in which their work has shaped understandings of essential concerns in psychosocial intervention.

Otto Rank

Rank's emphasis on relationship, will, and creativity has influenced a wide range of thinkers and psychotherapists, including Henry Murray, Carl Rogers, Rollo May, Esther Menaker, and Irving Yalom. His developmental psychology and his approach to psychotherapy served as the foundation for the functional school of social work, as we will see, and his core ideas have shaped basic principles of psychosocial intervention in the broader social work profession and models of brief treatment in contemporary psychotherapy.

Life and Work

Rank was born in Vienna on April 22, 1884, and died in New York on October 31, 1939, a month after Freud's death. He read widely in literature, art history, philosophy, and mythology; loved music; and wrote poetry and journals, seeing himself as an artist. Freud's *The Interpretation of Dreams* moved him to write about creativity from a psychoanalytic perspective; one of his biographers, James Lieberman (1998), speculates that the manuscript probably came to Freud through Adler, Rank's physician. Freud invited Rank to participate in the Vienna Psychoanalytic Society, of which he was appointed secretary in 1906, and encouraged him to pursue graduate study. Rank received his doctorate from the University of Vienna in 1912; he was the first doctoral candidate to complete a thesis on a psychoanalytic topic.

Rank emerged as an expert on philosophy, art, literature, and mythology in the psychoanalytic movement, and he worked closely with Freud, whom Lieberman (1998) describes as his mentor and foster father. He married Beata Mincer, a student of psychology, in 1918 and enlarged the range of his activities, providing psychotherapy, training clinicians, and writing. He was the founder or editor of three European journals on psychoanalysis. As he pursued his own lines of inquiry, however, his relationship with Freud became increasingly strained; like Adler and Jung, he too was forced to leave the inner circle in the 1920s and proceeded to establish his own school of thought. His marriage of three decades ended following his break with Freud.

Rank continued to teach, lecture, write, and conduct a clinical practice, developing a humanistic and briefer form of psychoanalytic psychotherapy that emphasized an egalitarian relationship between the therapist and client. Between 1926 and 1931 he wrote a series of works on developmental psychology and psychotherapy that anticipate developments in object relations psychology.

He moved to New York and taught at the University of Pennsylvania School of Social Work, where he analyzed several of the faculty members, including Virginia Robinson and Jesse Taft, and lectured at two schools of social work in New York City in the 1930s. Taft translated his major works into English.

Theoretical Perspectives

Like Adler and Jung, Rank rejected the mechanistic, deterministic explanations of behavior that characterized the Freudian system and introduced a humanistic perspective with an existentialist orientation. He viewed the person as an initiator of action and interpreter of meaning. He emphasized conscious rather than unconscious domains of experience; the present situation and anticipated future over past events; and notions of choice, responsibility, and action, in contrast to the classical Freudian focus on intellect and insight. The individual is conscious, choosing, self-determining, and purposive—what Rank (1945) describes as "a moving, effective cause" (p. xx).

He focused on the crucial functions of separation and individuation in development through the life course, and he came to see problems in living as a consequence of unsuccessful efforts to negotiate coexisting needs for union and dependency, on one hand, and separation and independence, on the other (Rank, 1936). He conceived of the will as an organizing, integrative force that facilitates efforts to negotiate basic existential dilemmas and promotes realization of potential and individuation of self. As Menaker (1982) explains in her account of Rank: "To be born means to be responsible for one's own separate existence and survival; and in this separateness man experiences his own finiteness; he comes to know death, to fear the loss of his hard-won individuality, and to perceive the connection between birth and death" (p. 64). The neurotic is constrained, bound by the fear of life and of death, unable to act. One restricts patterns of activity and ways of being in efforts to preserve self. Rank (1945) writes: "All symptoms in the last analysis mean fear" (p. 157).

Clinical Perspectives

The fundamental task of intervention, in Rank's view of the therapeutic endeavor, is to provide facilitating conditions and relational experiences that foster separation-individuation processes and empower the person to act and to create. Every individual carries the potential for constructive change and growth, in his humanistic conception of the person, and the aim of intervention is to foster "the acceptance of the self . . . with its volitional and emotional autonomy" (Rank, 1945, p. 97). The goal is not to alleviate neurotic symptoms as such but to help one bring self to bear and establish ways of being and relating that facilitate efforts to negotiate problems in living as they emerge over time. The individual is capable of making decisions, acting, and shaping his or her life.

For Rank, the therapeutic situation is a present experience rather than a reliving of the past. He assumes that maladaptive modes of functioning perpetuated by neurosis will emerge in the therapeutic relationship, providing opportunities to identify and change dysfunctional behavior. He argues that knowledge of the origin of problematic behavior does not necessarily facilitate change and observes that exploration of earlier events may encourage the client to deny responsibility for present behavior. Since the fundamental problem is one of will—becoming a self-determining, self-directed individual—the client must accept the responsibility for change.

Rank emphasizes the curative functions of the therapeutic relationship and experiential learning through the give-and-take of therapeutic interaction. Like Ferenczi, he sees the relationship as the central medium in efforts to identify problematic patterns of interaction, learn more adaptive modes of relating, and explore the application of new behaviors to representative situations following the end of treatment.

Rank encourages all signs of assertiveness and self-direction in the therapeutic situation. He rejects Freud's conceptions of resistance, believing that such behavior has the potential to reflect expressions of will and independence. The experience of ending provides a means of renegotiating issues of dependency, separation, and relatedness, and he sees termination as a crucial feature of the therapeutic process. Rank set the date for ending treatment, believing that it would foster self-direction and individuation. "The key aspect of this process," as O'Dowd (1986) explains, "is maintaining the connection, the sense of belonging and attachment, along with the new-found capacity to will and to create a separate individual" (p. 146).

Clinical Applications

Rank's conceptions of the helping process continue to shape principles of intervention in the field of social work and contemporary approaches to brief psychotherapy. The following section briefly reviews work in each of these areas, showing the ways in which clinicians have applied his theory and methods.

Functional School of Social Work and Contemporary Practice.   The functional school of social work emerged in the late 1920s and 1930s at the University of Pennsylvania School of Social Work. Jesse Taft and Virginia Robinson drew on his developmental and clinical theories in fashioning the functional model of social work practice. In doing so, they emphasized the crucial role of the client's participation in the therapeutic process, the helping relationship, and the social agency (see Dore, 1990).

The client, rather than the worker, identifies the focal problems, and the principle of starting where the client is affirms the importance of accepting the individual's interpretation of what is the matter. The client is responsible for change and growth. The individual's experience of will fosters efforts to individuate, and the larger aim of intervention is to strengthen the client's sense of volition and self-determination through the helping relationship.

Following Rank's conceptions of the therapeutic relationship, Robinson and Taft focused on the dynamics of interactive experience in the helping process. The clinician's understanding of the client emerges over the course of the relationship. The interactive experience of the helping process facilitates efforts to work toward change, growth, and individuation of self. Drawing on Rank's appreciation of time as a critical determinant of change and growth, functional theorists identified dynamic processes and tasks that shaped ways of working across the beginning, middle, and ending phases of the helping process.

In their efforts to distinguish social work practice from psychoanalysis, Taft and Robinson emphasized the function of the social agency (Dore, 1990). As they understood it, the social agency creates a dynamic context for the helping process. The interaction between the client and the worker is defined and limited from the beginning by the purpose and function of the agency, which determine the nature of the help provided and the requirements for conditions of service. The agency became "a symbolic representation of external reality," as Dore (1990) explains, "the reality of life against which the client struggled in the reach toward growth and change" (pp. 365–366).

The functional school has shaped basic principles and core concepts in contemporary social work practice, including conceptions of the client's right to self-determination, the notion of starting where the client is, appreciation of the crucial functions of the relationship in the helping process, and recognition of time as a facilitating condition in the therapeutic process (Dore, 1990).

Brief Psychotherapy.   Rank's theoretical perspectives have shaped conceptions of short-term intervention in contemporary psychotherapy, emphasizing the developmental contexts of problems in living and the role of the therapeutic relationship in efforts to facilitate change, growth, and individuation of self (Borden, 1999; Messer & Warren, 1995).

His influence is seen most clearly in the existential model of James Mann, which addresses problems in functioning precipitated by developmental transitions and loss. Mann assumes that "life consists of a never-ending series of reunions, separations, and losses," that "separation and loss are never fully mastered," and that "better resolution of the separation-loss problem leads to a greater sense of self and greater independence" (Mann & Goldmann, 1982, p. 28). He employs a fixed time frame in his model of brief intervention, limiting the therapy to twelve sessions. The larger aim of intervention is to help the individual process experiences of separation and loss in light of the anticipated end of the therapeutic relationship and to strengthen capacities to negotiate subsequent separation and individuation across the life course.

Case Illustration: Working through Loss

Virginia R., age seventy-four, had experienced the deaths of her husband, father, and mother within a nine-month period shortly after her fiftieth birthday. She explained that she had developed a pervasive sense of fear, deep sadness, and feelings of hopelessness after recently retiring from the job that she had begun shortly after the losses. Over the course of intervention the client realized that her retirement had precipitated earlier feelings of loss and grief.

Rank's existential perspective provided a frame of reference for the clinician in efforts to help the client process and integrate the experience of earlier losses, explore sources of purpose and meaning, and proceed with life tasks.

Rank in Context: Contemporary Perspectives

As we have seen, Rank's clinical perspectives have influenced contemporary models of social work practice and brief treatment, particularly through his conceptions of the helping relationship and interactive experience, his emphasis on the present rather than the past, and his use of time limits and termination as transformative elements in the therapeutic process. James Lieberman (1985) provides a scholarly account of his life and work. Peter Rudnytsky (1991, 2002) offers trenchant critiques of Rank's contributions in his writings on contemporary psychoanalysis.

Sándor Ferenczi

Sándor Ferenczi has been characterized as the most brilliant and intuitive member of Freud's inner circle, and he has emerged as a complex figure in recent accounts of his life and work following publication of his correspondence with Freud and his *Clinical Diary*, a private journal he kept in 1932, the year before his death. Freud (1937/1964a) himself memorialized Ferenczi as "a master of analysis" (p. 230), though their relationship had been taxed by strain, conflict, and rupture. Ferenczi's interest in trauma and early family life, his focus on the therapeutic relationship and the role of empathy in the helping process, his conceptions of transference and countertransference, and his efforts to develop more active, experiential methods of intervention anticipate fundamental concerns and developments in contemporary practice.

Life and Work

Ferenczi was born on July 7, 1873, in Miskolc, Hungary, and died on May 24, 1933, in Budapest. He grew up in a cultivated family, the eighth of twelve children. His father had emigrated from Poland and established himself as a socialist publisher; his mother served as president of the Union of Jewish Women. He developed a strong interest in the arts and humanities. After he received his medical degree in Vienna in 1894, he became head neurologist at the Elizabeth Poorhouse in Budapest and was appointed psychiatric consultant to the Royal Court of Justice. In addition to his work as a physician, he wrote essays and poetry and became a member of the Nyugat (Occident) circle, whose members included the composers Zoltán Kodály and Béla Bartók and György Lukács, the literary critic.

Ferenczi had first encountered Freud's writings as a medical student at the Burghölzli, where Jung and Karl Abraham had also trained. He met Freud in 1908 and was invited to join the inner circle; in time, he would become Freud's "favorite son" (Rachman, 2007). He accompanied Freud and Jung on their visit to Clark University in 1909. He founded the Hungarian Psychoanalytic Society in 1913 and emerged as the leading figure in the international psychoanalytic movement (see Grosskurth, 1991). He helped establish the *International Journal of Psychoanalysis*. Ferenczi's marriage to Gizella Pálos in 1919 was an outcome of his analysis with Freud. She was seven years his senior and had become his lover in 1900, while still married to her first husband (Rudnytsky, 2002).

Ferenczi was particularly attuned to the political and economic contexts of vulnerability and difficulty, and he passionately defended the rights of women and homosexuals as early as 1906 (Danto, 2005). "In our analyses," he wrote to Freud in 1910, "we investigate the real conditions in the various levels of society, cleansed of all hypocrisy and conventionalism, just as they are mirrored in the individual" (qtd. in Brabant, Falzeder, & Giampieri-Deutsch, 1994, p. 153). He established a free clinic in Budapest in 1929, seeking to make mental health services available to the poor, the unemployed, and other disenfranchised groups.

His major papers are collected in two volumes: *First Contributions to Psycho-analysis* (1952) and *Final Contributions to the Problems and Methods of Psycho-analysis* (1955). The *Clinical Diary of Sándor Ferenczi* was published in 1988.

Theoretical Perspectives

Ferenczi explored a range of theoretical concerns in the course of his work, enlarging conceptions of relational life and trauma, and he was a crucial influence in the development of object relations perspectives through his analyses of Melanie Klein and Michael Balint, and formulations of interpersonal theory through his analysis of Clara Thompson.

He broke with Freud over the issue of childhood sexual abuse, challenging his abandonment of the seduction theory, and he deepened appreciation of the role of actual events in the outer world in his formulations of psychopathology. In his last paper, "The Confusion of Tongues between Adults and the Child: The Language of Tenderness and Passion" (1933/ 1980), presented at the twelfth International Psychoanalytic Congress, he argued that neurotic problems in functioning originate in what really happens to people, not in fantasies of what could have occurred. He came to link neurotic symptoms and character disorders to lapses in attunement and responsiveness in earlier care, emphasizing the traumatic effects of empathic failure, deprivation, and overstimulation in relational life.

He increasingly focused on dynamics of caretaking experiences in the family surround in elaborating his understanding of the origins of traumatic experience. "In most cases of infantile trauma," he writes in his *Clinical Diary*, "the parents' cure is repression—'it's nothing at all'; 'nothing has happened'; 'don't think about it. . . .' The trauma is hidden in a deadly silence. First references are ignored or rejected . . . and the child cannot maintain its judgment" (Ferenczi, 1988, p. 25).

Although he had a deep interest in theory, Ferenczi was first and foremost a practitioner, ever focused on the concrete particularity of the clinical situation, most interested in the dynamics of the therapeutic relationship and technique. His growing understanding of the dynamics of traumatic experience revised his ways of working in treatment. He departed from the neutral stance that Freud had advocated and introduced "the rule of empathy," believing that the patient comes to register the reality of traumatic experience only through the clinician's expressions of emotion and empathic processing of experience (Ferenczi, 1933/1980). In another *Diary* entry, he reflects: "Patients cannot believe that an event really took place . . . if the analyst, as the sole witness of the events, persists in his cool, unemotional, and . . . purely intellectual attitude, while the events are of a kind that must evoke . . . emotions of revulsion, anxiety, terror, vengeance, grief and the urge to render immediate help" (Ferenczi, 1988, p. 24).

Ferenczi (1933/1980) increasingly focused on the importance of the practitioner's attunement, responsiveness, and flexibility in the therapeutic process, emphasizing the emotional connection between the client and the clinician, urging therapists to offer "maternal friendliness" rather than "intellectual explanations" (p. 160). He came to believe that the practitioner's empathy and attitude of loving acceptance are the most crucial elements in healing. He worked to revise conceptions of the therapeutic relationship, coming to see it as a collaborative, mutually supportive partnership. As we will see, his conceptions of the helping relationship influenced Ian Suttie in his understanding of love as the curative factor in psychotherapy.

Clinical Perspectives

Ferenczi emphasizes the role of interactive experience in the two-person field of the clinical situation. In his view, psychotherapy is not an intellectual reconstruction but an emotional reliving and renegotiation of earlier experience. "In the experiential reliving of the past," Aron (1996) explains in his account of Ferenczi, "a new present is both found and created—a new self, a new other, and new possibilities for what can occur internally and externally between self and other" (p. 164).

Ferenczi was increasingly troubled by the constraints of classical psychoanalytic methods, and he began to experiment with more active strategies of intervention in his clinical practice. In a collaborative project with Rank, he carried out significant revisions of psychoanalytic technique and therapeutic practice in their classic monograph, *The Development of Psychoanalysis* (1924). They believed that analysis of "living out" tendencies in the immediacy of the therapeutic relationship, without extended exploration of childhood antecedents to current problems, could be sufficient to facilitate growth and change (see Tosone, 1997).

They reasoned that earlier experiences of childhood conflict are inevitably carried forward and represented in current patterns of interaction. In their view, the relationship between client and therapist serves as a facilitating medium in efforts to revise problematic patterns of interpersonal behavior and develop more adaptive ways of being and relating (Tosone, 1997). Transference and countertransference states emerge as crucial sources of experience and understanding in efforts to represent and renegotiate the effects of earlier trauma (Ferenczi & Rank, 1924/1986). While Freud had regarded countertransference as a sign of the clinician's psychopathology and an intrusive threat to the therapeutic process, Ferenczi viewed it as a facilitating element, and he experimented with methods of disclosing countertransference states in efforts to deepen the client's understanding of earlier relational life and current problems in living.

Clinical Applications

Ferenczi's contributions have deepened our appreciation of essential concerns in the helping relationship and concepts of therapeutic action in brief psychotherapy.

The Therapeutic Relationship.   Ferenczi increasingly emphasizes the crucial functions of empathy, authenticity, and mutuality as he elaborates conceptions of the therapeutic relationship and interactive experience in his later writings, anticipating the contributions of Carl Rogers and Heinz Kohut. He urges the clinician to process interactive experiences with the patient and to acknowledge empathic lapses in responding to concerns and errors in interpreting content.

Ferenczi's interest in mutuality and collaboration in the therapeutic situation prefigures growing recognition of the ways in which the client and the clinician influence and help one another. More broadly, his work foreshadows a range of current concerns regarding the helping relationship, encompassing questions of authority, autonomy, and authenticity and the dilemmas of self-disclosure (see Aron, 1996; Fiscalini, 2004; Rachman, 2007).

Brief Psychotherapy.   Ferenczi increasingly experimented with more active ways of working in his efforts to shorten treatment and improve outcomes, and his work has shaped the contemporary understanding of core elements in brief psychotherapy (see Borden, 1999; Tosone, 1997). He emphasized the importance of the therapeutic alliance, the establishment of a focus on circumscribed difficulties and current life conditions, the confrontation of defensive behaviors, and the role of emotion as a transformative element of change and growth (Ferenczi & Rank, 1924/1986).

He used a variety of strategies in his efforts to intensify emotion in the therapeutic situation. At times, for example, he encouraged patients to face feared situations or prohibit certain patterns of behavior in efforts to delve more deeply into underlying issues. He introduced a range of methods, including the use of suggestion, advice, and relaxation techniques. His formulations anticipate contemporary integrative perspectives that link psychoanalytic and behavioral concepts, seen most clearly in Paul Wachtel's (2008) cyclical psychodynamic approach.

Ferenczi in Context: Contemporary Perspectives

The emergence of relational psychoanalysis has deepened appreciation of Ferenczi's contributions, and a growing number of thinkers have drawn on his writings in elaborating conceptions of relational life and trauma, the therapeutic relationship, transference and countertransference states, enactment, and interactive experience in the clinical situation (see Aron, 1996; Aron & Harris, 1993; and Rachman, 2007, for reviews of his contributions to contemporary psychotherapy and relational psychoanalysis).

Ian Suttie

Ian Suttie centered on the dynamics of relational life and the social surround in developing what some scholars have characterized as the first object relations perspective. Vincent Brome, writing in 1982, described Suttie's formulations as "a systematic account of man as a social being whose object-seeking behaviour was discernible from birth. It replaced Freud's dual instinct theory with a full object relations theory" (p. 144). Suttie saw Freud's views of individual and social development as authoritarian and patriarchal, and he offered a democratic and matriarchal perspective as an alternative, emphasizing the crucial role of love and relational life—rather than sex—in human experience.

He was deeply interested in religious and spiritual life as well. If Freud regarded religion as a "universal obsessional neurosis," Suttie saw religion as serving crucial functions in social life, arguing that religious forms of expression work to preserve health and well-being through love and relationship. In his view, the revered traditions and social institutions of religion constituted systems of psychotherapy in their own right, engaging a range of moral and ethical concerns in relational life and society. Broadly speaking, he writes, religion "is mainly concerned in its higher forms to better our affective relationships with others" (Suttie, 1935, p. 104). He offers a conception of the clinical situation that emphasizes the role of relational experience and the therapeutic functions of essential others in ordinary everyday life.

Life and Work

John Bowlby had hoped to write a biography of Ian Suttie, but he died before he could begin the project, and we know surprisingly little about Suttie's life and work. The account here is drawn largely from a brief essay by Dorothy Heard (a niece of Jane Suttie, his wife), prepared as an introduction to an edition of *The Origins of Love and Hate* published in 1988. Suttie was born in Glasgow, Scotland, in 1889 and died in London on October 23, 1935. Heard (1988) relates few details of his early family life; she explains that his father was a physician; that he had a sister and two brothers, all of whom trained as physicians; and that his mother was widowed in the 1920s.

Suttie completed medical school at Glasgow University in 1914, specializing in psychiatry. Beyond his medical training, he pursued interests in anthropology, comparative religion, and social thought. He served in France and the Middle East during World War I, after which he returned to the Glasgow Royal Asylum as a staff psychiatrist. He married Jane Robertson, a psychiatrist, and the couple moved to London in 1928. Suttie became a clinician at the Tavistock Clinic; his wife joined the staff in 1932. They lived in Bloomsbury, where they conducted their clinical practice. Jane Suttie translated Ferenczi's work into English, and Ferenczi became a major influence in the development of his ideas.

Suttie elaborated his theoretical perspectives in a series of papers between 1922 and 1926; he completed a second group of writings in the early 1930s. The latter papers were developed over the course of study groups and lectures he organized at the Tavistock Clinic, where the eclectic practitioners engaged in vigorous discussion of a range of psychological and social perspectives. The Tavistock Clinic sponsored his book, *The Origins of Love and Hate*, which appeared in 1935. The bombings of London during World War II destroyed Suttie's unpublished notes, the texts of his lectures, and plans for a second book that had been preserved in the Tavistock archives.

Heard (1988) describes Suttie as extroverted, energetic, generous, and playful—he wrote standing up "in between excursions up and down the room," she reports (p. xxxv)—but explains that he was ill through the latter half of his adult life, suffering from kidney disease and a duodenal ulcer. He completed *The Origins of Love and Hate* in the last year of his life, and he died only days before the book appeared in print.

Ernest Jones had rejected an article Suttie submitted to the *International Journal of Psychoanalysis* in 1923. Jones's biographer, Vincent Brome (1982), observes: "Critical material was one thing[,] revolutionary principles quite another" (p. 144). As Howard Bacal observes, Suttie's rejection of Freudian drive psychology undoubtedly contributed to his neglect in mainstream psychoanalytic literature (see Bacal & Newman, 1990, pp. 17–27).

Theoretical Perspectives

Suttie introduces an original relational perspective that challenges the individualism of classical psychoanalytic thought, emphasizing family, community, social life, and culture in his understandings of personality development, health and well-being, and problems in living. It is an optimistic, hopeful point of view, and his conceptions of the human situation are based on what he sees as innate needs for love, relationship, and social life.

He rejects Freud's drive psychology, offering a powerful critique of his dual instinct theory. He argues that the patterns of sexual development that Freud had assumed to be universal—seen most clearly in his formulation of the Oedipus complex—are shaped by the dynamics of family life and culture. "The most important aspect of mental development," he theorizes, "is the idea of others and of one's own relationship to them. . . . Man [for Freud] is a bundle of energies seeking to dissipate themselves but restrained by Fear. Against this I regard expression not as an outpouring for its own sake, but as an overture demanding response from others. It is the absence of this response, I think, that is the source of all anxiety and rage whose expression is thus wholly purposive" (Suttie, 1935, pp. 29–35).

Concepts of relationship, interdependence, and love are central in his understandings of personality development and social life. The child's most basic need is for love from parents and other caretaking figures, he emphasizes; the fundamental fear is loss of such love. He links the love of others and the dread of loneliness to the instinct of self-preservation, originating in the vulnerability and dependency of the infant at the start of life. In contrast to Freudian and Kleinian accounts of the infant as solipsistic and narcissistic, however, Suttie (1935) emphasizes what he sees as innate capacities for relationship at the start of life. "I consider that the child wakes up to life with the germ of parenthood, the impulse to 'give' and to 'respond,' already in it," he writes. "This impulse, with the need to get attention and recognition, etc., motivates the free 'give and take' of fellowship" (p. 58).

Accordingly, the infant is motivated not by sexual or aggressive instincts but by the need to establish connection and closeness and engage in give-and-take with essential others—independent of bodily need or sensory gratification. He emphasizes that "love, not selfish appetites, is the mainspring of social life" (Suttie, 1935, p. 125). He views interdependence and participation in social life as crucial markers of health and well-being across the life course.

In contrast to Klein, Suttie views aggressive behavior as the individual's response to lapses, failings, and constraints in relational life originating in experiences of refusal, rejection, and "nonresponsiveness." He writes: "Earth hath no hate but love to hatred turned, and hell no fury but a baby scorned" (Suttie, 1935, p. 23). At the start of life, he imagines, the infant experiences "only its pleasure and goodwill, and these it gives freely" (p. 42). However, when the child discovers that the benevolence of others is "conditional and that its own gifts in turn are apt to be criticized or rejected[,] . . . [its] frustrated social love turns to anxiety . . . and then to hate if the frustration is sufficiently severe" (p. 42). Anger, then, does not originate in instinctual process; it is a response to rejection—and, he stresses, "an insistent demand made upon the help of others" to respond. He views anger as "the maximal effort to attract attention, [which] . . . must be regarded as a protest against unloving conduct rather than aiming at destruction of the mother, which would have fatal repercussions on the self" (p. 23).

Here, however, the child faces a fundamental dilemma. Given the experience of vulnerability and dependency in early life, Suttie reasons, hatred of the loved object (meaning actual relation to other) is intolerable. Accordingly, the child does what he or she can in efforts to preserve the sense of a loving relationship "as a matter of life or death" (Suttie, 1935, pp. 43–45). In what may be the first relational conceptions of defense, Suttie describes four approaches by which the child may restore the other as good and loving.

First, the child may preserve a view of the primary caretaker as good by reasoning: "My parents are good and kind; if they do not love me it is because I am bad." Suttie links this approach to subsequent feelings of low self-esteem and the development of melancholia associated with feelings of unworthiness; he also makes reference to Adler's conception of the inferiority complex. Second, the child may use regression as a means of reactivating earlier states of self and other when the other *was* experienced as good and loving. Third, the child may search for a good substitute for the bad caretakers in other parenting figures. Suttie recognizes that this may be a healthy move in that dependency is transferred to others in the social environment. Finally, the child may use power to exact services for the lost sense of security in freely available love. Anger, coercion, and threat may be used to make the other demonstrate his or her love. This is seen in delinquent behavior and varying forms of narcissistic organization. In this formulation, as we will see, Suttie anticipates Winnicott's formulation of the antisocial tendency.

Suttie believes that the responsiveness of the caretaking experience and the character of the family environment influence ways of being and relating across the course of life, and he traces the capacity to engage and participate in social and cultural life to the nature of earlier relational experience. He describes a range of conditions and circumstances that may constrain caretakers in their efforts to provide love and care, including family demands, traumatic life events, poverty, and other adverse social conditions that constrain functioning. Unlike other psychoanalytic thinkers at the time, he engages biological, social, and anthropological perspectives in his efforts to deepen understandings of family life and community, emphasizing the ways in which essential others in the larger social surround serve crucial caretaking functions and facilitate development across childhood, adolescence, and adulthood.

Clinical Perspectives

Suttie anticipates fundamental concerns in contemporary research on curative factors in psychosocial intervention. He chooses to emphasize the therapeutic functions of relational elements over specific techniques, seeing psychotherapy as a healing relationship based on attunement and empathic responsiveness. He embraces Ferenczi's belief that it is the clinician's love more than anything else that heals the patient, the nature of love being understood as a "feeling-interest responsiveness" (Suttie, 1935, pp. 212–213).

Suttie traces a range of problems in living to disruptions in earlier relational life, arguing that the sense of feeling unloved or unwanted or the rejection of offerings of love can perpetuate demoralization, anxiety, guilt, frustration, and aggression. The fundamental aim of the therapeutic endeavor, in Suttie's (1935) rendering, is to strengthen capacities for giving and receiving love and to restore the individual to "full membership of society, to a feeling-interest integration with other minds" (p. 213).

The essential process in psychotherapy, he writes, is "to offer the patient the means of re-establishing free 'feeling-interest' relationships with his social environment in the person of the" clinician (Suttie, 1935, p. 213). His conception of the therapeutic process anticipates the relational perspectives of Winnicott, Fairbairn, and Kohut. Once the patient has established trust in the clinician, he theorizes, the individual re-creates problematic aspects of earlier lapses and failings in relational life through the transference; regressive behavior in the therapeutic situation constitutes an effort to return to the point at which one was failed.

Suttie is particularly attuned to resistant behavior, which he views as a protective effort to avoid retraumatization. The clinician replays the original role of the primary caretaker, helping the patient process and work through earlier failings, and becomes "the starting point of a broadening circle of anxiety-free relationships," where "feelings need not be inhibited or repelled" and "where interest responses are equally free" (Suttie, 1935, p. 213). Suttie writes: "Little by little suspicion and anger [negative transference] is dispelled as the patient ventures to attack the [clinician]-parent with . . . accusations of injustice and unkindness, and finds these protests sympathetically understood, admitted, and excused" (p. 252). For Suttie, cure lies not in "removal of gaps in memory" or "increase in insight," as orthodox Freudians believed, but in the helping relationship that strengthens the patient's sense of security and confidence that overtures to others will be received with the "feeling interest" one brings to the encounter.

Clinical Applications

Suttie's conception of resistance as fear of retraumatization deepens our appreciation of a range of behaviors in the clinical situation. As he shows in his discussions of psychotherapy, clients may deflect opportunities to develop the sustaining relationships they most need in efforts to protect themselves from the disappointment and rejection they have experienced earlier in life. The following account provides an example of the ways in which a client's fears of retraumatization challenged the establishment of the therapeutic alliance and engagement in the helping process.

Barbara K., age thirty-seven, was referred to a family service agency for a consultation by the social worker at her daughter's school following her husband's death after a heart attack. She apologized to the clinician at the start of the interview—"I'm sorry I have to see you"—and explained: "I've always been able to manage my life." In the course of the consultation she described herself as "a real problem solver" and appeared to take pride in the self-reliance and self-sufficiency that she had developed as a child following her mother's death.

Although Barbara's account of events was deeply moving, she kept a measured distance in her interaction with the clinician. She deflected his efforts to empathize with her experience and explore sources of support, saying, "Thanks, but I don't see what good talking about things is going to do. . . . I just have to deal with things on my own. . . . I'll figure it out." She decided not to proceed with ongoing psychotherapy. She did, however, initiate episodic consultations, at which she reviewed the course of her efforts to care for her children and negotiate practical demands.

While she remained reserved in the sessions, appearing to treat the clinician as if he had little to offer, she began to share more of her experience of vulnerability and loss. She appeared to be conflicted between her longings for greater connection and support in the therapeutic process and her need to remain self-reliant in order to avoid disappointment. The practitioner understood her presentations of self and detachment in the relationship as forms of resistance that reflected her underlying fears of connection and dependency in light of earlier loss and deprivation. Over time, as she continued to explore her experience of vulnerability, she increasingly suspended her protective sense of self-reliance and made growing use of the acceptance, support, and understanding in the therapeutic relationship.

Suttie in Context: Contemporary Perspectives

The contributions of Suttie remain oddly neglected in the psychoanalytic literature. As clinical scholars have emphasized, his conceptions of the therapeutic process foreshadow contemporary views on the crucial role of emotion and relational experience in change and growth (see Bacal & Newman, 1990, pp. 17–27). His theoretical contributions build on Ferenczi's formulations of trauma, relational life, and the therapeutic relationship, and they anticipate Winnicott's conceptions of the holding environment, the role of regression in efforts to work through earlier traumatic experience, and the antisocial tendency. As we will see, he also anticipates key concepts in the writings of Fairbairn and Kohut.

Chapter 6

Psychoanalysis in Great Britain: Melanie Klein and Beyond

I have always been primarily a clinician. It has never happened that I arrived at a concept theoretically and then allowed this concept to guide my clinical work. It has always been the other way round.

—Melanie Klein, Draft Statement, British Psychoanalytical Society Archives

Bold and imaginative thinkers in Great Britain enlarged the field of psychoanalysis beginning in the 1920s and elaborated compelling perspectives that would change the course of psychodynamic understanding. Having established himself as a member of Freud's inner circle in 1912, Ernest Jones founded the British Psychoanalytical Society in 1919, and the emerging psychoanalytic movement drew a divergent group of thinkers and practitioners under his leadership. Many of the early members came from humanistic backgrounds with liberal leanings, and the society included figures from the bohemian world of Bloomsbury. Among them were James Strachey, who would translate Freud's work into the English standard edition; Adrian Stephen, brother of Virginia Woolf; Ella Sharpe, a teacher of literature and head of a teachers' training college; Sylvia Payne, a physician who had been honored for her work with shell-shocked troops during World War I; and John Rickman, a Quaker who had organized medical services in Russia during the war. Melanie Klein and Donald Winnicott joined the society in the 1920s; W. R. D. Fairbairn and John Bowlby followed in the 1930s.

Other thinkers remained uneasy with the orthodoxy of the official psychoanalytic society, however, and came to embrace a more eclectic pluralist perspective, drawing on the work of Adler, Jung, and Ferenczi as well as writings in religion and anthropology and the other social sciences. Many of these practitioners were affiliated with the Tavistock Clinic, one of the first community settings in London to provide low-fee psychotherapy for the working class (for a history of the Tavistock Clinic, see Dicks, 1970). Known informally as "the parson's clinic," its practitioners sponsored the development of an independent depth psychology. Its credo was "No doctrine, only aims," and its "new psychology" came to center on the "whole person" (see Zaretsky, 2004, p. 253). As Peter Homans (1989) observes, many of the clinicians who joined the clinic had never accepted Freud's emphasis on sexuality; what is more, many of them were deeply religious and found Freud "insufficiently hopeful" in his neglect of religious and spiritual life.

The experience of vulnerability, turmoil, and death in the aftermath of World War I was a crucial force in the development of psychoanalytic understanding. England was in a state of mourning following the war, and clinicians were increasingly forced to address the widespread experience of separation, loss, and grief. More than three-quarters of a million men died, about a third of whom were married, leaving behind 248,000 widows and 381,000 children (Newcombe & Lerner, 1981, cited in Homans, 1989, p. 227). Clinical case records, journal articles, and literary evidence confirm that "pathological mourning or grief-related mental problems" were widespread (Newcombe & Lerner, 1981, p. 9).

Although many practitioners were familiar with Freud's classical thought, a growing number of clinicians found his ideas remote from the immediate concerns and problems of their patients, many of whom had been traumatized and lost family members in the war. Thinkers began to develop new theories and therapeutic perspectives that departed from orthodox Freudian thought and increasingly emphasized subjectivity, relational experience, and social life. Three figures, Winnicott, Fairbairn, and Bowlby, introduced original and compelling ways of seeing the human situation that continue to shape thinking in relational psychoanalysis and psychotherapy. The next chapters examine their theoretical perspectives and place their work in the broader context of the Independent Tradition, a group whose practitioners share essential concerns with the field of social work. In order to understand the development of psychoanalytic thought in Great Britain, however, we begin with the work of Melanie Klein, a crucial figure in the transition from drive psychology to relational understanding. With the exception of Suttie, her contributions influenced all the relational theorists in Great Britain—even those who rejected her perspective in toto. As we will see, we can understand the work of Winnicott, Fairbairn, and Bowlby largely as challenges to Kleinian theory.

By her own account, Melanie Klein embraced Freud's psychoanalytic system, emphasizing conceptions of innate instinct and the dynamic unconscious, and she saw her work as an elaboration of his dual drive theory, which he introduced in *Beyond the Pleasure Principle* in 1920. She drew on Freud's view that the infant is born with libidinal and destructive drives—Eros and Thanatos, in his conception—and came to see instinctual forces as core constituents in personality development and behavior. In doing, so, however, she introduced a radically different conception of mind that emphasized subjective experience, fantasy process, and personal meaning. In Klein's vision of the human situation, life is dominated by the urge to love and the urge to destroy, what Harry Guntrip (1971) would later characterize as "a mighty and mysterious inner struggle between the forces of creation and destruction" (p. 58). The fundamental conflict is between love and hate, between life and death, between care for others and their destruction. Aggression, greed, and envy threaten to destroy those whom we love, in her view of the human condition, and the balance between love and hate remains tenuous through life. A growing number of scholars have explored the moral implications of her work, arguing that she sets forth an ethic of responsibility that carries crucial implications for relational and social life (see, e.g., Alford, 1989, 1998; Zaretsky, 2004).

Klein's theory is complex, rendered in a dense, technical language, and a full review of her system is beyond the scope of this chapter. It is essential, however, to understand the defining features of her work and to appreciate the core concepts of her developmental and clinical perspectives, which have remained marginal in the American psychoanalytic literature until recent years. As we will see, her formulations provided key points of departure for Fairbairn and Winnicott in the development of their views, and her contribution continues to inform lines of inquiry in the broader fields of psychoanalysis, neuroscience, cognitive psychology, and social thought.

Life and Work

Klein was born Melanie Reizes in Vienna on March 30, 1882, and lived in London from 1926 until her death on September 22, 1960. Although her colleagues described her as a private and enigmatic figure, she began an autobiography in 1953, which she continued to work on until 1959, shortly before she died. It remained unpublished, however, and her biographer, Phyllis Grosskurth (1986), describes it as "cautious, repetitious, ingenuous, and evasive," reminding us: "Melanie Klein was the stuff of which myths are made" (pp. 3, 4).

Scholars have enlarged Klein's own version of her life over the last quarter century, drawing on unpublished documents and family letters that were discovered in the home of Klein's son in 1983, and recent writings provide careful accounts of her family life. Her father had rebelled against his family's Jewish orthodoxy, choosing to become a physician rather than a rabbi, and he devoted himself to knowledge and learning, reportedly mastering ten languages. Although he was highly educated, he struggled to support his family in Vienna and was forced to work in a dental practice and supplement his income as a medical consultant to a theater. Klein idealized her mother, whom she found more responsive and understanding than her father, and came to see her as a role model for her own development (Sayers, 1991). Grosskurth describes the complexities of her early family life and education, providing a moving account of the influence of her brother, Emanuel; Klein describes him as "my confidant, my friend, my teacher" (qtd. in Grosskurth, 1986, p. 16). She read widely through adolescence and was drawn to the works of Friedrich Nietzsche and Arthur Schnitzler, the playwright. Her dream, she later recalled, was to attend medical school and train as a psychiatrist. She met her future husband, Arthur Klein, when she was seventeen and married him four years later—a decision that she would later regret, she said, because it foreclosed her option to train as a physician. Her husband became a chemical engineer, and the couple settled in the Hungarian province of Liptau. They had three children: Melitta, Hans, and Erich. The marriage was deeply troubled from the beginning, by her accounts, and she left the relationship in 1924 after a long period of unhappiness.

Klein had been moved by Freud's essay "On Dreams" (1901) in 1914, and she pursued her interests in psychoanalysis, captivated by the idea of the unconscious, wanting to train as a clinician. She began an analysis in Budapest with Ferenczi, who encouraged her to pursue therapeutic work with children. She was the first psychoanalyst to use analytic approaches—rather than supportive, educational methods—with children (Alford, 1998). She became a member of the Hungarian psychoanalytic society in 1919 following the presentation of her first paper, "The Development of a Child." Shortly afterward at the invitation of Karl Abraham, a prominent analyst, she moved to Berlin, where she continued to work with children. In time, she began a second analysis with Abraham, which ended with his sudden death in 1926 after only eighteen months. She served as a member of the Berlin Psychoanalytic Institute from 1921 to 1926, when Jones invited her to continue her psychoanalytic work with children in London.

Her thinking and practice increasingly challenged views set forth by Anna Freud, who had continued to develop an ego psychological perspective in accord with her father's metapsychology. In time, Klein and her followers split the psychoanalytic movement into a London school and a Viennese school. Their initial differences centered on clinical technique in psychotherapy of children. Klein believed that children could be analyzed through interpretation of their play, much in the way that free associations were interpreted in psychotherapy of adults; she focused on what she saw as derivatives of instinctual process. Anna Freud argued that children's difficulties originate not in instinctual life but in external conditions—often in the context of the school setting—and held that they cannot make use of interpretive interventions focused on intrapsychic life; she advocated a pragmatic, educational approach. There were major theoretical differences as well, focused on divergent conceptions of mental activity in early infancy, the nature and content of early fantasy processes, defensive operations, and developmental markers and trajectories.

Following Anna Freud's immigration to London in 1938, tensions between the two women intensified, threatening to fracture the British Psychoanalytical Society. In an attempt to preserve the organization, Ernest Jones initiated a series of talks known as the Controversial Discussions, which were held in 1943 and 1944 and intended to clarify their theoretical and clinical differences. The proceedings, held in the midst of World War II, are documented verbatim in a volume edited by Pearl King and Riccardo Steiner (1991). Jones and the other facilitators of the discussions concluded that Anna Freud and Klein were each advancing varying aspects of Freud's thought in light of their particular domains of concern and clinical interests. In order for Anna Freud and Klein to continue their work within the psychoanalytic society, the British analysts decided to establish three independent training sequences: Group A consisted of followers of Klein, Group B those of Anna Freud. Members of the Middle or Independent Group refused to identify themselves with a particular thinker or theoretical perspective and drew on a range of ideas in the broader psychoanalytic landscape. Winnicott, as we will see, emerged as a major figure in this latter group, committed to a theoretical eclecticism, suspicious of dogma and orthodoxy.

Klein continued to conduct her clinical practice, train analysts, and write through the late 1950s. Her major papers are collected in *The Psychoanalysis of Children* (1932), *Contributions to Psycho-analysis, 1921–1945* (1948), *Developments in Psycho-analysis* (1952), *New Directions in Psychoanalysis* (1955), and *Envy and Gratitude* (1957). *Narrative of a Child Analysis* was published in 1961, a year after her death. Hanna Segal wrote a primer on Kleinian theory in 1964. Grosskurth's biography, *Melanie Klein: Her World and Her Work*, written in 1986, provides a scholarly account of her life and her contributions.

Theoretical Perspectives

Klein emphasizes biological drives and subjective domains of experience in her conceptions of psychic life and the development of the self. She believes that the life and death instincts—core constituents in the development of personality—predispose the infant to experience him- or herself and the world as good and bad. In her view of the human condition, life is dominated by the urge to love and the urge to destroy. By virtue of being human, we must negotiate fluctuations between loving, generative feelings originating in the life instinct, and hateful, destructive feelings issuing from the death instinct. As Stephen Mitchell and Margaret Black (1995) are careful to emphasize, Klein sees instinctual impulses as "entire ways of *experiencing* oneself, as 'good' (both loved, loving) or as 'bad' (both hated and destructive)" (p. 91).

The inner world, as rendered by Klein, is a fluid, phantasmagoric landscape of gratifying and frustrating objects; she seeks to offer "a new understanding of the unconscious and of internal relationships as they have never been understood before apart from the poets" (Klein, 1942, qtd. in Zaretsky, 2004, p. 256). In her conception of personality development, both good and bad experiences—originating in the life and death instincts—are projected outward. Projection of the life instinct generates the experience of good objects and gives rise to basic trust. Like Freud, Klein uses the term "object" to refer to an internal representation rather than to an interpersonal relation, as we find in the relational perspectives of Winnicott, Bowlby, and other theorists. The infant projects the experience of the death instinct onto the world of outer objects, which creates a world of malevolent and destructive others.

Good and bad objects—originating in the child's internal experience, independent of actual parental response—are then internalized (or introjected, in Klein's language) to create an inner representational world that is split into good and bad elements. The play of good and bad objects shapes Klein's view of self in early infancy. In Klein's view, real parents, and their loving or frustrating reactions to the child, play little role in the child's experience. Good objects and bad objects are generated from within and appear to operate independently of the actual caretaking experience. For Klein, the most fundamental relationships are internal, occurring between mental objects (see Alford, 1998, p. 121, for critical discussion of these points).

Klein describes two modes of psychic organization and functioning in her account of development: the paranoid-schizoid position, spanning the first six months of life, and the depressive position, which emerges over the second half of the first year. She uses the term "developmental position" to refer to the child's different ways of experiencing and relating to internalized objects and external objects; she defines position as "a specific grouping of anxieties and defenses" that constitute a stance or attitude of the self as a whole. She describes representative anxieties and defenses, specific types of psychological mechanisms, and modes of relating to objects associated with each period. Klein believes that the fundamental processes that characterize each period of development are reconstituted as modes of organizing and processing experience across the course of life. As such they serve defensive functions and influence ways of being and relating.

The paranoid-schizoid position is characterized by primary fears about the preservation of the self that take the form of persecutory anxiety. Klein hypothesizes that the trauma of birth and the loss of intrauterine security predispose the infant to feelings of anxiety and persecution, thus her use of the term "paranoid." She draws on Fairbairn's work in her use of the term "schizoid" to represent the splitting processes that characterize functioning during this period. Experience is fragmentary, fluid, and unstable in these early months, and one cannot yet speak of a core, subjective sense of self. There is not yet an "I" that can interpret experience. It is as if the infant is *lived* by his or her experience; feelings and thoughts are events that happen to the child rather than personal creations that are felt or thought (Ogden,1986). The child does not have the capacity to relate to an intersubjective, ethically meaningful world (Zaretsky, 2004).

The principal means of managing danger is splitting, a dichotomous organization of experience as good or bad that separates the endangered from the endangering. A second defensive process associated with this period is projective identification, an elaboration of the process of splitting, in which the child uses another person to experience that which he or she is unable to experience in him- or herself (for further discussion of these concepts, see Hinshelwood, 1989; Ogden, 1986, p. 65) The early ego is rudimentary, lacking cohesion and coherence, comprised of part-objects; strengths and vulnerabilities are determined chiefly by constitutional factors rather than by environmental conditions. As Ogden (1986) writes, "The relative constitutional endowment of life and death instincts is the major determinant of which code the infant will rely upon to process experience. Experience interpreted in accord with the death instinct will be attributed aggressive and dangerous meanings, whereas experience organized in terms of the life instinct will be understood in terms of nurturing, loving meanings" (p. 65).

In Klein's schema, then, the first developmental task of the infant is to manage the experience of danger that originates in the death instinct. Faced with the threat of internal destructiveness, the child uses the mental operations of splitting and projective identification as defenses and as modes of organizing experience. Splitting allows the child to love safely and to hate safely by holding good and bad objects apart, as if they exist in separate psychic worlds (see Ogden, 1986, pp. 44–45).

The second developmental configuration, emerging over the second half of the first year, is the depressive position, named for the depressive anxiety that marks this period. Conflict over loving and destructive impulses is the defining feature of this position. Splitting recedes as the child matures, and there is an inherent predisposition to integrate experience. Klein theorizes that the child's growing sense of reality brings about the realization that the good and bad objects are really one, and that the parent or primary caretaker—by virtue of being a whole object—has both good and bad elements. With a more developed sense of self, the child realizes that good and bad reside in the same person. The recognition that the good and the bad objects are one serves as the foundation of the depressive position. As Alford (1998) explains, "the world is not divided into black and white; only our primitive mental processes are" (p. 123). The child must come to terms with gray; the task is to develop the capacity for ambivalence. Klein emphasizes that the internal integration of the good and bad parent is a function of cognitive maturation rather than the relative responsiveness of the environment—an assumption that Fairbairn, Winnicott, Bowlby, and other thinkers reject in their relational formulations, arguing that the provisions of caretakers and the nature of the social surround are crucial conditions in the development of the self.

As splitting diminishes and the development proceeds, Klein believes, the child begins to register the cumulative experience of aggression he or she has felt toward the good object. In contrast to the persecutory fears of the paranoid-schizoid position, the predominant fear at this point is harm of the good object. The child begins to experience depressive anxiety, fearful that repeated fantasies of destruction have destroyed the good parent. As Neville Symington (1986) explains: "The baby feels bad and sad because an inner emotional realization dawns that its angry attacks are against not just some unfeeling object but a person with feelings and sensibilities" (p. 268).

The child negotiates the experience of depressive anxiety through reparation. Fantasies and actions that symbolize love and gratitude work to restore a sense of the good parent and reduce feelings of guilt for having felt aggression toward the good object. Expressions of concern and care reflect "a profound urge to make sacrifices," Klein believes (Klein & Riviere, 1964, p. 65). Continued reparative activities strengthen the child's experience of good objects and foster the development of empathy and concern for others, trust, and capacities to give and receive love.

The fundamental task of the depressive position, then, is to establish the other as a whole internal object. This realization constitutes the start of subjectivity. Subjectivity, for Klein, is linked with the recognition that one has harmed or destroyed the internal object on whom one depends. Whereas in the paranoid-schizoid position one forms relations to "part-objects," the depressive position entails efforts to represent "whole objects"—to recognize others as subjects. The essence of the depressive position is that one can achieve safety and security only through responsibility (see Alford, 1989; Ogden, 1986; Zaretsky, 2004, for discussions of the moral and ethical implications of her theory). Klein (1957/1975) writes: "When Goethe said, 'He is the happiest of men who can make the end of his life agree closely with the beginning,' I would interpret 'the beginning' as the early happy relation to the mother which throughout life mitigates hate and anxiety and still gives the old person support and contentment" (p. 204).

Clinical Perspectives

The aim of the therapeutic endeavor, from a Kleinian perspective, is to analyze the relationships between the self and its objects—internal and external—as they are influenced by unconscious instinctual processes. The clinician explores the individual's internal object relationships as they emerge in the therapeutic relationship. The content of interpretive work centers on object relations, anxieties, and defenses associated with the paranoid-schizoid and depressive positions. Conceptions of transference emphasize the unconscious instinctual process rather than patterns of expectation originating in earlier relational life; presumably, one experiences the therapeutic relationship in terms of the early object relations that continue to shape current states of self. The working-through process inevitably involves fluctuations between modes of organization associated with the paranoid-schizoid and depressive positions. At times, for example, the individual experiences the clinician as good, nurturing, and generative, in accordance with the life instinct; at other points, as bad, ruthless, and destructive, in accordance with the death instinct. The assumption is that unconscious organizations of experience generate oscillating periods of hope and dread over the course of intervention.

The clinician's capacity to contain and process the foregoing emotional states is a crucial condition of the therapeutic process. Following classical Kleinian views, clinicians assume that early and deep interpretation of unconscious fantasy reduces the persecutory and depressive anxiety associated with each of the developmental positions. The goals of treatment are to work through unresolved conflicts that have split the psyche, to modify pathological object relational configurations, to integrate and strengthen the self, and to foster development of life-affirming, generative activities. Alford (1998) argues: "For all its concern with greed, hatred, envy, and rage, Kleinian theory and practice are built on hope: that the power of love and gratitude is as natural and powerful as hatred, though infinitely more fragile" (p. 13).

Clinical Applications

Klein's conceptions of the paranoid-schizoid and the depressive positions and the defensive operations of splitting and projective identification deepen understandings of self-organization and modes of interaction in the clinical situation. The following cases illustrate the ways in which clients use splitting and projective identification as defensive operations and re-create internalized object relations through transference states and interactive experience in the therapeutic relationship.

Case Illustration: The Paranoid-Schizoid Position in the Clinical Situation

Allison R., age thirty-three, initiated psychotherapy following the onset of diffuse anxiety states and growing difficulties in managing frustration, anger, and destructive behavior; she was unable to identify precipitating conditions and described a history of global problems in functioning. She had been diagnosed with borderline personality disorder early in her twenties and had received brief periods of supportive psychotherapy in community mental health settings over the past decade.

She experienced fluctuating states of anxiety, dread, and anger and periods of engagement, hope, and possibility as she began psychotherapy. Most of the time, however, she felt a pervasive sense of hatred and destructiveness that she experienced as originating from within herself; she viewed the clinician as bad—"evil"—in these states and showed no capacity to summon alternate experiences of herself or the practitioner as good. From the Kleinian perspective, the mental operation of splitting generated distinct qualities of experience in which there was no middle ground between good and bad.

Allison could not engage an observing self and consider alternate ways of seeing, understanding, and acting. She was unable to process internal states of self or reflect on her behavior; there was no distinction between perception and interpretation of events. The therapist *was* bad in such impersonal, nonreflective states of experience; in Kleinian terms, the history of the therapeutic relationship was negated in order to preserve the split between the loving and hating experience of self and internalized object.

When Allison was identified with the experience of herself as good, however, she saw the clinician as caring, supportive, and helpful and did not recall having felt otherwise; she experienced the "good" clinician and "bad" clinician as different individuals. She had radically different experiences of herself, others, and the world that she could not connect.

From the perspective of the paranoid-schizoid position, Allison generated polarized forms of experience through her use of splitting, which allowed her to love safely and hate safely. There was no connection between her loving self and her destructive self; at her level of development, it was crucial that only one state of self exist at a time. She had not yet established a sense of self that would allow her to process internal states or reflect on her behavior. The practitioner's understanding of phenomena encompassed in Kleinian conceptions of the paranoid-schizoid position and the functions of splitting operations facilitated efforts to contain and process experience in the therapeutic situation; equally important, the developmental perspective helped the practitioner envision how the patient could work toward new modes of organization and enlarge ways of being, relating, and living.

Case Illustration: Splitting and Projective Identification in the Clinical Situation

Robert B., age twenty-eight, began psychotherapy after he was suspended from his job. His supervisor had placed him on leave because he was "unable to get along with people" and urged him to seek counseling to address his anger and interpersonal problems. He acknowledged growing feelings of frustration and anger in interactions with coworkers, whom he characterized as "incompetent" and "deadbeats," and described ongoing patterns of strain, rupture, and loss in his relational life, rendering his experience in absolute terms: "People are with you or against you."

Such splitting operations shaped his perceptions of the clinician, whom he alternatively experienced as "great" and "on my side" or as "useless" and "incompetent." From a Kleinian perspective, he split relationships into good and bad, protecting others from his rage, fearing they would not survive his destructive rage. The practitioner experienced fluctuating periods of vulnerability and aggression in countertransference states, which he understood as a function of the client's use of projective identification, a complex form of splitting where one uses others to experience states that one is unable or unwilling to experience oneself (for further discussion of this concept, see Ogden, 1986, p. 65).

The patient and clinician experienced repeated strain and rupture as they explored underlying vulnerabilities and fears that perpetuated use of such defensive strategies. As the therapeutic process continued, Robert was increasingly able to identify and suspend splitting operations, embody emotion that he had managed through projective identification, and tolerate coexisting experiences of destructive and loving feelings. In time, he began to express frustration and anger toward those whom he realized he also cared for and loved. In doing so, he experienced considerable anxiety, fear, and guilt, consistent with phenomena described in Kleinian conceptions of the depressive position. The clinician processed underlying fears and fantasies in efforts to help Robert enlarge the complexity of experience in his inner life and strengthen relationships in the outer world.

At this point in treatment, he related the following dream: "I am driving down the ramp in a parking garage. You [the clinician] are driving up the ramp. We have a head-on collision, and our cars roll over the edge and fall to the ground. We get out and realize we're not hurt. We've survived. We embrace one another and walk away together." In a Kleinian reading of the dream, Robert moves beyond his split experience of love and hate (represented in the head-on collision) and enters the realm of the depressive position, where self and other are vulnerable but potentially sustaining and enriching in a world of relationship and meaning.

The clinician understood Robert's use of splitting, projective identification, and interpersonal behavior as unconscious efforts to communicate features of early life in contemporary form; as in the preceding case, the developmental perspective helped the clinician engage new possibilities in old ways of being over the course of the therapeutic process (see Mitchell, 1993).

Klein in Context: Contemporary Perspectives

Klein introduced ways of thinking about human experience that anticipate essential concerns in our time focused on the nature of mind, self, and subjectivity. Over the course of her work, she introduced conceptions of internal representation, defensive processes, and self-organization that continue to enrich understandings of personality development, modes of organizing and processing experience, and states of self associated with more severe forms of psychopathology. A number of thinkers, notably Wilfred Bion (1988) and Heinrich Racker (1968), have elaborated core elements of this theoretical system. Thomas Ogden (1986) has argued that Noam Chomsky's concept of deep linguistic structure offers an analog for Klein's instinct theory. In his refashioning of her formulations, we understand her contribution as a theory of inborn codes, originating in the life and death instincts, that organize perception, meaning, and behavior. Ogden reconceptualizes Klein's formulations of the paranoid-schizoid and depressive positions as representative states of being that constitute fundamental aspects of inner life. Alford and Zaretsky have elaborated the moral and ethical implications of her theory. A number of analytical psychologists, including Andrew Samuels (1985) and Anthony Stevens (1990), have drawn parallels between Klein's drive psychology and Jung's concept of archetypes.

In the domain of clinical practice, a number of thinkers, notably Betty Joseph (1989) and Stephen Mitchell (1997), have deemphasized core features of classical Kleinian approaches and placed greater importance on patterns of interpersonal interaction and analysis of here-and-now experience in the therapeutic situation. These developments have generated growing interest in Kleinian thought among a range of interpersonal and relational thinkers (see Mitchell, 1997, for accounts of interactive experience from Kleinian perspectives).

Equally importantly, Klein's ideas have provided critical points of departure for a range of thinkers in the development of alternative relational perspectives. In this sense, she has had a powerful influence on the development of psychoanalytic thought—as much through the rejection of her theories as by their acceptance and elaboration.

Critics of Klein have focused on the implausible assumptions she makes about the inner life of the infant; her emphasis on aggression; her use of pathological terms to describe normative developmental processes; and her failure to take account of actual relationships, particular conditions of caretaking, and real-life experience in the outer world. Klein appears to have had little understanding of the infant-caretaker unit as the basic unit of development at the start of life, as Winnicott emphasizes, and she fails to appreciate the crucial role of the social environment in maturation, health, and well-being. Klein privileges the internal domain of fantasy and does not consider the contribution of social and cultural factors in the development of the self and relational life. As we will see, these concerns provide critical points of departure for Fairbairn and Winnicott in the development of their relational points of view.

As Mitchell and Black (1995) observe, Klein enlarged "the palette of symbols to themes of internality and externality, life and death, blossoming and depletion, thereby making it possible to paint more contemporary themes on the interpretive canvas, for both the individual and social movements in our time" (p. 111).

Chapter 7

W. R. D. Fairbairn: Inner Experience and Outer Realities

I suffered from all the disadvantages of working in comparative isolation; but perhaps a sojourn in the wilderness is not without its advantages.

—W. R. D. Fairbairn, "Object-Relationships and the Dynamic Structure"

William Ronald Dodds Fairbairn introduced what he characterized as an object relations psychology in a series of seminal papers in the 1940s. Although he presented his formulations as if he were extending Freud's work, he challenged the very foundations of classical psychoanalytic theory, carrying out a radical critique of drive psychology. In Fairbairn's view, as we will see, the person is a social being, inherently oriented to others from birth, and the cardinal motivation in human experience is to establish connections with others and preserve relationships across the course of life. The aim of libido is not tension reduction and fulfillment of instinctual desire, as Freud theorized, but the creation of gratifying and meaningful relations with others. For Fairbairn, libido is object seeking, not pleasure seeking. "The clinical material on which this proposition is based," Fairbairn (1946) explains, "may be summarized in the protesting cry of a patient to this effect—'You're always talking about my wanting this and that desire satisfied; but what I really want is a father'" (p. 30).

Although Fairbairn brought a brilliance of mind to psychoanalysis, he worked in what he referred to as the "comparative isolation" of Edinburgh, Scotland, making only brief visits to London, which was rapidly becoming the center of the psychoanalytic movement in Europe, and his contributions remained peripheral for many years. His body of work is highly schematized, intricate, and abstruse, and he appears to have been more interested in reworking psychoanalytic theory than in developing methods of therapeutic practice. Only toward the end of his life, depleted by illness, did he begin to focus on the concrete applications of his ideas in psychosocial intervention. Most clinicians failed to recognize the practical implications of his theorizing.

Over the last quarter century, however, the emergence of relational psychoanalysis has generated considerable interest in his contributions. Jay

Greenberg and Stephen Mitchell (1983) provide a trenchant analysis of his theoretical formulations in their classic study of relational thought, predicting that his work would have "a lasting place and seminal role in the history of psychoanalytic ideas" (p. 176). The Fairbairn Conference, organized by Mitchell and other psychoanalytic scholars in 1996, continued to explore the implications of his ideas for contemporary psychotherapy, philosophy, and the humanities (see Skolnick & Scharff, 1998, for edited versions of conference papers).

Fairbairn's formulations have come to influence conceptions of personality development, self, and social life, and they have informed scholarly work in religious studies, literature, and the arts. In the domain of clinical practice, his perspectives have enlarged understandings of the role of the therapeutic relationship, interpersonal interactions, and experiential learning in efforts to negotiate a range of problems in functioning precipitated by neglect, abuse, and trauma (see, e.g., Borden, 1997, 2000; Celani, 1993; Davies, 1998; Seinfeld, 1990, 1996). His work has deepened ways of understanding subjectivity, defensive processes, transference and countertransference phenomena, and curative factors in psychosocial intervention. The following sections examine the course of Fairbairn's life and work, the core concepts of his developmental psychology, and the implications of his theoretical formulations for psychosocial intervention.

Life and Work

Fairbairn was born in Edinburgh, Scotland, in 1889 and died there on December 31, 1964. He was the only child of a middle-aged couple, and biographical accounts emphasize the austere environment of his family life, which was influenced by the Calvinist values that had shaped Scotland since the Reformation. His father was Presbyterian; his mother was Anglican, having come from a Yorkshire farm family that traced its origins to the Norman times. Both of his parents appear to have to have been devoted to his care and his intellectual development, but they were formal and distant. John Sutherland (1989), his principal biographer, writes that "much of the joyful spontaneity of the ordinary family was missing" in his childhood home (p. 332). In time, Fairbairn would come to see his parents as having failed to establish themselves as strong, loving figures, and were unable to support his natural development.

He entered the Merchiston Castle School at age nine, following a Latin and Greek curriculum, and completed his secondary education there. He developed a deep interest in philosophy and enrolled in Edinburgh University, where he received a master's degree with honors in 1911. Although he was introverted by nature, reserved, and diffident in his manner, he took part in student organizations devoted to social concerns and developed close friendships with those who shared his interests. His practical Christianity was deep rooted and authentic, Sutherland (1989) observes, and it motivated his voluntary activities with youths in impoverished areas of Edinburgh. After he received his master's degree, he pursued postgraduate studies in Hellenistic Greek and divinity at the universities of Kiel, Strasbourg, and Manchester, following his plan to become a Presbyterian minister.

His preparation for the ministry was interrupted, however, by the First World War. He entered the Royal Garrison Artillery and then volunteered for overseas service in Egypt, taking part in the Palestinian campaign. In the course of the war, he discovered the writings of Freud and Jung and developed an interest in depth psychology and practical means of helping others. He abandoned his plan to enter the ministry and decided to enroll in medical school, intending to train as a psychotherapist. Just as Suttie's experience of war was a formative experience in his move into psychiatry, Fairbairn's military service clearly shaped his decision to study psychotherapy; the most powerful influence, according to his daughter, appears to have been his visit to the W. H. R. Rivers Hospital for shell-shocked soldiers in 1916 (see Fairbairn Birtles, 1998).

Fairbairn began medical school in 1918 and received his degree in 1923. That same year he entered psychoanalysis with Ernest Connell, a Jungian-oriented psychotherapist who had been analyzed by Ernest Jones, and began a psychiatric residency at the Royal Edinburgh Hospital. In 1926, at the age of thirty-seven, he married Mary More Gordon, a medical student. They had five children between 1927 and 1933; two of them, twins, died at birth. Fairbairn began an independent practice in psychotherapy shortly after he was married and took a position as psychiatrist at the Edinburgh University Psychological Clinic for Children; he also served as a lecturer in psychology at the university from 1927 to 1935.

In the course of his education he had been deeply influenced by ancient Greek philosophy—Aristotle was particularly important—and by the Continental philosophers, including Immanuel Kant, G. W. F. Hegel, Gottfried Wilhelm Leibnitz, and Friedrich Nietzsche. His thinking was also shaped by the English philosophers Thomas Hobbes and George Berkeley, David Hume, and William James (see Grotstein, 1998). Having been trained in philosophy, Fairbairn brought an intellectual rigor to his study of personality and social problems, rejecting the impersonal methods of scientific materialism in favor of humanistic approaches that carried the potential to account for the unique qualities of the person as an individual (Sutherland, 1994).

Fairbairn became an associate member of the British Psychoanalytical Society in 1931, on the basis of a clinical paper he had presented to the group, and he was made a full member several years later. He kept his distance from the society, however, limiting his contact largely to episodic communications with Ernest Jones and Edward Glover. Jones encouraged him to establish a clinical practice in London, but he chose to remain in Edinburgh. Fairbairn (1946) reflected: "I suffered from all the disadvantages of working in comparative isolation; but perhaps a sojourn in the wilderness is not altogether without its compensations. For, if the isolated worker lacks the stimulus that comes from exchanges of thought with his fellow-workers, at any rate he does not lack the stimulus that comes from the necessity to work out for himself the problems which he encounters. . . . He is thus afforded an unusual opportunity to reconsider classic problems from a new approach" (p. 36). In spite of his geographic isolation, he was deeply influenced by the work of Melanie Klein. As we will see, he drew on core concepts of her theoretical perspective in forming his relational point of view.

Like Suttie, Fairbairn was particularly attuned to the ways in which adverse social conditions perpetuate problems in living. His clinical practice was guided by a social consciousness and a deep commitment to service, and he cared for vulnerable families from the impoverished areas of Edinburgh. As we will see, his work with abused and neglected children informed the development of his theoretical perspective in crucial ways.

Fairbairn's wife died suddenly in 1952. Although their relationship had been taxed by growing strain and conflict as a result of his wife's alcoholism and his emotional distance and absorption in professional activities, he was deeply attached to her, and he experienced intense grief following her death. He remarried in 1959 and died in 1964 from Parkinson's disease. Sutherland, whom Fairbairn had analyzed in the 1930s, and Harry Guntrip, who provided a moving account of his analysis with him in the 1950s, would develop his concepts and attempt to introduce his work to the wider psychoanalytic community. Even so, his work remained poorly understood and largely unappreciated until the emergence of relational psychoanalysis in the 1980s.

Fairbairn published his major papers in *Psychoanalytic Studies of the Personality,* which appeared in 1952. As he explains, the work does not provide the "systematic elaboration of an already established point of view, but the progressive development of a line of thought" (Fairbairn, 1944/1952a, p. 133). The collection contains a series of essays written in the early 1940s that form the core of his theoretical system, including "Schizoid Factors in the Personality" (1940), which describes his conception of the splitting processes that shape the development of the self; "A Revised Psychopathology of the Psychoses and Psychoneuroses" (1941), which outlines phases of dependence that mediate the development of personality; "The Repression and Return of Bad Objects (with Special Reference to the 'War Neuroses')" (1943), which explores defensive organizations of self that allow children to preserve attachments to parental caretakers by blaming themselves for bad experiences (see Fairbairn, 1940/1952d); and "Endopsychic Structure Considered in Terms of Object-Relationships" (1944), which examines the ways in which the vicissitudes of dependency in the caretaking situation influence the development of the self. Other papers, including an autobiographical account and his only essay on the implications of his theory for therapeutic

practice, are collected in a volume edited by David Scharff and Elinor Fairbairn Birtles, *From Instinct to Self: Selected Papers of W. R. D. Fairbairn*
(1994). The most comprehensive biography is Sutherland's work, *Fairbairn's Journey into the Interior* (1989). Judith Hughes (1989) provides a
brief but engaging biographical account in her historical study of Fairbairn,
Winnicott, and Klein.

Theoretical Perspectives

Fairbairn introduced conceptions of personality development, mental structure, and psychopathology that constituted the most radical break with
Freudian thought since the writings of Suttie, his Scottish predecessor. According to Freud's drive psychology, as we have seen in chapter 2, the infant
is born unrelated to others, seeking pleasure; the baby comes to form connections with others only because they reduce tensions and gratify instinctual longings. Fairbairn offers an alternative conception of the child. The
baby is a social being, oriented to others from the start of life, and the ego,
present at birth, structures efforts to engage others and form relationships.
The self, the core of the person, is constructed in the give-and-take of relational life, and the need for connection and relationship continues to shape
behavior across the life course.

Fairbairn had become a member of the British Psychoanalytical Society
as Melanie Klein was developing her ideas, and he drew on her conceptions
of internal objects and internalized object relations in fashioning his theoretical system. In doing so, however, he rejected her drive psychology and
introduced a relational point of view, seeing inner representational worlds
not as a function of instinctual process but as an outcome of interpersonal
experience. For Klein, as we have seen, internal objects originate in the life
and death instincts and serve as primary modes of processing experience. In
Fairbairn's schema, however, the self is constituted and structured through
internalization and representation of interpersonal experience. The "badness" of an object, Fairbairn emphasizes, is an internalized aspect of others
whom the child has *experienced* as inadequate, withholding, hostile, rejecting, alluring, or abusive. He thereby departs from the intrapsychic one-body
psychology of Klein and engages the particularity of relational life, for good
and for ill, in the social surround.

Personality Development

In his developmental psychology, Fairbairn centers on the experience of
dependency in the parent-child relationship and the ways in which interactions with caretaking figures shape the organization of the ego and the configuration of internalized object relations. Like Suttie, he conceives of personality development as a maturational sequence of relations with others,

focusing on progressive experiences of dependency, interdependence, and individuation over the course of parental caretaking (Fairbairn, 1946). He describes three phases in the development of the self, which are summarized briefly here. The first period, the stage of infantile dependence, is characterized by the "one-way dependence" of the child on the parental caregiver and the attitude of "taking"; the infant is merged in a "primary identification" with the caretaking figure. As maturation proceeds, the child increasingly relates to others as differentiated objects in the transitional stage. The third phase, mature dependence, is characterized by mutuality, giving and receiving, and the capacity to recognize and value difference in relational life.

Fairbairn emphasizes the individuality of the infant and the crucial role of attunement, empathy, and responsiveness in the caretaking experience. The child must feel loved in a deeply personal way, he believes, and come to know that his or her love is received and valued by others. Although the child generally experiences the caretaker as good, in his account of development, there are inevitable lapses, disruptions, and deprivations in relational life that generate frustration, rejection, and trauma. Under such conditions, the child experiences the parental caretaker as bad. Such failings create a dilemma for the infant, as the baby cannot tolerate coexisting experiences of the caretaker as good *and* bad. The vulnerability and the dependency of early life force the child to search for a solution that preserves the experience of the caregiver as good and protects him or her from the consequences of unmet needs.

In Fairbairn's schema, the child negotiates the vicissitudes of the caretaking situation by internalizing the experience of inadequate caretakers; the child "incorporates" the object as a first defense in an effort to manage the pain of frustration (Fairbairn, 1944/1952a). The infant cannot control the behavior of unresponsive or depriving parental figures, he reasons, but the child *can* attempt to control the "badness" by relocating it within the self, where it assumes the form of "internal objects" that serve as substitutes for problematic relationships with actual people (for elaboration, see Greenberg & Mitchell, 1983, p. 159). A sector of the ego or self remains related to real figures in the outer world, but other parts of the ego or self are bound to internalized objects that represent unresponsive features of parental caretakers. Ongoing internalization processes, precipitated by the experience of unavailable or depriving caretakers, foster splitting operations that structure the ego in a tripartite fashion. Fairbairn is proposing, then, that the frustrations and failings inherent in the caretaking situation activate universal defensive processes—internalization and splitting—that shape the development of inner structures within the ego.

He describes the structuring of the ego as the "basic endopsychic situation" (Fairbairn, 1944/1952a, p. 112). The ego is split into three sectors, each of which corresponds to a different experience of the caretaking figure. By dividing the caregiver into good and bad elements, the child is able to maintain dependent ties with parental figures and split off distressing features of the relationship; the infant can love safely and hate safely. The outcome is an inner world that is divided into good and bad internal objects, each of which corresponds to gratifying and frustrating features of the caretaker.

The good internal object or "ideal object" embodies the comforting and rewarding aspects of the caretaker that foster the experience of feeling loved and worthy. The bad object takes two potential forms, both of which are repressed in efforts to manage the anxiety and pain of rejection. One version is the "exciting object," which emerges out of interactions with the caretaker who generates expectation and hope but fails to follow though and fulfill needs and desires; the child comes to feel frustrated and empty. The second version is the "rejecting object," created through interactions with the caretaking figure whom the child experiences as hostile and withdrawing. The child feels unloved, unwanted, and angry. These two renderings of bad inner objects and the ideal object constitute a tripartite organization of the child's inner world.

Each of the foregoing inner objects generates states of self through a process that Fairbairn calls parallel ego splitting. As the child internalizes the features of parental caretakers and establishes them as inner objects, he theorizes, sectors of the ego are split off from their original unity and bound in an internal object relationship. Ego and object are inextricably linked. "The ego is unthinkable except as bound up with objects. It grows through relations with objects, both real and internal, like a plant through contact with soil, water and sunlight. Objects are necessary for the ego to survive and flourish" (Greenberg & Mitchell, 1983, p. 165). The alluring experience of the caretaker, associated with the "exciting object," fosters the development of the "infantile libidinal ego." In this mode of organization, the child is ever longing but never satisfied and feels perpetually frustrated and deprived. The rejecting experience of the caretaker generates the development of the "internal saboteur" or "anti-libidinal ego"; in this mode of organization, the child longs for love and acceptance but feels hateful, fearing that he or she is unlovable.

The "central ego," linked with the gratifying aspects of the caretaker, is the complement to the ideal object. The central ego mediates interaction with real people in the outer word. For Fairbairn, health is realized in the capacity to establish relationships and to engage in give-and-take with actual individuals in the social surround; the individual is oriented to external reality and lives in the world of others (see Mitchell & Black, 1995, for further development of these points).

Although Klein's work was a major influence on the development of his thinking, his theoretical formulations were also shaped by his clinical practice. In the course of his work with abused and neglected children, he was moved by the intensity of their attachment to the parental caretakers who had harmed them (Fairbairn Birtles, 1998). He writes: "At one time it fell to my lot to examine quite a large number of delinquent children from homes which the most casual observer could hardly fail to recognize as 'bad' in the crudest sense—homes, for example, in which drunkenness, quarreling and physical violence reigned supreme. It is only in the rarest instances, however[,] . . . that I can recall such a child being induced to admit, far less volunteering, that his parents were bad objects" (Fairbairn, 1943/1952b, p. 64).

In spite of their traumatic experience, he found, many of the children failed to recognize or acknowledge the implications of their neglect and abuse; instead, they excused their parents' violations and put forth their own moral shortcomings as justification for their parents' neglect and abuse. He saw such strategies as desperate attempts to preserve self-bonds with parental caretakers (Fairbairn, 1943/1952b).

In a move that closely follows Suttie's thinking, Fairbairn theorized that the child attempts to deny the parents' badness by internalizing the destructive elements and preserving the parent as good. This strategy allows the child to sustain the illusion of control in a situation in which he or she is relatively helpless. Fairbairn (1943/1952b) writes: "It is better to be a sinner in a world ruled by God than to live in a world ruled by the Devil. A sinner in a world ruled by God may be bad; but there is always a certain sense of security to be derived from the fact that the world around is good. . . . In a world ruled by the Devil, the individual may avoid being a sinner; but he is bad because the world around him is bad. Further, he can have no sense of security and no hope of redemption" (pp. 66–67).

He theorized that children come to experience abusive behavior as a mode of connection; as Mitchell and Black (1995) observe, "children become powerfully attached to and build their subsequent emotional lives around the kinds of interactions they had with early caregivers" (p. 116). Fairbairn described the paradox by which the child preserves the integrity of inner life by perpetuating destructive ties that continue to threaten his or her well-being.

Psychopathology

The splitting of the ego is universal in Fairbairn's developmental psychology, and all people suffer varying degrees of psychopathology as a consequence of constraints and failings in the caretaking experience. The greater the fragmentation of the ego, Fairbairn assumes, the more severe the psychopathology. In an effort to deal with the pain of unavailable, unresponsive, or abusive caretakers, he theorizes, the child establishes internal objects that serve as substitutes for unfulfilling relationships with actual figures. Fairbairn (1941/1952c) views these objects as compensatory; the greater the degree of disruption and deprivation in relationships with "natural objects"—real people—the greater the need to establish relationships with inner objects.

Although the internalization process restores an experience of the other as good, Fairbairn (1943/1952b) emphasizes that outer security is achieved at the price of fragmentation and inner insecurity, "since it leaves the ego at the mercy of internal persecutors" (p. 65). The sense of safety that follows from the internalization of inadequate caretakers, Fairbairn explains, is compromised by the pernicious elements that have been relocated within the self: the child attempts to manage the pain through repression, the earliest form of defense—the bad objects are "banished to the unconscious" (p. 65). If repression fails, however, the individual must resort to other defensive operations that generate a range of symptoms, taking the form of "paranoid," "hysterical," "obsessive," and "phobic" behavior (Fairbairn, 1951/1952e, p. 163). He regards such symptoms not as psychopathology per se but rather as techniques of managing disruptions in relational life.

In Fairbairn's schema, the inner structuring of the ego or self influences actual behavior in the outer world. He envisions the basic endopsychic structure, or split ego, as a closed system. Representative ways of being and relating, established in interactions with early caretakers, are projected in contemporary relational life, skewing perceptions of self and others, perpetuating constricted patterns of functioning that generate vicious circles of behavior.

The most severe psychopathology, in Fairbairn's view, assumes the form of schizoid states, which originate in the unresponsiveness of parental caretakers during the earliest phase of dependency. In his schema, as we have seen, the child's most fundamental need at the start of life is to love and to be loved; the first object relationship is organized around this task. If the infant's love is rejected, however, the child comes to feel that his or her love is unacceptable—a tragic turn in Fairbairn's developmental psychology. The experience of deprivation intensifies the child's need for the object; the desire may be so strong, Fairbairn imagines, that the child wants to devour the object in order to possess it.

In his conception of the schizoid dilemma, every move toward the object generates the fear of destroying it because of the intensity of the need; one can protect and preserve the object only by withdrawing from it. The schizoid situation—the intense need for the object and fear of destroying it through connection—predisposes the individual to a range of vulnerabilities and problems in functioning.

Fairbairn describes the most prominent features of the schizoid character as preoccupation with inner reality, a sense of omnipotence, and an attitude of detachment and isolation. In time, however, he would trace a wide range of problems in living to unfulfilled longings for dependence and schizoid sectors of the self.

Clinical Perspectives

The fundamental task of psychoanalytic psychotherapy, from Fairbairn's perspective, is to restore the integrity of the self and to strengthen the capacity for core-to-core connection with actual people in the outer world. In "On the Nature and Aims of Psychoanalytic Treatment" (1958), his only writing on the implications of his object relations theory for clinical practice, Fairbairn emphasizes the ways in which the traumatic failings of relational life predispose individuals to problems in living. The person has preserved internal representational worlds as defensive, closed systems, deflecting contemporary relational experience that carries the potential for actual connection, closeness, and growth. One interprets new situations along the lines of old problematic relationships, and the ongoing cycle of projection and re-internalization of self-other configurations perpetuates maladaptive modes of functioning.

Fairbairn (1958/1994) emphasizes the protective functions of resistance in the therapeutic situation: "I have now come to regard . . . the greatest of all sources of resistance [to be] the maintenance of the patient's internal world as a closed system" (p. 84). One has come to feel connected to others, in the real world and in internal presences, through painful states of self and maladaptive patterns of behavior. The fear is that renunciation of such ways of being and relating will lead to annihilation of the self and abandonment by others. The task of therapeutic intervention, he continues, is to "effect breaches of the closed system which constitutes the patient's inner world, and thus to make this world accessible to the influence of outer reality." The therapeutic process, then, seeks to open the system and restore the unity of the self.

In Fairbairn's view, the person must experience the "badness" of his or her internal objects, renegotiate pathological attachments, and establish more fulfilling ways of being and relating with actual people in the outer world. Transference states provide crucial points of entry into the individual's inner world of object relations; he describes transference as the patient's "counter effort" to bring the clinician into his or her inner world. As long as this world remains self-contained, he explains, it is not amenable to change, and the result is a "static internal situation" (Fairbairn, 1958; see Summers, 1994, p. 47).

In Fairbairn's conception of the therapeutic situation, then, as Stephen Mitchell and Margaret Black observe, the patient inevitably experiences the clinician as a familiar bad object. The basic modes of connection established in the past, preserved in representations of self and others, shape one's view of the clinician. On one hand, if the psychotherapist is not experienced through old patterns, the clinician is not important, and one is not deeply engaged in the therapeutic process. On the other hand, they wonder, if the clinician is experienced *only* along the lines of old problematic relationships, how can anything new and different follow? One cannot relinquish powerful addictive bonds to old objects unless one believes that new and better connections to others are possible; one must come to believe in responsive and generative modes of relationship (Mitchell & Black, 1995).

Fairbairn came to see the relationship between the patient and the therapist as *the* crucial element in change and growth, and he viewed it as far more influential than interpretive work focused on genetic reconstruction or analysis of transference phenomena. He was increasingly critical of the impersonal style of interpretation that characterized classical psychoanalytic practice. "In my own opinion," he writes, "the really decisive factor is the relationship of the patient to the analyst, and it is upon this relationship that the other factors . . . depend not only for their effectiveness, but for their very existence, since in the absence of a therapeutic relationship with the analyst, they simply do not occur" (Fairbairn, 1958/1994, pp. 82–83).

Fairbairn's work increasingly pointed to the importance of the human qualities of the clinician and the real relationship in the therapeutic situation (Skolnick & Scharff, 1998). He reasons that one cannot expect inner object configurations to change through interpretive work alone; interpretations can be transformative only in the context of a relationship with "a reliable and beneficent parental figure" (Fairbairn, 1958, p. 379). Such an individual provides an attuned, responsive object relationship that can mediate the effects of earlier traumatic relationships. In time, Fairbairn revised his methods of intervention in efforts to strengthen the therapeutic relationship. He ended his use of the traditional analytic couch because he believed that it undermined the establishment of the relationship, replacing it with facing chairs, and he challenged what he saw as the restrictive conditions of the classical psychoanalytic frame, arguing that clinicians should use flexible individualized approaches that address the changing needs and capacities of the client. The attuned, empathic figure of the clinician facilitates the release of internalized bad objects without threat of attack or abandonment.

Clinical Applications

Although Fairbairn's theoretical formulations are framed in abstract philosophical terms, his formulations have practical implications for the ways we understand self-defeating or destructive patterns of behavior, process interactive experience in the clinical situation, and facilitate change and growth over the course of psychosocial intervention.

Presumably, conditions of deprivation and trauma over the course of development undermine efforts to establish adequate representations of good object experiences, and the absence of sustaining others within creates particular challenges in therapeutic efforts to address the deficits, defenses, and conflicts that have limited development of the self and constricted interpersonal functioning. As Jeffrey Seinfeld (1996) observes in his applications of Fairbairn's theory, individuals who have been subject to trauma can "feel the dread of falling into a psychic black hole when they lack a securely held internal good object. Thus in separating from internal bad objects they are left with a void. The tenacious clinging to bad objects implies the lack of a good internal object to hold the space of separation" (p. 14).

If those who have suffered lapses in care and trauma are to release themselves from their internal persecutors, he writes, they must come to internalize their clinician as a good-enough object. Seinfeld, like Fairbairn, believes that interpretive work deepens the patient's understanding of the traumatic effects of earlier experience and, in doing so, facilitates efforts to separate from bad internal objects. The decisive factor in the therapeutic process, however, as Fairbairn stresses, is the therapeutic relationship itself. Seinfeld emphasizes the importance of holding and containment in the therapeutic situation as individuals negotiate their experience of rage and despair. Over time, Seinfeld believes, the patient internalizes the therapist as a containing object, thereby strengthening efforts to mediate the destructive features of bad object representations, integrate split-off sectors of inner experience, and proceed with the development of more sustaining and responsive relationships.

Case Illustration: The Moral Defense

Loren S. initiated a therapeutic consultation at a family service agency shortly after her twenty-sixth birthday. She related that she had been involved in a series of conflicted and abusive relationships following graduation from high school and had just left her boyfriend of nearly a year after he initiated an affair with her close friend. She felt a pervasive sense of helplessness and hopelessness in reflecting on the end of the relationship and wanted to understand why she continued to find herself involved with abusive partners.

In the course of the interview, she related that her stepfather had sexually abused her in early adolescence. She emphasized, however, that she was responsible for the experience. She characterized her father as "a good, loving man" and described herself as flawed: "I have not lived the right life. . . . I deserved what I got. . . . I asked for it." In spite of her idealized accounts of her stepfather and mother, she described a history of deprivation and abuse through childhood and adolescence.

As Fairbairn observed, children whose parents abuse and neglect them seldom have access to attuned, responsive caretakers who can help them process the experience of violation and trauma. In his understanding, they turn to their abusers for comfort instead and often continue this pattern of relationship into adulthood, searching for partners who perpetuate earlier ways of being and relating.

As Fairbairn shows in his formulation of the moral defense, children assume that a bad parent is better than no caretaker at all and believe that they were treated badly because they *are* bad. They appear to be devoted to the abusive internal object, seemingly unable to relinquish their attachment. As he explains, the individual's internalized badness has been used as a defense against the realization of how badly he or she has been treated. In light of this dynamic, a central task in intervention is to help the individual locate the "badness" in others who have harmed him or her rather than carry it within as an experience of self.

In anticipating the course of Loren's psychotherapy, the clinician realized that it would be crucial to help her reconstruct critical events from her family life and explore the ways in which she felt responsible for the violation and deprivation that had occurred. The clinician would challenge her experience of "badness," contrasting her conclusions with alternate interpretations of events. In the course of the process, the practitioner expected, it was likely that Loren would develop intense transference states, given the strength of the bond with her stepfather and mother. It would be crucial to analyze transference enactments and continue to process family experience in light of her reactions in the clinical situation. Over the course of intervention, the practitioner would seek to help Loren understand the origins of her destructive relationships with men, develop a more affirming view of herself, and strengthen her capacities to establish and develop constructive, fulfilling relationships.

Case Illustration: Reworking Internal Representations

The case of Anne A. provides an illustration of the ways in which the therapeutic situation challenges connections to internalized objects that perpetuate problems in living. In the middle phase of the therapeutic process, she related that she had felt "deeply understood" by the clinician in the preceding session. She had decided to initiate a job search, overriding her parents' view that she should remain in her current position because it was secure, "a sure thing." She explained, however, that on leaving the clinic, she had found herself disoriented and frightened. On arriving home, she related, she had stuck her fingers down her throat, making herself vomit. She felt an "odd calm" afterward.

Exploration of her experience revealed a fundamental conflict between two different modes of experiencing herself in the therapeutic situation. When she felt the clinician understood her "real self" and encouraged her to pursue her interests and goals, she felt a sense of hope and possibility; at the same time, she found herself frightened—"I'm not myself"—and restored a familiar experience of herself as "my mother's daughter." In this state, she would suspend her deepest experience of need and desire—"Who do I think I am, anyway, to imagine finding a new job?"—and comply with her parents' version of who she should be. The more authentic she was in her expressions of self, the more threatened she felt.

As Mitchell and Black (1995) observe, it is only in living through such moments in the therapeutic situation, "moments that stand outside old patterns, containing states of mind that are 'out of character,' that the patient gradually begins to believe in and become able to commit herself to new modes of relatedness" (p. 123).

In the context of Fairbairn's thought, the clinician had challenged her attachment to internalized objects in encouraging her to pursue her personal goals, and she struggled to mediate the conflict between her devotion to the internalized experience of her parents and her growing need to individuate and give expression to more authentic, fulfilling ways of being, relating, and living.

Fairbairn in Context: Contemporary Perspectives

Fairbairn introduced an original perspective that offers a radical alternative to Freud's drive psychology, placing relationship, rather than instinctual process, at the center of human life. In refashioning Kleinian concepts from a relational perspective, he introduced new conceptions of internal representation, defensive processes, and self-organization, emerging as the principal architect of contemporary object relations theory. He has deepened appreciation of the subjective nature of relational life and provided ways of conceptualizing interactive features of the therapeutic process that present challenges in psychosocial intervention with a range of vulnerable groups.

Sutherland (1994) extended Fairbairn's work over the course of his writing, exploring the ways in which individuals elaborate relational involvements through participation in family, group, and community life. Guntrip (1971) provided careful accounts of Fairbairn's work and introduced significant revisions and elaborations of his theory of the self and object relations concepts (see Greenberg & Mitchell, 1983, for analysis of Guntrip's theoretical contributions). In the field of social work, Seinfeld has explored the implications of Fairbairn's contribution for psychosocial intervention, focusing on the dynamics of the therapeutic process and use of relational elements in treatment of psychotic, borderline, schizoid, and depressive states of self. His contributions are explored by James Grotstein and Donald Rinsley in *Fairbairn and the Origins of Object Relations* (1994) and in a series of papers presented at the Fairbairn Conference in New York entitled *Fairbairn, Then and Now* (1998), edited by Neil Skolnick and David Scharff.

Chapter 8

D. W. Winnicott and the Facilitating Environment

Psychotherapy is not a matter of making clever and apt interpretations; by and large it is a long-term giving back what the patient brings. It is a complex derivative of the face that reflects what is there to be seen. I like to think of my work this way, and to think that if I do this well enough the patient will find his or her own self, and will be able to exist and feel real.

—D. W. Winnicott, *Playing and Reality*

Donald Woods Winnicott was a pediatrician before he trained as a psychoanalyst, and he continued to practice medicine as he carried out his work as a psychotherapist, writer, and educator in London. His colleagues estimate that he saw more than 60,000 cases over the course of his career. His theoretical formulations are grounded in the concrete particulars of the clinical situation, following his empirical disposition and pragmatic sensibilities. His "experiments in adapting to need," as he called his therapeutic interventions, are shaped by a deep interest in observation and empathy (Phillips, 1988). As a leading representative of the Independent Tradition in Great Britain, he was uneasy with grand theory, ever suspicious of abstraction and dogma, refusing to ally himself with the orthodoxy of Melanie Klein or Anna Freud.

Winnicott elaborated a series of concepts that have shaped ways of understanding crucial features of human development: the "good enough" caretaker, the "holding environment," and the "transitional object," a term he used to characterize the special blanket, teddy bear, or toy that children use to comfort themselves early in life. When Winnicott introduced the concept of the transitional object, André Green (1978) has observed, he saw "what had been escaping everyone's attention" and discovered the unnoticed obvious (p. 179). Over the course of his teaching and writing he set forth a series of developmental perspectives that have enlarged conceptions of self and personality development; vulnerability, problems in living, and psychopathology; health, well-being, and the common good; and curative elements in therapeutic practice.

He is increasingly recognized as one of the most creative thinkers in psychoanalysis since Freud, and his theories have informed contemporary lines of inquiry in child development, family studies, sociology, education, the humanities, philosophy, religion, and social work. This chapter provides an introduction to Winnicott's life and work, the core concepts of his developmental psychology and corresponding formulations of vulnerability and psychopathology, and the implications of his theoretical formulations for psychosocial intervention. The biographical overview and summary of his contributions is an expanded version of an earlier synopsis (Borden, 2001).

Life and Work

Winnicott was born on April 7, 1896, in the English coastal city of Plymouth, Devon, a stronghold of the Wesleyan tradition, and he died in London on January 22,1971. He was the only son of Frederick and Elizabeth Winnicott, who had two daughters, ages five and six, at the time of his birth. His father, a merchant, was twice mayor of Plymouth and knighted for civic work, and Winnicott developed a strong appreciation of public service and community life through his father's example. One biographer, F. Robert Rodman (2003), characterizes Winnicott's early life as "an idyllic, turn-of-the century English provincial childhood" and sees him as having had "deep roots in a nurturing environment, leading logically to the good-natured and clever pediatrician-psychoanalyst who understood children, mothers, and deeply disturbed patients" (p. 11).

He was drawn to literature, music, and natural history as an adolescent. At the age of fourteen, he entered the Leys School, a Methodist public school in Cambridge described in James Hilton's novel *Goodbye, Mr. Chips*. He developed a strong interest in Darwin that would lead him to study the life sciences in college. Winnicott recalled his discovery of *The Origin of the Species* as a youth in a talk for students at St. Paul's School shortly before this fiftieth birthday: "I could not leave off reading it. At the time I did not know why it was so important to me, but I see now that the main thing was that it showed that living things could be examined scientifically with the corollary that gaps in knowledge and understanding need not scare me. For me this idea meant a great lessening of tension and consequently a release of energy for work and play" (qtd. in Davis & Wallbridge, 1981, p. 24).

He received a degree in biology from Cambridge University, and he began medical studies at Jesus College, Cambridge. His training was interrupted by World War I, however, and he served as a medical officer in the navy before completing his education at St. Bartholomew's Hospital in London. He married Alice Taylor in 1922. She was a painter, sculptor, and musician, and they shared artistic and cultural interests. She began to show signs of mental illness soon after the wedding, however, and he would eventually leave the relationship, having been depleted as her caretaker.

Winnicott became interested in psychoanalysis in his early twenties after reading Freud's *The Interpretation of Dreams*, and he decided to pursue analytic training at the start of his medical practice. He was the first pediatrician to train as a psychoanalyst in Great Britain. His first analysis, with James Strachey, lasted a decade. Strachey himself had been analyzed by Freud, and he would prepare the standard translation of his writings into English. Winnicott completed a second course of analytic treatment lasting six years with Joan Riviere, a devoted follower of Klein. He worked closely with Klein herself in the 1930s. Although he initially regarded Klein as a mentor and treated her son in psychoanalysis from 1935 to 1939, he eventually rejected her intrapsychic model of human development in view of his growing belief in the crucial role of actual relationships and the conditions of the social surround in the maturation of the child. He continued to elaborate his developmental perspectives in the course of his clinical practice, teaching, and community service and, in doing so, would come to challenge classical psychoanalytic views of personality, psychopathology, and psychotherapy.

More than six million people were evacuated from England's cities and relocated in the countryside following the Blitz in 1940. Winnicott documented the emotional problems of children who had been separated from their parents during the evacuations and was appointed psychiatric consultant to the Government Evacuation Scheme in Oxfordshire. Working with Clare Britton, a social worker whom he married in 1951, Winnicott helped organize evacuation hostels for homeless children, many of whom had experienced earlier deprivation and loss. His supervision of psychosocial intervention with troubled adolescents during this period shaped his formulation of the "antisocial tendency." He traced the origins of antisocial behavior to disruptions in the caretaking environment and understood delinquent behavior as a symbolic attempt to compensate for earlier deprivations of love and care.

Winnicott emerged as the leading representative of the Independent Tradition in British psychoanalysis in the late 1940s and served two terms as president of the British Psychoanalytical Society. Britton became a social work educator and served on the faculty of the London School of Economics, where she headed the child concentration. She arranged for Winnicott to join the faculty as a lecturer, teaching courses on human development and mental health in the social work program.

In 1923 Winnicott had joined the medical staff of Queen's Hospital for Children and Paddington Green Hospital for Children, where he would practice as a pediatrician and child psychiatrist for forty years. His prominence as a pediatrician is frequently compared to that of Benjamin Spock in the United States, and his radio broadcasts, sponsored by the British Broadcasting Corporation between 1939 and 1962, helped generations of parents attend to the emotional needs of their children.

He focused on the central importance of the infant-mother relationship in his talks and emphasized the crucial functions of empathic attunement and responsive caretaking in the development of health and well-being. He believed that mothers are naturally prepared to foster their child's maturational processes, and his use of such terms as "ordinary devoted mother" and "good enough mother" reflected his faith in caretakers' abilities to recognize changing needs and respond accordingly. The father provides ongoing support and care for the mother-child couple in his conceptions of parenting and thereby strengthens the holding environment.

In addition to his broadcasts, he lectured widely on child development for parents, policy makers, social workers, teachers, clergy, judges, physicians, nurses, midwives, and psychotherapists. He published more than six hundred papers between 1931 and 1970. A number of his collections of writings, most notably *The Maturational Process and the Facilitating Environment* (1965), *Playing and Reality* (1971), and *Therapeutic Consultations in Child Psychiatry* (1971), have become classic works in the fields of psychoanalysis and social work. Among his best-known writings for general readers are *Babies and Their Mothers* (1987) and *Human Nature* (1988). Adam Phillips (1988) has written the best introduction to his life and work. F. Robert Rodman's biography, *Winnicott: Life and Work* (2003), provides the most comprehensive account of his life.

Theoretical Perspectives

Although Winnicott elaborated a complex theory of human development, over four decades of clinical practice, he did not codify his formulations in a systematic manner. He preferred to present his ideas in ordinary everyday language, explaining that he wanted his understanding to be accessible to a wide audience, and wrote in a personal idiom that remains distinctive in the psychoanalytic literature. His style is often characterized as poetic and evocative, though some critics see him as vague and elusive in his refusal to define his most fundamental concepts in the technical empirical language of the behavioral and social sciences. The authority of experience and tentativeness that mark his theoretical writings, as Jan Abram (1997) observes, suggest an elusive duality, "as if he feared creating theory that might turn into dogma" (p. 2).

The talks he prepared for social workers, teachers, and lay audiences, on the other hand, in which he tried to communicate essential concerns in human nature and helping, carry a freedom of expression. We see his independence of mind as he explains his method at the start of a talk on early emotional development: "I shall not first give an historical survey and show the development of my ideas from the theories of others, because my mind does not work that way. What happens is that I gather this and that, here and there, and settle down to clinical experience, form my own theories, and then, last of all, interest myself in looking to see where I stole what" (Winnicott, 1945/1975d, p. 145).

Although Winnicott documented his work in a casual and conversational voice, he set forth orienting perspectives, basic assumptions, and core concepts that provide an encompassing view of human development, psychopathology, and psychosocial intervention. The following sections explore the core concepts and essential concerns that shape his developmental formulations, understandings of psychopathology, and principles of psychosocial intervention.

Developmental Formulations

Winnicott's conceptions of the maturational process and the facilitating environment serve as the foundation for his developmental psychology. In his view, we are born with an inherent drive to realize our potential as we work toward development of self; he characterizes this drive as the maturational process, viewing it as a biologically based constitutional force inherent in life itself. While our predisposition to actualize potential is a defining feature of human development, it can be arrested, blocked, or undermined if the conditions of the facilitating environment fail to foster the maturational process. He writes: "The mind has a root, perhaps its most important root, in the need of the individual, at the core of the self, for a perfect environment" (Winnicott, 1954/1975c, p. 246). The maturational process and the facilitating environment are closely linked.

Winnicott realizes that environments are never ideal, but he emphasizes that they must be "good enough" in order to facilitate the maturational process. If they are not, he theorizes, development is undermined and individuals are at risk for psychopathology, dysfunction, and problems in living; he speaks of "a freezing of the failure situation" that arrests the development of the self (see Winnicott, 1954/1975b, p. 281). Winnicott links a range of problems in functioning, including psychotic states, disorders of the self, psychosomatic conditions, and neurotic behavior, to disruptions of the maturational process that have compromised the emergence of the person.

More than any other psychoanalytic thinker, Winnicott focuses on the ways in which the mother and primary caretakers facilitate the development of the self. "There is no such thing as a baby," Winnicott (1952/1975a) writes, emphasizing the relational, interactive features of care. "If you show me a baby," he explains, "you certainly show me also someone caring for the baby, or at least a pram with someone's eyes and ears glued to it. One sees 'a nursing couple'" (p. 99). Although he assumes that there is an innate drive to realize what he calls the "true self," he believes that tendencies toward growth are established only through attuned, responsive caretaking. His conceptions of personality development and health, accordingly, emphasize the continual interplay between maturational processes and the empathic provisions of caretakers over the course of infancy, childhood, and adolescence.

In fashioning his account of human development, Winnicott would base his understanding of maturation on the child's experience of dependency over the course of the caretaking experience. Like Fairbairn, he describes three phases of dependence in the child-caretaker relationship: absolute dependence, relative dependence, and moves toward independence (Winnicott, 1960/1965f). As he elaborated his theory, he formulated three core processes that foster the development of the self—integration, personalization, and object relating—and three corresponding environmental provisions that facilitate maturation: holding, handling, and object presenting.

The first process, integration, refers to the infant's gradual gathering together bits and pieces of experience into a sense of continuity, or "going on being." Winnicott describes this as the synthetic function of the developing ego, originating in what he sees as a primary drive toward individuation of self, which he refers to as "unit status," or "I am." The environmental provision that facilitates integration of self is holding.

His conception of holding encompasses not only "the actual physical holding of the infant, but also the total environmental provision prior to the concept of living with. . . . It includes the management of experiences that are inherent in existence[,] . . . processes which from the outside may seem to be purely physiological but which belong to infant psychology and take place in a psychological field, determined by the awareness and empathy of the mother" (Winnicott, 1960/1965f, pp. 43–44). He continues: "The holding environment has as its main function the reduction to a minimum of impingements to which the infant must react with resultant annihilation of personal being. Under favorable conditions the infant establishes a continuity of existence" (p. 47). The primary function of the holding environment at the start of life, then, is to limit environmental impingements and preserve conditions that foster the growth of the self.

The second process, personalization, refers to the integration of self and body—what Winnicott calls "psychosomatic collusion," or "psyche indwelling in the soma." Since the infant has yet to distinguish "me" from "not me" in the phase of absolute dependency, Winnicott reasons, the child does not experience a sense of him- or herself as a subject at the start of life and cannot personalize sensations, feelings, and needs as "my" experience. Experience is not yet "localized" within the self, he theorizes. "The ego is based on a body ego," he writes, "but it is only when all goes well that the person of the baby starts off linked with the body and the body-functions, with the skin as the limiting membrane. I have used the term personalization to describe this process" (Winnicott, 1962/1965d, p. 59). The basis for personalization—the embodiment of self, or "indwelling of psyche in soma," Winnicott explains, "is a linkage of motor and sensory and functional experiences with the infant's new state of being a person. . . . There comes into being what might be called a limiting membrane, which to some extent (in health) is equated with the surface of the skin, and has a position between the infant's me and not-me. So the infant comes to have an inside and an outside, and a body scheme. . . . It becomes meaningful to postulate a personal, or inner psychic reality for the infant." With continued development, then, the child experiences a new sense of an internal "me."

The environmental provision that facilitates personalization is handling, which refers to the physical forms of care the baby receives that contribute to the child's sense of him- or herself as a person. "In favourable conditions," Winnicott (1962/1965d) writes, "the skin becomes the boundary between the me and the not-me. In other words, the psyche has come to live in the soma and an individual psycho-somatic life has been initiated" (p. 61).

In the caretaker's empathic attunement and devotion to the child—what Winnicott calls "primary maternal preoccupation"—the good-enough mother creates a holding environment at the start of life that organizes the infant's fragmentary world of experience. The mother figure's empathic presence, ongoing responsiveness, and constancy of care foster the infant's sense of a primary creative omnipotence, allowing the child to experience him- or herself as the source of all creation, seemingly in possession and control of the world. Her devotion and accommodation to the child's needs in the early months of life strengthen the infant's emerging sense of self, Winnicott believes, and he views this early experience of omnipotence as a critical phase of healthy development.

As maturation proceeds, however, the caretaker increasingly limits her accommodations to the child's wishes, fostering the transition into the phase of relative dependence. Winnicott (1988) explains: "The baby begins to need the other to fail to adapt—the failure being also a graduated process that cannot be learned from books" (p. 8). Such incremental failures in adaptation help the child move beyond the illusory experience of omnipotence and consolidate capacities to negotiate the experience of other people and activities in the outer world. In time, the infant's illusion of magical creation and control yields to extended periods of disillusionment and optimal frustration, facilitating adaptation to reality.

The third process in Winnicott's schema is the development of a sense of reality, designated by the terms "realization" and "object relating," that is fostered by the environmental provision of "object presenting," which refers to the ways in which caregivers bring the world to the child. The child establishes a growing sense of autonomy and develops capacities for interdependence and relationship, moving "toward independence," in Winnicott's schema, experiencing others as having an independent existence beyond the bounds of magical control.

In Winnicott's theory of human development, then, the emergence of the self involves a movement from a state of "illusory omnipotence"—where the infant, through the mother's facilitation, experiences him- or herself as creating and controlling the world—to a state of "objective perception," where the child accepts the limits of its powers and becomes aware of the independent existence of others. Paradoxically, it is the sustained experience of illusory omnipotence at the start of life—in which the child negates the experience of separateness and the independent existence of others—that leads to growing recognition of external reality.

In the course of his work with babies and parents, Winnicott observed that many children become attached to a particular object, often a blanket or teddy bear, that provides comfort and restoration during times of vulnerability, transition, and stress. He regards such an object as the child's first possession and theorized that the use of transitional objects leads to the establishment of intermediate states between subjectivity and outer reality. In his view, the transitional object is neither fully a part of the self nor completely separate from the self; it functions as an intermediate object in the transition from inside to outside. He sees transitional objects as serving a critical role in the establishment of healthy functioning and encouraged parents to support the child's use of such toys through infancy and childhood.

Winnicott continued to develop his conception of the transitional object in his later writings, forming what we can regard as a developmental theory of object relations. He describes developmental shifts in the transition from omnipotence and the growing development of relations with others in the outer world. In his schema, the first object is a subjective object—an object "created" by the child that essentially has no independent existence. The second stage is the phase of object relating; here, the object remains under the omnipotent control of the child but is perceived as outside the self. The third stage is seen in the establishment of the transitional object—as we have seen, an object that is "created" but was waiting to be found. The fourth stage is seen in the capacity for object use, where the child perceives the object as an external aspect of outer reality and therefore capable of offering "other than me" experience. This transition is facilitated by the subject's fantasied destruction of the object and the object's survival of the destruction (Winnicott, 1971a).

In his later work, Winnicott increasingly explored the functions of illusion, creativity, and play in human development and their place in the ordinary experience of everyday life. He used the term "transitional phenomena" to designate categories of activity characterized by extended periods of illusion, heightened emotion, imaginative involvement, and reverie. Representative examples include participation in play, artistic activity, religious or spiritual practices, participation in cultural experiences, and psychotherapy. He viewed the process of symbolization as essential in the development of health, creative living, and cultural life (Winnicott, 1971a).

For Winnicott (1971a), then, playing, creativity, transitional phenomena, psychotherapy, and cultural experience all have a place in which they occur: "an intermediate area of experiencing, to which inner reality and external life both contribute" (p. 2).

Psychopathology

Winnicott's conceptions of psychopathology are closely linked to his developmental formulations. He traces a range of problems in functioning to failings in the facilitating environment that have undermined the maturational process and compromised the development of the self. The effects of environmental failures depend upon the nature of the traumatic disruptions and the stage of development. He theorizes that impingements during the phase of absolute dependence have the potential to lead to the most severe forms of psychopathology because they disrupt "going on being" and undermine the development of core structures in the emerging self, predisposing the individual to psychotic states. He links failings during the stage of relative dependence to disorders of the self. Disruptions in care at later points predispose one to neurotic problems in functioning.

Winnicott characterizes disruptions during the phase of absolute dependence as "privation" because caretaking conditions have failed to meet the infant's fundamental needs. In the absence of good-enough care, the child cannot negotiate the tasks of integration, personalization, and realization. Omnipotent states and the experience of illusion, so crucial in the emergence of the self, may be undermined by empathic lapses and traumatic conditions in the caretaking surround, Winnicott theorizes, forcing the child into a premature awareness of separateness. Failings at this point in development disrupt the experience of "going on being," leading to annihilation anxiety—"unthinkable anxiety," Winnicott (1962/1965d) speculates, comparing it to "going to pieces," "falling forever," "having no relationship to the body," and "having no orientation." The alternative to *being* is *reacting*, he writes, "and reacting interrupts being and annihilates. Being and annihilation are two alternatives" (Winnicott, 1960/1965f, p. 47). In efforts to manage the experience of anxiety, the infant relies on defensive use of omnipotent fantasy, thus compromising efforts to engage actual experience in the outer world. The more severe the impingement, the more the child resorts to omnipotent defenses that distort reality and have the potential to predispose him or her to psychotic states. Winnicott links a range of problems in functioning to impingements in the stage of absolute dependence.

Environmental failings in early stages of dependence can lead to the development of a "false self." In his developmental perspective, the good-enough caretaker "meets the omnipotence of the infant and to some extent makes sense of it. . . . A true self begins to have life" (Winnicott, 1960/1965c, p. 145). The inadequate caretaker, however, fails to "implement the infant's omnipotence, and so repeatedly fails to meet the infant's gestures." Instead, caretakers substitute their own gestures, which are "to be given sense by the compliance of the infant." This compliance, Winnicott says, is the earliest stage of the false self, arising out caretakers' failures to sense the child's needs.

In the face of such empathic lapses and impingements, the core of subjectivity is suspended, and the child attempts to negotiate the constraints of inadequate caretaking situations by adopting a reactive, adaptive way of being that complies with requirements for conditions of care. The child thereby protects the true self by establishing an outer adaptive layer of the self that negotiates the give-and-take of the outer world. In doing so, however, the individual forecloses a primary experience of the self and is predisposed to states of emptiness, deadness, demoralization, hopelessness, and helplessness. Winnicott speaks of a split between the true self—the source of aliveness, personal agency, and the authentic experience of desire and meaning—and the compliant false self formed by the premature necessity to adapt to the outer world. The individual is unable to bring self to bear in day-to-day life.

The developmental basis for feeling real, Winnicott, explains, lies in the true self. In a further conceptualization of the true self, he writes: "At the earliest stage the true self is the theoretical position from which comes the spontaneous gesture and the personal idea. The spontaneous gesture is the true self in action. Only the true self can be creative and only the true self can feel real. Whereas a true self feels real, the existence of a false self results in feeling unreal or a sense of futility" (Winnicott, 1960/1965c, p. 148). Feeling real, he writes, "is more than existing; it is finding a way to exist as oneself, and to relate to objects as oneself, and to have a self into which to retreat for relaxation" (Winnicott, 1971a, p. 117).

More than any other thinker, Winnicott focuses on personal subjectivity, emphasizing the role of the true self in health, well-being, and relational life. "Living creatively is a healthy state, and compliance is a sick basis for life," he writes. "It is creative apperception more than anything else that makes the individual feel that life is worth living. Contrasted with this is a relationship to external reality which is one of compliance, the world and its details being recognized but only as something to be fitted in with or demanding adaptation. Compliance carries with it a sense of futility for the individual and is associated with the idea that nothing matters and that life is not worth living" (Winnicott, 1971a, p. 65).

Although the infant has achieved some measure of integration by the stage of relative dependence, the child remains vulnerable to disruptions in the facilitating environment. If good-enough caretaking is disrupted and not restored, Winnicott theorizes, the child experiences deprivation and attempts to recover what he or she has lost. He comes to view various forms of antisocial behavior, such as stealing, as efforts to restore the lost caretaker by laying claim to the world. In his clinical reports he makes other connections between inadequate caretaking conditions and subsequent problems in functioning, including the lack of capacity to be alone and addictive behavior.

Clinical Perspectives

The fundamental task of the therapeutic endeavor, from the perspective of Winnicott's developmental psychology, is to foster the emergence of the self, and his conceptions of maturational process and the facilitating environment inform his understanding of basic tasks and core elements in psychosocial intervention. He compares the role of the psychotherapist to that of the caretaker: the clinician must recognize the point at which development has been compromised and create conditions that facilitate growth and development. "I am concerned with the search for the self," Winnicott (1971a) writes, "and the restatement of the fact that certain conditions are necessary if success is to be achieved in this search. These conditions are associated with what is usually called creativity" (p. 54). The challenge of intervention, from his point of view, is to recognize emerging needs and engage facilitating elements that reinstate the maturational process.

Winnicott's conceptions of developmental arrest, regression, and transference shape his understanding of essential concerns and facilitating conditions in the therapeutic situation. The arrest in the development of the self is recorded in what he calls the "freezing of the failure situation" (Winnicott, 1954/1975b, p. 281). The individual has suspended the experience of living, following impingements in the caretaking situation, through defensive operations. Although growth has been compromised, Winnicott theorizes, the individual continues to search for facilitating conditions that carry the potential to reinstate developmental processes. In the holding environment of the therapeutic situation, he believes, the individual can suspend defensive behaviors, return to points of trauma through regression, and generate experience that will foster the emergence of the true self. If healing is to occur, however, the patient must return to dependency on the actual living care of the clinician. The therapeutic setting, in Winnicott's (1954/1975b) understanding, "reproduces the early and earliest mothering techniques" (p. 286).

Winnicott believes that the patient shapes the therapeutic situation to generate the environmental conditions that were absent or compromised in earlier caretaking, and he compares the developmental provisions of holding, handling, and object presenting to facilitating elements in the therapeutic process, including the practitioner's attunement, constancy of care, and responsiveness as well as the frame of intervention.

The therapeutic situation, then, as conceived from Winnicott's developmental perspective, seeks to restore personal subjectivity. Like the good-enough caretaker, the clinician creates a holding environment that allows the individual to suspend defensive behavior, return to points of trauma in earlier caretaking environments, and generate experience that fosters the emergence of the true self.

Regression is a crucial element in the therapeutic process: "the tendency to regression," Winnicott (1959/1965a) writes, reflects "the capacity of the individual to bring about self-cure" (p. 128). From his perspective, regressive experience facilitates efforts to discover, feel, consciously suffer, and work through the effects of omissions, lapses, and failings in early care.

In his rendering of the therapeutic situation, the patient tests the reliability of the setting, including the person of the clinician and particular ways of working. If the clinician provides a constancy of care and holding, the individual suspends defensive behaviors and moves into the vulnerability of dependency. Over time, there is an emerging sense of the clinician as a caretaker who provides a more responsive, reliable holding than earlier environmental provisions. The clinician is increasingly useful as the patient locates his or her experience of the person in the real and contemporary world.

Winnicott emphasizes the importance of creativity and spontaneity in clinical practice, seeing psychosocial intervention as "experiments in adapting to need." The art of psychotherapy lies in the clinician's ability to recognize and respond to emerging needs that facilitate maturation. "The only companion that I have in exploring the unknown territory of the new case," he explains, "is the theory that I carry around with me. . . . This is the theory of the emotional development of the individual which includes for me the total history of the individual child's relationship to the child's specific environment. One could compare my position with that of a cellist who at first slogs away at technique and then actually becomes able to play music" (Winnicott, 1971b, p. 6). His theory gives him a probable map of the depths, he says, which allows him to work all the more effectively at the surface of things.

In his later work, Winnicott is increasingly concerned about the ways in which the clinician's interpretations may preempt the individual's discovery of self and realization of potential. He comes to say that he interprets experience in order to let the patient know the limits of his understanding. "It appa[l]ls me to think how much deep change I have prevented or delayed in patients . . . by my personal need to interpret. If only we can wait, the patient arrives at understanding creatively and with immense joy. . . . I think I interpret mainly to let the patient know the limits of my understanding. The principle is that it is the patient and only the patient who has the answers" (Winnicott, 1971a, pp. 86–87). It follows, then, that there are "few dazzling feats of interpretation or knowingness," as Adam Phillips (1988, p. 11) writes, and his concern for the patient is expressed without irony.

Winnicott's formulations of transitional phenomena, potential space, and play offer ways of conceptualizing the process of psychosocial intervention. In his discussions of psychotherapy, Winnicott increasingly relates notions of play and communication to transitional functioning in the potential space. "Psychotherapy," he says, "is done in the overlap of the two play areas, that of the patient and that of the therapist. If the therapist cannot play, then he is not suitable for the work. If the patient cannot play, then something needs to be done to enable the patient to be able to come to play, after which psychotherapy may be done" (Winnicott, 1971a, p. 38).

In Winnicott's (1971a) third region, "the intermediate area of experiencing," the "potential space between the individual and the environment" (p. 100), we experience the pluralism of reality, moving in and out of self, withdrawing, advancing, merging, finding the patterns that connect, making meaning out of self and non-self elements. In this domain, the transitional object is nether fully self nor other; success (i.e., experiences of merger and emergence, return and departure) leads to a sense that what is needed can be created or found. Eigen (1981/1993) describes the experience as "quickening and enhancing the subject's sense of aliveness. It opens the way for a new kind of freedom, one because there is radical otherness, a new realness of self-feeling exactly because the other is now felt as real as well" (p. 112).

Psychotherapy, Winnicott (1971b) comes to believe, "is not a matter of making clever and apt interpretations; by and large it is a long-term giving back what the patient brings. It is a complex derivative of the face that reflects what is there to be seen. I like to think of my work this way, and to think that if I do this well enough the patient will find his or her own self, and will be able to exist and feel real" (p. 117).

Clinical Applications: Development and Psychopathology

The following cases illustrate the ways in which Winnicott's conceptions of development and psychopathology inform understanding of facilitating conditions and use of various approaches over the course of psychosocial intervention.

Case Illustration: Developmental Arrest

Mary J., age twenty-nine, had received supportive services in a psychiatric rehabilitation program for three years following diagnosis of borderline personality disorder. Hopeful that she could strengthen her capacities to manage problems in functioning, form relationships, and engage in social life, her case manager referred her to a community mental health clinic for psychotherapy.

Winnicott's conceptions of developmental arrest and the facilitating conditions of the holding environment informed the clinician's understanding of essential concerns over the course of the intervention. In the first phase of treatment, Mary experienced the clinician as a subjective object, relating to him through omnipotence states and the experience of illusion: "You are my toy," she said, as if she were in possession and control of the clinician. "You speak when I want you to speak. . . . You move when I want you to move. . . . What *good* are you if you don't do what I want you to do?"

In Winnicott's schema, as we have seen, traumatic impingements during the phase of absolute dependence disrupt the formation of core structures in the emerging self, leading to the most severe forms of psychopathology. Mary's mother, who was mentally ill at the time of her birth, was unable to care for her. She was placed in foster care in infancy and experienced disruptions in caretaking arrangements across the course of childhood. In a Winnicottian reading of the case, traumatic conditions at the start of life had undermined her efforts to negotiate the tasks of integration, personalization, and realization and consolidate a core sense of self. Her reliance on omnipotent defenses to manage "unimaginable terror" distorted her experience of reality and compromised her ability to engage actual experience in the outer world.

The constancy of care in the holding environment of the therapeutic situation fostered her efforts to re-create crucial features of her early life in contemporary form, documenting the ways in which "going on being" had been undermined. Over time, the clinician's attunement, responsiveness, and empathic processing of her experience helped to reinstate developmental processes. Mary was increasingly able to move beyond the bounds of her encapsulated world of omnipotent fantasy and relate to the clinician as an objective object, as a separate individual with an independent center of thought, feeling, and action. "When I ask you a question," she told the therapist, "I want to know what *you* think. I know what *I* think. . . . What good are you if you don't offer something different?" Her illusions of magical creation and control continued to recede as she strengthened her capacities to make use of the clinician's provisions ("reality presenting") and engage in a give-and-take with actual experience in the outer world. She was developing capacities for object use—"other than me experience," in Winnicott's phrase. Over time, she continued to consolidate a sense of self and identity, established friendships, and initiated engagement in social life.

Case Illustration: True Self and the Relational Surround

Martha D., age thirty-eight, initiated psychotherapy following surgery for breast cancer. She had completed a course of chemotherapy and radiation and expected a full recovery. Even so, she explained, her parents wanted her to process her experience of the illness; she thought that it had been more traumatic for them than for her: "They said, 'How can you put us through this at our age?' and I decided I should talk with someone about it—if only for their sake." Martha was responsive to the clinician's efforts to explore concerns in the initial interview, and she provided detailed accounts of the illness experience and the events that followed, unusually attuned to the practitioner's expectations. As the therapeutic process proceeded, however, the clinician realized that she seldom reflected on her inner life. She deflected the practitioner's attempts to explore her feelings, thoughts, and reactions, instead providing accounts of recent activities with her parents and extended family. She became increasingly preoccupied with the clinician's reactions to her accounts.

Drawing on Martha's reports of family life and her behavior over the course of the sessions, the practitioner hypothesized that she had suspended her authentic experience of self in order to meet requirements for conditions of care in early family life. Her parents had failed to create an environment that fostered her explorations of subjectivity. As the psychotherapy continued, the practitioner realized that she had developed an adaptive mode of organization within the constraints of the caretaking surround in her family that perpetuated reactive, accommodating ways of being and relating. She had learned to generate false-self experience in order to fulfill her parents' needs but was unable to engage her inner life and bring self to bear in the give-and-take of day-to-day life. Martha came to see herself as living out her parents' life rather than her own, remote from her vitality and a sense of herself as alive and real. As she continued to process her earlier experience and current behavior, she was increasingly able to identify her deepest concerns and distinguish her interests from those of others. Over time, she began to express the core features of her true self in spontaneous ways of being, relating, and living.

From Winnicott's point of view, as we see in this account, lapses and failings over the course of caretaking can precipitate a radical split between the true self and an adaptive, compliant version of the self, which originates in the premature need to monitor and manage experience in the outer world. The aim of the therapeutic endeavor is to foster the development of the true self, reflected in a greater experience of aliveness, spontaneous gestures and play, and authenticity in relational life.

Case Illustration: The Antisocial Tendency

Winnicott's developmental formulations help clinicians understand resistant behavior and aggressive reactions as adaptive attempts to restore a sense of hope and possibility following trauma and loss. In a classic paper on character disorders, Winnicott (1963/1965e) reviews his conception of the antisocial tendency and describes the following cases:

> A boy of thirteen years, at a public school a long way from his good home, was stealing in a big way, also slashing sheets and upsetting the school by getting boys into trouble and by leaving obscene notes in lavatories. . . . In a therapeutic consultation he was able to let me know that he had been through a period of intolerable strain at the age of six when he went away to boarding school. I was able to arrange for this boy (middle child of three) to be allowed a period of "mental nursing" in his own home. He used this for a regressive phase, and then went to day school. Later he went to a boarding school in the neighbourhood of his home. His antisocial symptoms ceased abruptly after his one interview with me and follow up shows that he has done well. . . . [What] he needed was for the facts to be acknowledged and for an attempt to be made to mend, in token form, the environmental failure. (pp. 213–214)

In another account, Winnicott (1963/1965e) describes his consultation with an eight-year-old boy after he began stealing.

He had suffered relative deprivation (in his own good home setting) when he was two, at the time his mother conceived, and became pathologically anxious. The parents had managed to meet (his) special needs and had almost succeeded in effecting a natural cure of his condition. I helped them in this long task by giving them some understanding of what they were doing. In one therapeutic consultation when the boy was eight it was possible for me to get this boy into feeling-contact with his deprivation, and he reached back to an object relationship to the good mother of his infancy. Along with this the stealing ceased. (p. 213)

Clinical Applications: Transitional Objects

Winnicott's conceptions of transitional objects and transitional phenomena focus our attention on crucial domains of experience in assessment and intervention. Jeffrey Applegate and Jennifer Bonovitz (1995) show how educational efforts to help parents understand and facilitate the child's attachment to transitional objects can foster functioning and development through infancy and childhood. By way of illustration, they relate the following case.

Case Illustration: Parenting and Transitional Objects

Mrs. K. found herself struggling to manage her fifteen-month-old son's wakefulness at night. When the child awakened, he called, "Mommy, Mommy" until she came. The social worker asked her what happened if she did not respond, and she explained that she always attended to him, for her husband feared that their child would feel abandoned if she failed to go to him. When the practitioner asked Mrs. K. about the child's use of his baby blanket at night, the mother explained that she did not allow him to sleep with it for fear he would suffocate. The worker explored her worries further and learned that her mother had passed on a list of dangers to avoid in child rearing.

As the interview proceeded, the practitioner learned that Mrs. K's mother had spent her adolescence in a concentration camp. Applegate and Bonovitz (1995) relate that "she lived in terror of losing any of her family, and, during Mrs. [K.'s] childhood, compulsively checked on her whereabouts and safety" (p. 161). As the practitioner explored and processed the origins of Mrs. K's fears, she began to leave the child's blanket with him at night. He stopped calling for her, sleeping through the night.

While capacities for transitional relatedness originate in infancy, Winnicott emphasizes that transitional objects and phenomena serve crucial functions across the course of life, serving as sources of restoration and solace during times of disruption and loss. The following case illustrates the role of transitional objects in efforts to facilitate coping and adaptation following progressive loss in later life.

Case Illustration: Transitional Phenomena in Later Life

Curt S., age eighty-three, developed insomnia, anxiety, and signs of depression shortly after deciding to enter a nursing home. His wife had died four years earlier, and he was unable to care for himself in the home where they had lived for nearly half a century. He acknowledged a pervasive sense of loss as he anticipated the transition, but he explained that he was particularly distressed because he would not be able to take certain possessions with him. As a child, Curt had received his father's mineral collection following his death, and he had continued to enlarge it over the years, having developed a passion for the earth sciences. The practitioner understood the sustaining functions of transitional objects during times of disruption and loss in later life and realized that his continued involvement with the collection could potentially facilitate adaptation to the nursing home setting. Accordingly, he consulted with the administrator of the nursing home and made arrangements for Curt to take his most prized specimens with him.

As Winnicott emphasizes, various elements in the clinical situation have the potential to serve as transitional objects or transitional phenomena as individuals resume developmental processes over the course of intervention. Mary, for example, asked to take a plant home from the office between sessions as she began to symbolize her experience of the clinician. She also found it comforting to hear his voice on his answering machine, which reflected her growing capacities to make use of transitional phenomena (see Applegate & Bonovitz, 1995, for further illustration of the functions of transitional objects and phenomena in case management and other forms of psychosocial care).

Winnicott in Context: Contemporary Perspectives

Social workers and other helping professionals have increasingly realized the relevance of Winnicott's theoretical formulations and clinical perspectives—his "experiments in adapting to need"—in their efforts to carry out the diverse forms of psychosocial intervention. Jeffrey Applegate and Jennifer Bonovitz (1995) make connections between Winnicott's developmental formulations and orienting perspectives and core values in the social work tradition, showing how his ideas inform agency-based treatment of vulnerable and disenfranchised clients. In a series of writings and case reports, Joel Kanter (1990, 2004) has documented the ways in which the work of Winnicott and his wife, Clare Winnicott, deepen understandings of facilitating conditions and sustaining processes in community care of the mentally ill. Kanter has developed a model of clinical case management that emphasizes Winnicott's conceptions of holding, transitional phenomena, play, and management of the clinical situation.

The emphasis on subjectivity and relational life in Winnicott's renderings of the human situation has deepened our appreciation of the formative role of caretaking experience and the social surround in the emergence of self. His developmental formulations link lapses in care and environmental impingements to sources of vulnerability, cumulative trauma, and a range of problems in living.

Winnicott's focus on subjective domains of concern and interactive experience in the therapeutic situation has transformed our understanding of facilitating processes and curative factors in psychotherapy. As we have seen, he came to understand regressive experience as an effort to return to the point at which one had been failed by the social environment: "the tendency to regression reflects the capacity of the individual to bring about self cure" (Winnicott, 1959/1965a, p. 128). His conceptions of transference and countertransference states show how the clinician is compelled to relive the dynamics of the individual's history in the medium of the relationship; accordingly, transference and countertransference phenomena emerge as crucial sources of experiencing and understanding in the therapeutic process.

Winnicott's appreciation of ambiguity and paradox allows him to approach the therapeutic endeavor from multiple points of view, without privileging one position over another, without recourse to orthodoxy or notions of absolute truth (see Borden, 1994, 1998). Ever concerned about the dangers of omniscience, Winnicott (1987) works to undermine "the impression that there is a jigsaw of which all the pieces exist" in his observations on clinical theory and practice (p. 35).

Chapter 9

John Bowlby: Self, Others, and the Relational World

I was training to be a child psychiatrist, and I was working with two social workers. . . . They were very alive to the importance of real-life events and the way in which parents' problems impinge on children. I've always said I learned more from them than anyone else.

—John Bowlby, Interview

John Bowlby's conceptions of attachment, shaped by Darwinian thought, developmental biology, and cognitive psychology, have brought about major reformulations of personality development, relational life, and psychopathology. Bowlby believed that classical psychoanalytic thought had failed to take account of crucial aspects of interpersonal behavior in the social surround, and he brought an ecological perspective to his studies of children and caretakers. He had a deep appreciation of scientific inquiry as well, and he attempted to link psychoanalytic studies with empirical research in a range of disciplines, including evolutionary biology, ethology, and anthropology. In the course of his work he deepened understandings of the bond between children and primary caretakers; the impact of trauma, separation, and loss in early life; and the process of mourning. In the domain of clinical practice, his contributions have enlarged ways of understanding modes of connection, patterns of interpersonal behavior, and the critical functions of the helping relationship over the course of intervention. More broadly, his work has shaped empirical research in the behavioral sciences and informed the development of child welfare programs and social policy.

Like Fairbairn and Winnicott, Bowlby had close ties to Melanie Klein. He was introduced to her ideas through his personal analyst, Joan Riviere, then a follower of Klein, and he saw Klein herself for clinical supervision during his psychoanalytic training while working at the London Child Guidance Clinic. In light of his empirical turn of mind and his commitment to scientific inquiry, however, he eventually rejected Klein's drive psychology and began to elaborate a relational perspective that emphasized interdisciplinary study of behavior. Like Sullivan, he was interested in what actually happens between real people in the outer world. He had a brilliance of mind, generated testable hypotheses, and linked his concepts with empirical research in scientific disciplines. "I am with the object relations school," Bowlby explained, "but I have reformulated it in terms of modern biological concepts. It is my own independent vision" (qtd. in Grosskurth, 1986, p. 404). This chapter provides an introduction to Bowlby's life and work, examines the core concepts of his attachment theory, and considers the implications of his theoretical formulations for psychosocial intervention.

Life and Work

Bowlby was born on February 26, 1907, in London and died at the Isle of Skye, Scotland, on September 2, 1990. His father, Sir Anthony Bowlby, was a physician and served as surgeon to the royal family. He was the fourth child in a family of three girls and three boys. In his biographical account, Robert Karen characterizes his parents as reserved and self-absorbed, removed from the day-to-day concerns of their children, leaving their care to a governess and nannies. They were "conventional upper-class people of their day," he writes, "with a belief in intellectual rigor and a stiff-upper-lip approach to all things emotional" (Karen, 1994, p. 30). Although Bowlby characterized his early life as "stable," Karen emphasizes that his use of the term should "not be taken to mean warm, secure, emotionally responsive, or any of the other qualities that Bowlby believed were so important to a developing child" (p. 30). He explains: "Almost everything he wrote in later years about the needs of young children could be seen as an indictment of the type of upbringing to which he'd been subjected and to the culture that had fostered it" (pp. 30–31).

At age eight, following the start of World War I, Bowlby was sent to boarding school, where he distinguished himself as a strong student. He attended Trinity College at Cambridge University, intending to follow his father's example and train as a physician. In the third year of his studies, however, he began to explore the field of psychology and developed a particular interest in progressive education. Educators had begun to establish residential treatment programs for troubled youths—the most prominent example was A. S. Neil's Summerhill—and Bowlby decided that he wanted to serve as a volunteer in such an institution and reconsider his decision to train as a physician. Karen (1994) observes: "This amalgam of anarchism, utopian socialism, and Freudianism must have struck the proper young Bowlby as quite a good mix, for it remained a cornerstone of his own views for the rest of his life" (p. 31).

Bowlby actually worked in two schools; at the second institution, he met John Alford, a war veteran and artist who had developed a deep interest in psychoanalysis following his own treatment. Alford became a mentor, helping him consider potential connections between the troubled behavior he was observing in the children and traumatic events in their early family life. Two children in particular had a deep impact on Bowlby. One was an adolescent, described as isolated and inaccessible, who had been expelled from his previous school for stealing. Bowlby realized that the youth had never had the care and support of a stable, continuous parenting figure. A second child, an anxious boy, followed Bowlby closely and came to be known as his shadow (Ainsworth, 1974). Bowlby and Alford spent many hours exploring the ways in which earlier experience influenced vulnerability and problems in functioning. Late in his life, Bowlby would trace the origins of attachment theory to his work in the school.

With Alford's encouragement, Bowlby enrolled at University College Hospital Medical School in 1929, intending to train as a psychiatrist. At the same time, he began psychoanalytic training. Riviere and Klein introduced him to psychoanalytic thought, but he developed reservations about Kleinian approaches to child psychotherapy in the course of his training. As we have seen, Klein traced problems in functioning to fantasies originating in conflict between the life and death instincts. Bowlby, in contrast, focused on actual events and particular conditions of the outer world. Klein would not allow Bowlby to speak with the mother of a three-year-old whom he treated under her supervision. This was deeply problematic for Bowlby, who saw family experience and life events as crucial determinants of problems in functioning (Bretherton, 1992).

In 1938, Bowlby married Ursula Longstaff, who brought a love of literature to their relationship; she collaborated with him in his final work, a biography of Darwin, published shortly before he died in 1990. They had four children. The Bowlby family shared their household with the Labour politician Evan Durbin and his family, and later with John Sutherland and his family.

Although he continued to pursue his interests in children and family life over the course of his training in psychiatry and psychoanalysis, biographical accounts suggest that his teachers and clinical supervisors appear to have had little impact on his thinking. The social workers at the London Child Guidance Clinic, where he worked on completion of his training, were far more influential. They included James Robertson and Christopher Heinicke, who shared his interests in the social contexts of development, and Molly Lowden and Nance Fairbairn, who focused on practical applications of psychoanalytic concepts in family mental health settings.

Bowlby increasingly believed that psychoanalysis placed too much emphasis on intrapsychic domains of experience and failed to recognize the impact of real people, actual events, and social conditions on problems in living. In an early paper, "The Influence of Early Environment in the Development of Neurosis and Neurotic Character," published in 1940, he explored the influence of the early family environment on the emergence of neurotic problems. He wrote: "Psychoanalysts like the nurseryman should study intensively, rigorously, and at first hand, the nature of the organism, the properties of the soil and the interaction of the two" (Bowlby, 1940, p. 155).

When he became an army psychiatrist in 1940, his colleagues included Sutherland and Wilfred Bion, both of whom shared his interest in psychoanalytic thought. At the end of World War II, Sutherland was appointed director of the Tavistock Clinic. Bowlby became his deputy. He established the Department for Children and Parents and joined Esther Bick, a Kleinian, in organizing the child psychotherapy training program. In his role he began to carry out research with Robertson, whom he hired in 1948 to help him observe hospitalized and institutionalized children who were separated from their parents. Mary Ainsworth joined the research unit in 1950; in time, she would operationalize Bowlby's formulations in empirical study of mothers and children, documenting different types of attachment styles activated by controlled separations from the caretaking figure.

Bowlby introduced the core concepts of attachment theory in a series of presentations to the British Psychoanalytical Society in London, summarized in the following section, beginning in the late 1950s. Although he located himself in the psychoanalytic tradition, he became increasingly critical of core concepts of Freudian thought, and his ideas were poorly received by his colleagues, most of whom responded with indifference, hostility, or rejection. As Lavinia Gomez (1997) observes: "There was a temperamental and cultural chasm between the upper class Englishman and the traumatized, European Jewish contingent who, together with the British Independents, were more at home with art, emotion, and imagination than science, facts and statistics" (p. 153).

Bowlby increasingly distanced himself from the British Psychoanalytical Society, continuing to focus on development of his theory, research, and social policy concerns. Between 1969 and 1980 he published three seminal volumes, *Attachment, Separation,* and *Loss,* that linked attachment theory with evolutionary biology, developmental psychology, anthropology, cognitive studies, and systems theory. His thinking increasingly influenced work in a range of disciplines, including developmental psychology, social psychology, ethology, anthropology, sociology, and social work, and he was recognized as a major theoretician in the last decade of his life. His final work, a biography of Darwin, published shortly before his death in 1990, was widely praised; Frank Sulloway, the historian of science, described it as a model psychobiography. Bowlby felt a deep connection to Darwin and came to see the development of love as one of the greatest achievements of human evolution (see Karen, 1994, for further discussion of this work).

Theoretical Perspectives

Over the course of his thinking Bowlby (1969) formulated what he called "a new type of instinct theory" in his attempts to refashion psychoanalytic understanding from an evolutionary perspective (p. 17). He assumed that instinctive behavioral systems have been developed over time by natural selection for purposes of survival and adaptation. This evolutionary perspective provides the context for his conceptions of attachment, relational life, and social functioning.

Bowlby's initial formulations of attachment theory, which drew on concepts from psychoanalysis, developmental psychology, and ethology, were presented to the British Psychoanalytical Society in a series of talks, as noted earlier. The first paper, "The Nature of the Child's Tie to His Mother," published in 1958, challenged Freudian explanations of the child's libidinal tie to the mother, based on drive psychology, and introduced an alternative biological perspective. He describes a series of instinctual responses that facilitate attachment in infancy, including sucking, clinging, and following; he also includes the signaling behaviors of smiling and crying. In his report, he drew on his experience as a facilitator of a weekly support group for young mothers in London and empirical studies of cognitive and social development in infancy, including reports by Jean Piaget. He also introduced ethological conceptions of sign stimuli that facilitate activation or suspension of specific behavioral responses.

Bowlby's thinking had been expanded by his participation in an interdisciplinary child study group organized by Ronald Hargreaves at the World Health Organization. The meetings, conducted between 1953 and 1956, were attended by Julian Huxley, Konrad Lorenz, Margaret Mead, Ludwig von Bertalanffy, and Erik Erikson (see Bretherton, 1992).

In his second paper, "Separation Anxiety," which appeared in 1959, Bowlby focused on the primary attachment of infants and children to mother figures and their reactions to separation. He drew on Harry Harlow's classic studies of maternal deprivation in Rhesus monkeys and observational studies of children and mothers carried out by Robertson and Heinicke, arguing that psychoanalytic drive theory failed to explain the nature of the infant's attachment to caretaking figures and their responses to separation and loss. In the following paper, "Grief and Mourning in Infancy and Early Childhood," published in 1960, Bowlby continued to explore the infant's experience of grief and mourning following extended separations from mother figures. In doing so, he challenged classical Freudian assumptions about the nature of the infant-caretaker relationship. Anna Freud had argued that infants experience mother figures as need-gratifying objects and that the early caretaking relationship lacks the specificity and emotional ties that distinguish true love (for further discussion, see Greenberg & Mitchell, 1983, p. 185).

Bowlby (1979) came to describe attachment theory as a way of conceptualizing "the propensity of human beings to make strong affectional bonds to particular others," and he viewed it as a way of accounting for "the many forms of emotional distress and personality disturbance, including anxiety, anger, depression, and emotional detachment, to which unwilling separation and loss give rise" (p. 127). He emphasizes the following ideas in developing his conceptions of attachment: First, the infant is born with a predisposition to form attachments with primary caregivers. Second, the child organizes thinking and behavior so as to preserve attachment relationships, which are crucial to physical survival and psychological health and well-being. Third, the child maintains such relationships at great cost to his or her functioning and well-being. Fourth, disturbances in attachment—reflected in distortions in thinking, feeling, and acting—originate in parents' inability to address the child's needs for comfort, reassurance, and security (see Slade, 1998, for review of core concepts).

In spite of his criticisms of Freud and psychoanalytic theory, Bowlby's formulations were shaped by psychodynamic understanding, and he acknowledges overlapping thinkers in Great Britain and America, including Suttie, Fairbairn, Winnicott, and Sullivan. He is particularly appreciative of the contributions of the Hungarian school, citing the work of Michael and Alice Balint, who theorized that the infant has a primary, active relationship to the mothering figure from birth onward, and the formulations of Imre Hermann, who described a primary instinct to cling. In developing his point of view, however, Bowlby (1973) moves beyond the domain of psychoanalysis and integrates conceptual work and empirical research from developmental biology, ethology, neuroscience, and cognitive psychology, seeking to recast psychoanalysis in terms of modern evolution theory.

He views attachment as the defining feature of the relationship between the child and the mother figure. By virtue of heredity, he theorizes, the infant promotes attachment to a primary figure who provides care, support, and protection. Attachment behaviors facilitate efforts to establish and preserve closeness to a "differentiated and preferred individual" who is perceived as stronger and "better able to cope with the world" (Bowlby, 1979, p. 129). He discusses a range of phenomena in his descriptions of attachment behavior, including sucking, clinging, crying, smiling, and following. He draws on empirical studies of separation and loss to support his view that early disruption of the relationship precipitates grief and mourning.

Bowlby employed cybernetic models in his efforts to explain the regulation of attachment behavior. Subjective states of self and changing conditions in the social surround activate internal behavioral systems that, in turn, foster attachment behavior. He describes a variety of activating conditions, including hunger, fatigue, strangeness, and frightening situations. Behaviors recede following sight or sound of the mother figure.

While Bowlby focuses largely on the behavioral features of attachment, he also considers the emotional aspects of the bond. He likens the formation of the attachment relationship to the experience of falling in love and writes that the "unchallenged maintenance of a bond is experienced as a source of security and the renewal of the bond as a source of joy" (Bowlby, 1979, p. 130). Threats to the attachment relationship precipitate anxiety, Bowlby observes, and actual loss is followed by grief and mourning.

Although his formulations of attachment theory emphasize interactive experience with actual people in the outer world, Bowlby also explores intrapsychic domains of experience. Drawing on cognitive psychology, he theorized that individuals develop "working models" of self and others in the context of attachment relationships through internalization of interpersonal experience. He acknowledges that representations of mother figures, formed over the course of the attachment relationship, could be characterized as internal objects. He remains uncomfortable with the term, however, because he believes that it fails to link the inner representation to the living presence of another person (see Bowlby, 1986, pp. 36–64).

According to Bowlby's concept of working models, inner representations or schemas encompassing self, others, and modes of interactive experience shape the individual's perceptions of people and influence particular modes of behavior in the interpersonal field. He explored the role of internal working models in the intergenerational transmission of attachment patterns and came to see maladaptive patterns of interaction in family life as major determinants of dysfunction. He writes: "There is a strong causal relationship between an individual's experience with his parents and his later capacity to make affectional bonds, and . . . certain common variations in that capacity, manifesting themselves in marital problems and trouble with children as well as in neurotic symptoms and personality disorders, can be attributed to certain common variations in the ways that parents perform their roles" (Bowlby, 1979, p. 135).

Drawing on Bowlby's formulations, Mary Main (1995) has studied attachment behavior across generations, exploring potential connections between the parent's early attachment experiences and his or her child's attachment status as assessed by the "strange situation" method introduced by Ainsworth.

Like Suttie and Fairbairn, Bowlby views the person as a social being, and we work to establish and preserve connection and closeness across the course of life. He concludes the third volume of his study of attachment: "Intimate attachments to other human beings are the hub around which a person's life revolves, not only when he is an infant or a toddler or a school child but throughout his adolescence and his years of maturity as well, and on into old age" (Bowlby, 1980, p. 422).

As we have seen, Bowlby's conceptions of attachment and relational life influence his understandings of health, vulnerability, and psychopathology. The expression of attachment needs is a crucial determinant of well-being, from his point of view, and he challenges psychoanalytic perspectives that characterize "natural desires to be loved and cared for" as regressive or pathological (Bowlby, 1979, p. 157).

He views separation anxiety as a "basic human disposition" that follows potential loss of the primary caretaking figure. The observational studies of James and Joyce Robertson documented the traumatic effects of the child's separation from the mother, informing conceptualizations of representative stages in the child's reaction to the loss as follows: protest, despair, and detachment.

He described four patterns of pathological attachment originating in the caretaking relationship that can emerge over the course of childhood, adolescence, or adulthood: anxious attachment; compulsive self-reliance, compulsive caregiving, and detachment. In patterns of anxious attachment, Bowlby explains, individuals fear they will lose their primary caretaking figure; they may be described as overly dependent and have the potential to develop a range of neurotic symptoms under stress. Parental caretakers may have rejected basic needs for love and care or threatened to abandon the child. Failings in the attachment relationship may also lead to a compulsive self-reliance, where one protects oneself from rejection by withdrawing from connection and closeness with others; compulsive caregiving, where one disavows personal needs for care and instead extends concern and help to others; and emotional detachment, where one fails to establish stable bonds with others following more severe forms of maternal deprivation or parental rejection. In his efforts to explain such patterns of behavior, Bowlby emphasizes the ways in which the actual events and conditions of relational life in childhood shaped working models or representations of self and attachment figures that continue to guide functioning.

Clinical Perspectives

Although Bowlby's interests focused largely on research, child welfare, and social policy, he maintained a clinical practice and described basic principles of psychosocial intervention from the perspective of attachment theory. The task of the therapeutic endeavor, broadly understood, is to help individuals revise rigid, inadequate working models of self and others and modes of interaction that perpetuate problems in living and assist them in developing more adaptive ways of being and relating. He urged practitioners to develop "an extensive knowledge of deviant patterns of attachment and care-giving behaviour and of the pathogenic family experiences believed commonly to contribute to them" (Bowlby, 1979, p. 144).

Like Suttie, Winnicott, and Fairbairn, Bowlby compares the role of the clinician to that of the caretaker. The practitioner must provide what Bowlby termed a "secure base"—an attuned, empathic, responsive relationship—that fosters explorations of subjective experience and relational life. The patient and clinician work in a collaborative fashion to understand the origins of dysfunctional working models, exploring the ways in which adverse events, separations, and losses have shaped current patterns of behavior. In doing so, the clinician encourages the individual to consider "both the situations in which he nowadays tends to find himself with significant persons, and the parts he may play in bringing them about, and also how he responds in feeling, thought, and action when in these situations" (Bowlby, 1979, p. 146).

Transference phenomena in the therapeutic situation provide opportunities to connect working models of relational life with earlier patterns of attachment and conditions of care. Bowlby (1979) reminds clinicians: "The more unfavourable the patient's experiences with his parents were[,] the less easy it is for him to trust the therapist now and the more readily will he misperceive, misconstrue, and misinterpret what the therapist does and says" (p. 146). The clinician helps the patient consider "how the situations into which he typically gets himself and his typical reactions to them, including what may be happening between himself and the therapist, may be understood in terms of the real-life experiences he had with attachment figures during his childhood and adolescence (and perhaps may still be having) and of what his responses to them were (and may still be)."

Although Bowlby views provision of support, interpretation of transference phenomena, and reconstruction of past experience as core elements in psychodynamic psychotherapy, he brings what he calls "new points of emphasis" in his applications of attachment theory, including his focus on real-life experiences rather than on intrapsychic fantasy, his detailed exploration of the ways in which parental caretakers have actually behaved across the course of development and patterns of family functioning, and his use of disruptions in the therapeutic relationship over the course of intervention to observe reactions to separation and explore the ways in which earlier relational life has influenced current functioning (Bowlby, 1979). He affirms notions of self-determination and the patient's natural capacities for change and growth, emphasizing that "the psychotherapist's job . . . is to provide the conditions in which self-healing can take place" (Bowlby, 1988, p. 152).

Clinical Applications

Although Bowlby seldom presented accounts of his own clinical work in his writings or talks, his formulations of attachment, separation, and loss focus our attention on crucial domains of concern in assessment and intervention. The following account expands a brief case report (Borden, 2008b) in order to show how Bowlby's conceptions of early loss and modes of attachment inform understandings of vulnerability and patterns of behavior over the course of treatment.

Case Illustration: Early Loss and Attachment

James L., age sixty-three, developed diffuse anxiety, signs of depression, and dissociative states nine months after he was injured in an automobile accident. He had completed a course of rehabilitation in a nursing home following his recovery from life-threatening injuries and had recently returned to his apartment. He described a range of symptoms that met diagnostic criteria for post-traumatic stress disorder.

Beyond the impact of the traumatic event, underlying sources of vulnerability emerged in review of his developmental history. His mother had died shortly before his second birthday, following an aneurism, and he described ongoing disruptions in caretaking across the course of childhood and adolescence. He reported difficulties in establishing and preserving relationships in adulthood and described only distant, limited contact with extended family and acquaintances. His experience of dependency and isolation following the accident had intensified longings for closeness and connection, but he was reluctant to reach out to others for reasons he could not explain.

While the focus of intervention centered on problems in functioning precipitated by the traumatic event, the clinician realized that his history of early loss, disruptions in caretaking, and subsequent modes of attachment had the potential to limit his ability to establish a therapeutic alliance and engage in the interactive process of intervention. In the assessment interview, James had asked the practitioner if he would be available to speak by telephone between sessions in the event that he found himself overwhelmed by anxiety. The clinician was responsive to his concerns and encouraged him to call. He did not initiate contact before the next appointment, however, and failed to appear for the session. When the practitioner called him, he explained that he "must have forgotten about the meeting." When James did appear for the second session, he appeared detached, seemingly indifferent in his interaction with the practitioner.

Although James remained distant in the therapeutic relationship, he became increasingly engaged in the core activities of intervention and made use of cognitive and behavioral strategies in efforts to address problems in functioning associated with the post-traumatic stress syndrome. The clinician understood his pattern of behavior as a function of his anxious and resistant mode of attachment.

In time, the practitioner's attunement and responsiveness to his vulnerabilities and fears fostered his experience of acceptance, understanding, and support. Over the course of the psychotherapy James strengthened his capacities to identify and disrupt vicious circles of behavior that had perpetuated his isolation, deepen connections with others, and engage in the give-and-take of relational life.

Bowlby in Context: Contemporary Perspectives

Bowlby challenged core concepts of classical psychoanalysis, as we have seen, focusing on observable behavior in the outer world rather than on internal domains of experience that had been so central to Freud and Klein. His work has shaped an empirical research tradition in developmental psychology, and contemporary relational thinkers increasingly link his formulations with conceptions of mentalization (Fonagy, 2001) and intersubjectivity in contemporary theory and practice (see Mitchell, 2000).

Chapter 10

Harry Stack Sullivan, Karen Horney, and the Interpersonal Tradition

Life itself still remains a very effective therapist.

—Karen Horney, *Our Inner Conflicts*

The interpersonal tradition in American psychoanalysis encompasses the views of a divergent group of thinkers who came to share essential concerns and basic assumptions in their conceptions of personality development, problems in living, and therapeutic practice. The principal theorists, Harry Stack Sullivan, Karen Horney, and Eric Fromm, introduced original perspectives that emphasized relational views of human experience and placed growing importance on social, cultural, political, and economic conditions in their understandings of vulnerability, need, and dysfunction. Although their views differed considerably, they pursued overlapping lines of inquiry and elaborated an interpersonal perspective that enlarged the field of psychodynamic understanding.

They were united in their rejection of Freud's drive psychology, arguing that the intrapsychic focus and emphasis on biological factors that defined his classical thought failed to take account of the crucial role of relational life and the broader influence of social and cultural experience on personality development and problems in living. Fromm (1941/1965), writing in *Escape from Freedom*, explains: "We believe that man is primarily a social being, and not, as Freud assumes, primarily self-sufficient and only secondarily in need of others to satisfy his instinctual needs. In this sense, we believe that individual psychology is fundamentally social psychology, or in Sullivan's terms, the psychology of interpersonal relationships: the key problem of psychology is that of the particular kind of relatedness of the individual toward the world, not that of satisfaction or frustration of single instinctual desires" (p. 290).

Beyond their theoretical challenges, they argued that Freudian theory failed to provide a foundation for effective clinical practice, and they were troubled by the limitations of classical psychoanalytic methods. As clinicians they wanted to engage vulnerable, disenfranchised groups and address a wider range of problems in living in their clinical work than the classical analytic frame would allow. Sullivan, moved by the example of Jane Addams, wanted to democratize psychotherapy and broaden its relevance to social concerns. Over time, practitioners working in the interpersonal tradition introduced therapeutic approaches that centered on immediate, real-life concerns rather than on exploration of past experience; came to emphasize the interpersonal, social, and cultural contexts of problems in living; and began to employ brief, active modes of intervention.

Sullivan and Horney provide the most comprehensive theories of personality and psychopathology, and their core concepts have increasingly influenced discussion in relational psychoanalysis. In this chapter I review their theoretical systems and explore the ways in which interpersonal perspectives have shaped practice in contemporary psychotherapy.

Harry Stack Sullivan

Although Sullivan has been characterized as one of the most influential thinkers in contemporary psychotherapy (Havens & Frank, 1971), most of the books published under his name are based on transcriptions of notes from lectures and talks, and his original writings are seldom cited in the clinical literature. Sullivan demands more of his readers than most psychoanalytic thinkers, as Greenberg and Mitchell (1983) observe in their account of his theory, explaining: "He tries to startle them, to jar them from habitual and unwitting obfuscatory thinking and communicating. He wants the audience to realize that the manner in which they usually view human experience and difficulties is fundamentally misconceived, based on erroneous yet comforting illusions" (p. 81).

His work is better known through the integrative presentations of his colleague Clara Thompson, a brilliant thinker and clinician who fashioned her own interpersonal perspective by linking Sullivan's formulations with the contributions of Ferenczi and Fromm. Patrick Mullahy, who worked with Sullivan and Thompson, also helped to introduce Sullivan's interpersonal perspective to the mental health disciplines through his writings and edited works, starting in the late 1940s. More recently, reappraisals of Sullivan's work in relational psychoanalysis by Stephen Mitchell, Paul Wachtel, and other writers have deepened appreciation of his developmental views and renewed interest in a range of interpersonal concerns.

Life and Work

Sullivan was born near Norwich, New York, on February 21, 1892, and died in Paris on January 14, 1949, while returning from a meeting of the World Federation for Mental Health in Amsterdam. His grandparents had emigrated to the United States from Ireland, and he grew up on a farm in rural upstate New York. His was the only Roman Catholic family in a Yankee

Protestant community, and he felt isolated and out of place as a child. Clara Thompson, in her memorial address, described him as lonely from his earliest childhood. He developed a curiosity about the natural world around him, however, and read widely, developing an interest in medicine in adolescence.

He graduated from the Chicago College of Medicine and Surgery in 1917 and served with the armed forces in World War I. He became a medical officer with the Federal Board for Vocational Education and then worked as a physician in the U.S. Public Health Service. He went to Saint Elizabeth's Hospital in Washington, D.C., where he worked closely with William Alanson White, a major figure in American neuropsychiatry. He held appointments at the University of Maryland Medical School and Sheppard and Enoch Pratt Hospital in Towson, Maryland, from the early 1920s to the early 1930s.

The first period of his clinical work focused on therapeutic approaches to schizophrenia, and he introduced modes of intervention that offered alternatives to traditional forms of custodial care, based on Emil Kraepelin's biological approach, limited largely to diagnostic classification and management of symptoms (see Greenberg & Mitchell, 1983). In time, he shifted the focus of his practice from inpatient psychiatric hospitals to outpatient clinics. In the early 1930s, he moved to Manhattan, where he established an independent clinical practice.

Sullivan was analyzed by Thompson, whom he had encouraged to initiate a training analysis with Sándor Ferenczi in the late 1920s. She spent two months in treatment with Ferenczi in the summer of 1928 and returned for two more courses of analysis before his death in 1933 (Perry, 1982). Sullivan was appointed president of the William Alanson White Foundation and in 1933 became director of the Washington School of Psychiatry, the training institution of the foundation. In 1938 he became coeditor of *Psychiatry*, a journal devoted to development of his interpersonal perspectives.

Like Adler, Sullivan developed a deep interest in social problems, including poverty and racism, and he sought to democratize mental health services and broaden their relevance to contemporary concerns. In 1939 he made a trip to the South to study black youths in rural communities and later carried out research on black adolescents in Washington, D.C. Following the bombing of Hiroshima in 1945, he intensified his involvement in world peace efforts. He served as consultant to the United Nations in efforts to address international tensions and was a member of the commission that established the International Congress of Mental Health.

Sullivan began to develop his interpersonal perspective in 1929 and consolidated his thinking through the 1930s. He drew on a range of disciplines in elaborating his interpersonal point of view. A group of intellectuals associated with the Chicago School of Sociology that included George Herbert Mead, W. I. Thomas, Edward Sapir, and Harold Lasswell was especially influential. He established a close relationship with Sapir, who urged practitioners to integrate work in anthropology and sociology with psychoanalytic thought.

Sullivan published only one work presenting his theory, *Conceptions of Modern Psychiatry*, which appeared in 1947, two years before his death. However, he kept detailed notebooks and recorded many of his lectures to trainees at the Washington School of Psychiatry. Five books based on this material have been published. *The Interpersonal Theory of Psychiatry*, published in 1953, and drawing on lectures Sullivan gave in 1946–1947, provides the most comprehensive account of his interpersonal perspective. *The Psychiatric Interview* (1954) and *Clinical Studies in Psychiatry* (1956) are drawn from lectures given between 1943 and 1945. Other works include *Schizophrenia as a Human Process*, published in 1962, and *The Fusion of Psychiatry and Social Science*, published in 1964. Helen Swick Perry provides the most comprehensive account of his life in her biography, *Psychiatrist of America: The Life of Harry Stack Sullivan* (1982).

Theoretical Perspectives

Sullivan introduced a new framework for understanding personality development, problems in living, and methods of therapeutic intervention. He locates personality or self in the social field. "All organisms live in continuous, communal existence with their necessary environment," he writes, emphasizing the mutual, reciprocal influence of person and the social surround (Sullivan, 1953, p. 31). In departing from structural models of the individual, he defines personality as "the relatively enduring pattern of recurrent interpersonal situations which characterize a human life" (pp. 110–111). He conceives of self as process, shaped by interactive experience in relational fields. Personality, he argues, can "never be isolated from the complex of interpersonal relations in which the person lives and has his being" (Sullivan, 1940, p. 10).

In Sullivan's developmental schema, the nature of early interactions with primary caretaking figures shapes the organization of personality and representative ways of negotiating need and vulnerability in the interpersonal field. His conceptions of motivation emphasize fundamental needs for satisfaction and security, which are initially negotiated in the infant-caretaker dyad. His "tenderness theorem" explains the ways in which the infant's expressions of need evoke complementary responses in caretaking figures that foster personality integration. Needs for satisfaction operate as "integrating tendencies," he explains, theorizing that the needs of the infant are "ingrained from the very beginning of things as an interpersonal need" (Sullivan, 1953, p. 40).

According to his developmental theory, however, the infant's vulnerability, dependency, and conditions of care in early relational experience inevitably generate anxiety and restrict ways of negotiating need. He theorizes that the child internalizes caretakers' anxiety through "empathic linkage"; a second source of anxiety is inherent in the child's experience of dependency. Because of the noxious and inescapable character of anxiety, Sullivan reasons, the need for security is a crucial factor in the child's development; he defines security as freedom from anxiety. The child elaborates repetitive patterns of interaction in ongoing efforts to reduce anxiety and adapt to the requirements of particular interpersonal environments, maximize satisfaction and security, and preserve connections with others. Like Suttie, Fairbairn, Winnicott, and Bowlby, Sullivan believes that the actual characteristics of caretakers have a major impact on the child, and he is particularly attuned to the relative balance of anxiety-free and anxiety-filled domains of experience in the social surround.

His formulations of psychopathology, or "dynamisms of difficulty," center on defensive behaviors and self-defeating, maladaptive ways of relating. To avoid or reduce potential anxiety, he theorizes, the individual develops protective strategies and controls over behavior. One avoids punishment by suspending expressions of need or desire that have the potential to threaten others and complying with their expectations; for example, one may conform to parents' wishes in order to meet requirements for conditions of care. Safety and security measures make up the "self-system" that sanctions certain forms of behavior (the good-me self), prohibits other forms of behavior (the bad-me self), and excludes from consciousness those that are too threatening to be considered (the not-me self). Through these defensive operations, the self-system functions as a filter for awareness. Sullivan uses the term "selective inattention" to describe the unconscious refusal to register anxiety-generating feelings and experiences.

The self-system limits anxiety, to be sure, but it also constrains one's ability to process experience, negotiate need, and participate in relational life. Sullivan theorizes that the self-system fails to take account of information that challenges its present organization. Accordingly, one fails to register internal and external information that could potentially help one learn from experience. Sullivan (1953) called the self-system "the principal stumbling block to favorable changes in personality" (p. 169).

Sullivan places particular importance on the place of cognition in his conceptions of experience. He distinguishes three modes of experience: prototaxic, parataxic, and syntaxic. Prototaxic experience "may be regarded as the discrete series of momentary states of the sensitive organism" (Sullivan, 1953, p. 29). Hall et al. (1998) compare this mode to what William James called the "stream of consciousness," raw sensations, images, and feelings that flow through the mind of a sensate being. This type of experience characterizes the early months of life and is a precondition for the emergence of the other two forms. The parataxic experience consists of seeing causal relationships between events that occur at the same time but are not logically related; they are associative connections. The third and most developed mode of thinking is the syntaxic experience, which consists of consensually validated symbol activity, especially that of a verbal nature (for further discussion, see Hall et al., 1998)

Clinical Perspectives

Although Sullivan's interpersonal perspective originated in his work with schizophrenic patients, he increasingly addressed a wider range of problems in living in his clinical practice. He framed the diagnosis not in the language of psychiatric taxonomies but in interpersonal terms. People are defined largely by their relational life, he reasons, and what matters more than particular symptoms are the interpersonal strategies that one develops to negotiate the vicissitudes of ordinary every life. His emphasis on the interpersonal contexts of problems in functioning led to greater awareness of the central role of the helping relationship in the therapeutic process.

Concepts of therapeutic action center on the interactive nature of psychosocial intervention. Sullivan (1950/1964) views the clinician as a "participant-observer" in the interactive field of the therapeutic situation: "The theory of interpersonal relations lays great stress on the method of participant observation, and relegates data obtained by other methods to a most secondary importance. This in turn implies that skill in the face to face, or person to person, psychiatric interview is of fundamental importance" (p. 122). The clinician not only is an observer focusing on representative patterns of interaction but is engaged in the interpersonal process as "subject" and "object" (see Wolitzky & Eagle, 1997, p. 63).

Sullivan used the term "psychiatric interview" to characterize the interpersonal, face-to-face context of therapeutic interaction. In *The Psychiatric Interview* (1954), he describes it as "a system, or series of systems, of interpersonal processes, arising from participant observation in which the interviewer derives certain conclusions about the interviewee" (p. 128). For Sullivan, the interview is a "vocal communication" between two individuals; the interviewer attends not only to the content of the communications but also to the ways in which it is rendered—intonations, rates of speech, and other expressive behaviors. The interviewer is alert to subtle shifts in vocalizations because these may reveal clues about the focal problems, defensive operations, and attitudes toward others.

In the inception stage, the interviewer limits questions and maintains an attitude of observation, trying to understand *why, now,* the person is seeking help and what is the matter. In the reconnaissance stage, the clinician explores essential concerns that have shaped the individual's past and present experience, trying to understand the ways in which earlier ways of being and relating, established in the context of the family, influence current modes of functioning. Sullivan is active and direct in his efforts to clarify earlier patterns of interaction, as he demonstrates in the following illustrations of his method: "Let us see where in the world these patterns begin of presuming the other fellow is taking a slice when he is saying something that is approximately complimentary. Where did that begin?" (Sullivan, 1956, p. 280). In another consultation, Sullivan (1940) explores the patient's reactions to him: "This impression that you have had about me must have a history, must be the recollection of some such a person who was really important to you—perhaps you can recall someone?" (p. 235). By the end of the first two stages, the clinician has formed hypotheses about the person's problems and their origins (see Mitchell, 1997, for an extended account of Sullivan's approach to assessment in the psychiatric interview).

Therapeutic intervention continues to explore problematic aspects of interaction with others, including the clinician, and provides opportunities for experiential learning that enlarge ways of being and relating. From the interpersonal perspective, the individual engages the clinician in representative ways of being and relating. The practitioner draws on the give-and-take of interactive experience in efforts to identify security operations.

The more the individual learns about internal processes and interpersonal behavior, Sullivan (1940) believes, the more he or she can disrupt maladaptive patterns and develop more adaptive and fulfilling ways of being and relating: "Until a patient has seen clearly and unmistakably a concrete example of the way in which unresolved situations from the distant past color the perception of the present situations and overcomplicate action in them, there can be . . . no therapeutically satisfactory expansion of the self" (p. 205).

Clinical Applications

From the perspective of contemporary interpersonal understanding, as Mitchell and Black (1995) explain, the clinician assumes that he or she will inevitably participate in the dynamic patterns of the individual's most problematic ways of being and relating. The practitioner's experience serves as a crucial source of understanding in efforts to identify, challenge, and revise maladaptive patterns of functioning ("dynamisms of difficulty"). The following account provides an illustration of the ways in which Sullivan's ideas inform the clinician's understanding and use of interactive experience in the clinical situation.

The case of Robert B., explored from a Kleinian perspective in chapter 6, illustrates essential concerns in interpersonal conceptions of the therapeutic endeavor. By way of review, Robert initiated psychotherapy after he was suspended from his job. He acknowledged growing frustration and anger in interactions with coworkers and described ongoing patterns of strain and rupture in his relational life. In the course of the assessment interview, he grew increasingly impatient and argumentative, challenging the clinician's attempts to explore concerns beyond the workplace, coming to see the session as "useless." He pressured the practitioner to "come up with a solution" for his difficulties.

In approaching the case from an interpersonal perspective, the clinician would focus carefully on Robert's accounts of relational experience, pressing for concrete detail, trying to understand what happens between him and others in the context of particular relationships and settings. In light of Sullivan's emphasis on developmental history in diagnostic evaluation, the clinician would selectively explore the ways in which earlier conditions of care and formative experience in family life had shaped ways of being and relating, seeking to identify the antecedents of current behavior. Equally importantly, the practitioner would closely observe patterns of interaction during the sessions, exploring Robert's experience of the therapeutic relationship, defensive operations, and potential enactments of dysfunctional behaviors in therapeutic interaction, seeking to identify central "dynamisms of difficulty" that perpetuate problems in living.

Exploration of earlier family experience revealed that Robert had been the object of his father's anger, bullying, and teasing through childhood and adolescence. He had developed a deep sense of inadequacy, and his aggressive modes of behavior served as security operations that reduced his sense of vulnerability and fear. Ironically, these attempts to mediate his experience of vulnerability intensified his sense of inadequacy, precipitating strain and rupture in relational life, and perpetuating further expressions of aggression and grandiosity in interactions with others. This vicious circle of behavior emerged in the therapeutic process as the practitioner attempted to explore his underlying feelings of fear and inadequacy.

As Wachtel (1993, 2008) emphasizes in his interpersonal formulations of problems in functioning, the individual will repeat dysfunctional patterns of behavior so long as he or she continues to carry out familiar ways of being, relating, and living. One cannot relinquish reflexive patterns of behavior because the intensity of the fear overrides whatever understanding of difficulties one may have achieved. The clinician must address the underlying anxiety if the client is to disrupt reflexive patterns of behavior and establish new ways of being and relating.

Robert's efforts to maintain security in his reflexive ways of negotiating interpersonal life had undermined his efforts to establish relationships that could potentially sustain him over time. The cycle of strain, rupture, and repair in the therapeutic relationship served as crucial sources of experiential learning, providing opportunities for Robert to process earlier trauma, deepen understanding of defensive processes, and develop skills in managing his vulnerability, inadequacy, and fear.

Karen Horney

Karen Horney rejected Freud's biological system of thought and introduced an interpersonal perspective that emphasizes the role of culture and relational life in conceptions of personality development and problems in living.

Although she explored a range of concerns over the course of her work, she is increasingly recognized as having fashioned a distinctive psychology of the self. Scholars identify three distinct periods in the development of her thought, broadly focused on feminine psychology, culture, and relational life (Paris, 1994).

In the first phase of her work, extending from the 1920s to the early 1930s, she challenged Freud's formulations of feminine development. In a series of forceful essays, she emphasized the role of cultural factors as sources of gender identity and explored the ways social conditions restrict women's opportunities to develop capacities, assume roles, and realize their potential. Although her writings on gender remained outside the mainstream of psychoanalytic thought for many years, they were republished in 1967 as *Feminine Psychology*, and she is increasingly recognized as the first major psychoanalytic feminist. Nancy Chodorow (1989) traces the political and theoretical origins of psychoanalytic feminism to her work, which continues to shape understandings of gender in contemporary psychoanalysis.

Her second period of work was carried out in the late 1930s during her time as a member of the so-called cultural school, which included Harry Stack Sullivan, Eric Fromm, and Clara Thompson. Two major works, *The Neurotic Personality of Our Time* (1937) and *New Ways in Psychoanalysis* (1939), deepened appreciation of the role of cultural conditions in psychopathology and generated studies of culture from psychodynamic perspectives.

In her third period of work, the products of which were introduced to a general readership in two books, *Our Inner Conflicts* (1945), and *Neurosis and Human Growth* (1950), she theorized that maladaptive conditions in relational and social life predispose individuals to defensive, constricted modes of functioning. She described a series of defensive strategies encompassing intrapsychic and interpersonal domains of experience and emphasized interactive experience in her conceptions of therapeutic practice. As we will see, her approach to psychotherapy focused on present conditions rather than on past events and tried to help individuals suspend defensive, neurotic ways of being and bring their "real" selves to bear in day-to-day life. Paris (1994) provides a careful review of the development of her thought, in which he comes to see her as one of the founders of humanistic psychology in light of her emphasis on self-realization as the source of health, well-being, and the good life.

Life and Work

Horney was born Karen Danielsen in a suburb of Hamburg, Germany, on September 15, 1885, and died in Manhattan on December 4, 1952. She provides moving accounts of her family life in the diaries she began to keep at the age of thirteen, revealing her sense of inadequacy and suffering (Horney, 1980). She decided during her adolescence that she wanted to become a physician and pursued her education in spite of her father's objections (Paris, 1999).

Horney was one of the first women in Germany to be admitted to medical school. She studied at the universities of Freiburg and Gottingen before graduating from the medical school at University of Berlin. In 1910 she married Oskar Horney, a social scientist, whom she would divorce in 1938. She entered analysis with Karl Abraham and decided to train as a psychoanalyst. She was one of six founding members of the Berlin Psychoanalytic Institute. She taught there from 1920 until 1932, when Franz Alexander invited her to serve as associate director of the Chicago Psychoanalytic Institute. Two years later, she moved to New York, where she taught at the New York Psychoanalytic Institute.

Like Sullivan and Fromm, however, she was deeply troubled by the orthodoxy of Freudian thought, and publication of *New Ways in Psychoanalysis* precipitated her break with the Freudian-oriented New York Institute in 1941. She founded the American Institute for Psychoanalysis that same year and established the *American Journal of Psychoanalysis*, which she edited.

The last fifteen years of her life were extraordinarily energetic and creative, as Paris (1994) shows in his biographical account. She published five books that would be recognized as seminal works; continued to carry out her work as clinician, supervisor, and lecturer; served on the faculty of the New School for Social Research and participated in the intellectual circles of New York; learned how to paint; and read widely. She had developed an interest in Zen in the late 1930s and visited Zen monasteries in Japan with D. T. Suzuki, the Zen scholar, shortly before her death.

Her major works are *The Neurotic Personality of Our Time* (1937), *New Ways in Psychoanalysis* (1939), *Our Inner Conflicts* (1945), and *Neurosis and Human Growth* (1950). Paris (1994) provides a full account of Horney's theories in his character portrait. Susan Quinn (1987) describes the social and cultural conditions that shaped Horney's life in her biography, and Marcia Westkott (1986) shows how Horney's thought enlarges understandings of feminist concerns.

Theoretical Perspectives

Horney believed that Freud had placed too much emphasis on biology and failed to take account of actual experience in the outer world, and she saw his drive psychology as reductive and mechanistic: "My conviction, expressed in a nutshell, is that psychoanalysis should outgrow the limitations set by its being an instinctivistic and genetic psychology" (Horney, 1939, p. 8). Freud incorrectly assumed that the feelings, attitudes, and relationships in his particular culture were universal, she argued. Horney understood neurotic conflict as an outcome of pathogenic relationships, adverse environments, and cultural conditions that constrain efforts to negotiate needs and realize potential.

Like Adler and Sullivan, she believed that Freud had failed to appreciate the crucial role of relationships, social life, and culture in human experience. In time, she elaborated a cultural perspective, proposing that we internalize negative cultural stereotypes in the form of basic anxiety and inner conflicts. "There are certain typical difficulties inherent in our culture," she writes, "which mirror themselves as conflicts in every individual's life and which, accumulated, may lead to the formation of neuroses" (Horney, 1937, p. 284). She describes a series of trends in social life that predispose people to neurotic conflict, including social isolation and the principle of individual competition in economic life. At the root of psychic disturbance, she believes, are "neurotic trends," or "unconscious strivings developed in order to cope with life despite fears, helplessness, and isolation" (Horney, 1942, p. 40).

Horney challenges Freud's conception of the Oedipus complex, framing it as an interpersonal dilemma originating in the child's experience of rejection, overprotection, or punishment in relationships with caretaking figures. Further, she departs from Freud's view of aggression as an innate constituent of human experience. Like Suttie, she comes to see aggressive behavior as a means of preserving self. Finally, she understands narcissism as inflation and over-evaluation of the self originating in feelings of vulnerability and insecurity (for further discussion, see Hall et al., 1998; Paris, 1994).

Like Winnicott, Horney emphasizes the role of the social environment in the development of the person. Relational provisions and facilitating conditions over the course of infancy and childhood foster the emergence of the self. These include "an atmosphere of warmth" that allows children to express their own thoughts and feelings, and the "healthy friction with the wishes and will" of others around them (Horney, 1950, p. 18). If parents and other caretaking figures are unable to meet basic needs and recognize the child as an individual, the child develops a sense of "basic anxiety" that prevents him or her from "relating himself [or herself] to others with the spontaneity of his [or her] real feelings," perpetuating defensive strategies (Horney, 1950, p. 18).

Following Sullivan, Horney views anxiety as a core constituent in human experience, and she assumes that children must inevitably negotiate vulnerability and feelings of helplessness over the course of development. If caretaking figures fail to provide loving support, security, and guidance, she theorizes, children are predisposed to a "basic anxiety" that constrains ways of living. She defines "basic anxiety" as "the feeling a child has of being isolated and helpless in a potentially hostile world. A wide range of adverse factors in the environment can produce this insecurity in the child: direct or indirect domination, indifference, erratic behavior, lack of respect for the child's individual needs, lack of real guidance, disparaging attitudes, too much admiration, or the absence of it, lack of reliable warmth, having to take sides in parental disagreements, too much or too little responsibility, overprotection, isolation from other children, injustice, discrimination, unkept promises, hostile atmosphere, and so on" (Horney, 1945, p. 41). She characterizes such adverse factors as "basic evil."

In her dynamic formulations of development, the child's experience of "basic evil" precipitates feelings of resentment or "basic hostility." This creates a dilemma for the child, however, because expressions of hostility have the potential to threaten or destroy existing conditions of love and care. She theorizes that the child deals with hostility by repressing it, perpetuating anxiety and hostility. She describes a series of strategies that the child may engage in efforts to manage the experience of anger and resentment: "I have to repress my hostility because I need you," "I have to repress my hostility because I am afraid of you," "I have to repress my hostility for fear of losing love" (Horney, 1937, p. 86; see Hall et al., 1998, and Paris, 1994, for extended accounts of core concepts and dynamic processes summarized here).

The repression intensifies the conflict, precipitating vicious circles of thought, feeling, and behavior. The experience of vulnerability generates needs for affection and reassurance. When these needs are not fulfilled, the child feels rejected, which intensifies anxiety and hostility. The growing hostility must be repressed in order to preserve the child's sense of security, anxiety grows, and the need for more repression generates more hostility. The individual is embedded in a cycle of intensifying distress and self-defeating, destructive behavior.

In formulations that parallel Suttie's relational perspective, Horney theorizes that the insecure, anxious child develops various approaches to deal with the experience of helplessness, alienation, and isolation. The child may assume a hostile stance and attack those who have mistreated or rejected him or her. Or the child may assume a submissive stance in efforts to restore the lost love. He or she may develop an unrealistic, idealized view of him- or herself in order to compensate for a deep sense of inferiority. The child may make threats or engage in coercion in efforts to force expressions of love or may turn aggression inward and undermine the self (Horney, 1937, 1950; see Hall et al., 1998).

As she developed her relational perspective, Horney (1945) described three patterns of interpersonal defense in approaches to neurotic conflict, broadly classified in the following conceptions of behavior: (1) moving toward others, seen in irrational needs for love and approval; (2) moving away from others, marked by withdrawal and isolation; and (3) moving against others, represented in unchecked need for power. She theorizes that in the first category, the individual attempts to deal with vulnerability through compliance and self-efficacy, reasoning: "If you love me, you will not hurt me." The second is characterized by withdrawal, resignation, and seeming indifference: "If I withdraw, nothing can hurt me." The third strategy, moving against people, is an aggressive approach. The individual assumes, "If I have power, no one can hurt me."

Each of the foregoing "neurotic trends" emphasizes varying aspects of basic anxiety—helplessness in moving toward others, isolation in moving away from others, and hostility in moving against others. As such, they represent basic orientations toward self, interpersonal interactions, and relational life (see Hall et al., 1998; Paris, 1994).

She understands neurotic conflict as a matter of degree. By virtue of being human, all of us struggle with our experience of vulnerability and need. However, requirements for conditions of care over the course of development, marked by periods of rejection, neglect, or abuse, predispose us to neurotic conflict that constrains ways of being and relating. The neurotic individual, having to negotiate greater degrees of anxiety, must rely on irrational solutions. She writes: "The person who is likely to become neurotic is one who has experienced the culturally determined difficulties in an accentuated form, mostly through the medium of childhood experience, and who has consequently been unable to solve them, or has solved them only at great personal cost to his personality. We might call him a stepchild of our culture" (Horney, 1937, p. 290).

In a further development, paralleling Winnicott's conception of the false self, Horney theorizes that neurotic conditions may force the individual to repudiate the "real self" and embrace an idealized version of him- or herself. Here, Horney assumes, the person experiences his or her "real self" as inadequate, unlovable, and unworthy; in an effort to mediate this sense of self as bad, the child creates an idealized image of the person the child feels he or she should be. This "idealized self" is closely linked to unrealistic expectations, leading to what Horney calls "the tyranny of the should" and the "search for glory." The individual pursues the esteem he or she is lacking in efforts to achieve an unrealistic version of the self (see Paris, 1999).

Neurosis, for Horney (1950), is a "special form of human development antithetical to human growth" (p. 13). She writes: "The neurotic process . . . is a problem of self. It is the process of abandoning the real self for an idealized one; of trying to actualize this pseudoself instead of our given human potential; of a destructive warfare between two selves; of allaying this warfare the best, or at any rate the only way we can; and finally by having our constructive forces mobilized by life or by therapy, of finding our real selves" (p. 371).

Horney (1945) describes other solutions to neurotic conflict that overlap with Sullivan's formulations of defensive operations. She observes that one may develop "blind spots" or protectively compartmentalize experience that challenges one's idealized views of self. One may engage in "rationalization," "cynicism," or "excessive self-control." The foregoing efforts to negotiate neurotic conflict, operating out of awareness, inevitably fail.

Anxiety and the search for safety are the core constituents of neurotic development, which constricts the individual's options of choice and reaction and limits realization of the individual's potential. Horney's understanding of neurotic process is closely linked to her concept of the "vicious circle."

She explains: "Any protective device may have, in addition to its reassuring quality, the quality of creating new anxiety" (Horney, 1937, p. 136). By way of illustration, she schematizes the vicious circle generated by the neurotic need for affection as follows: anxiety; intense need for affection, including demands for unconditional love; a feeling of rejection if these demands are not fulfilled; reaction to the rejection with intense hostility; need to repress the hostility because of fear of losing affection; the tension of diffuse anger; increased anxiety; and increased need for reassurance. The very means that reduce anxiety also create new hostility and new anxiety, she explains. "The formation of vicious circles is the main reason why severe neuroses are bound to become worse, even though there is no change in external conditions" (p. 138).

Clinical Perspectives

Horney came to view the essential feature of neurosis as alienation from the core authentic self as a consequence of pathogenic conditions in the social environment. The fundamental task of the therapeutic endeavor is to relinquish neurotic ways of living and "restore the individual to himself, to help him regain his spontaneity and find his center of gravity in himself" (Horney, 1939, p. 11). Following her conception of the "vicious circles" that perpetuate neurotic functioning, the clinician seeks to identify the individual's defensive strategies and understand their functions and consequences and facilitate efforts to establish more fulfilling ways of being, relating, and living.

She increasingly centered on the functions of the helping relationship and the role of interactive experience in her conceptions of the therapeutic process. Like Winnicott, she saw the clinician-client relationship as collaborative, mutual, and democratic in nature; the practitioner is not an authoritative translator of the unconscious. In her teachings on therapeutic techniques, she asserted that intellectual insight is but one aspect of understanding. She feared that "a detached, purely intellectual attitude" would lead to "a mechanical classification of the patient's personality according to our preexisting ideas" (qtd. in Paris, 1999, p. 199) and stressed the importance of intuition and emotion as modes of knowing. Like Ferenczi, Horney views the clinician as a real person with vulnerabilities and shortcomings, and she emphasizes the crucial functions of self-analysis in the practitioner's efforts to understand reactions to clients and foster change and growth (Paris, 1999).

Clinical Applications

The following case reports illustrate central concerns in Horney's theoretical system.

Case Illustration: Challenging Vicious Circles of Behavior.   Martha D., introduced in chapter 8, initiated psychotherapy following treatment for breast cancer because her parents wanted her to process the illness experience. Drawing on her reports of family life and her behavior in the sessions, the practitioner came to realize that she had suspended core authentic experiences of self in order to meet requirements for conditions of care. From the perspective of Horney's formulations, the practitioner would explore the constellation of "neurotic needs" that emerged from her family experience, reflected in her search for approval and her wish to please others and meet their expectations. The foregoing needs would be seen as unrealistic and irrational, generating inner conflict and perpetuating vicious circles of behavior. Horney realizes that neurotic conditions force the individual to repudiate the "real self," which is experienced as inadequate, unlovable, and unworthy. Martha's experience of anxiety and her search for safety constricted her ways of being, relating, and living. The aim of intervention, from the perspective of Horney's formulations, is to restore the authenticity of the self.

Case Illustration: Stages of Understanding.   Horney (1942) illustrates what she describes as "representative stages of understanding" in psychoanalytic psychotherapy in her account of Clare, who initiated psychotherapy at age thirty in an effort to deal with a lack of confidence and a paralyzing fatigue that limited her ability to carry out her work and engage in social life. She distinguishes three phases in Clare's treatment: the discovery of her compulsive modesty, the discovery of her compulsive dependence on a partner, and the realization of her compulsive need to force others to recognize her superiority.

In the first phase of treatment, Horney (1942) explains, Clare tended to minimize her own value and capacities: "not only was she insecure about her assets but she tenaciously denied their existence, insisting that she was not intelligent, attractive, or gifted" (p. 77). She viewed others as superior to herself, reflexively assuming that others were right if there was a dissension of opinion. Horney concludes that she had developed a "compulsive modesty" that violated her most fundamental experience of self and constricted her ways of living. She experienced a "progressive lowering of self-confidence" and a "diffuse discontentment with life" (p. 79).

In time, Clare came to recognize the real, intense anxiety underlying her facade of modesty when she brought an authority of self to bear in the work setting. In asserting herself, she moved beyond "the narrow artificial precincts that she had anxiously preserved. Only when she recognized the truth of this observation did she become fully convinced that her modesty was a face to be maintained of the sake of safety" (Horney, 1942, p. 80). The outcome of this first phase of work, Horney explains, was the beginning development of faith in herself and the courage to "feel and assert her wishes and opinions" (p. 80). The next period of intervention focused on her dependency on a partner. Horney observes that she felt "completely lost, like a small child in a strange wood," when she was temporarily separated from a partner or when a relationship ended. In their analysis of underlying issues, they identified her "unconscious wish to feed on the partner, to expect him to supply the content of her life, to take responsibility for her, to solve all her difficulties and to make her a great person without her having to make efforts of her own" (p. 82).

As Horney observes, this alienated her from her partner and other people as well, because her unrealistic expectations generated disappointment when they were inevitably unfulfilled. "Since she could not defend herself she needed someone else to defend her. Since she could not see her own values she needed someone else to affirm her worth" (Horney, 1942, p. 83). In time, through the processing of her experience, she overcame her sense of helplessness and initiated greater activity. She developed more authority of self, reflected in a dream in which she drives with a friend to a strange country and realizes that she, too, could apply for a driver's license. For Horney, the dream symbolizes a growing realization that she had rights of her own and "need not feel like a helpless appendage" (p. 84). The final phase of psychotherapy explored her ambitious strivings. Horney describes how she disrupted the vicious circles that perpetuated her self-defeating behavior.

In her reflections on the case, Horney observes that it illustrates three fundamental tasks in the therapeutic process: recognition of neurotic trends; discovery of their causes, manifestations, and consequences; and discovery of their interrelations with other parts of the personality. Such understandings inform concrete interventions to identify, disrupt, and revise vicious circles of behavior.

The Interpersonal Tradition in Context: Contemporary Perspectives

The contributions of Sullivan and Horney have shaped the development of relational theory, and their views continue to influence the practice of psychotherapy. Both thinkers emphasized the social, cultural, political, and economic contexts of problems in living. Sullivan's focus on the interactive field of psychosocial intervention and the practitioner as a participant-observer has informed the development of clinical theory and practice across the major schools of thought. Interpersonal perspectives have shaped conceptions of brief psychotherapy (McCaughan, 1999), integrative models of treatment (Wachtel, 2008), and interactive experience in evidence-based practice (Borden, 2008b). The pragmatism and pluralism of contemporary interpersonal thought are exemplified in the writings of Edgar Levenson (1972, 1983), Benjamin Wolstein (1987), and John Fiscalini (2004).

Heinz Kohut and the Emergence of Self Psychology

I'm trying to grasp what makes this man tick. I have no interest at this particular moment to help him tick differently. I don't even know yet how he ticks. This is my general attitude.

—Heinz Kohut, *Kohut Seminars*

In fashioning his psychology of the self, Heinz Kohut engaged domains of human experience that Freud had failed to encompass in drive psychology, forming what he would come to see as a new paradigm in contemporary psychoanalysis. Although Kohut did not make connections between his theoretical formulations and the contributions of earlier relational thinkers, we find clear antecedents in the work of Suttie, Fairbairn, Bowlby, and Winnicott, all of whom emphasize the crucial ways in which caretaking figures facilitate or undermine the emergence of the self and relational life. There are striking parallels with the humanistic perspective of Carl Rogers as well. Kohut had been trained as a classical psychoanalyst, and his early thinking was based on the fundamental assumptions of Freudian ego psychology. He cultivated friendships with important figures in the field, establishing close relationships with Heinz Hartmann and Anna Freud. Freud, iconic in her symbolic significance, "pinned very many hopes for the future of analysis on him," Charles Strozier (2001, p. 170) writes in his biography of Kohut. In developing his theoretical formulations, however, he realized that the classical psychoanalytic paradigm failed to address the implications of his clinical work, in which he had explored problems in functioning that he traced to arrests in the development of the self.

In *The Restoration of the Self*, which appeared in 1977, Kohut characterized his perspective as "the psychology of the self," presenting it as a comprehensive system of personality development, psychopathology, and psychotherapy. In this work he defined the self as the organizing force in personality development and the center of being. The self is "the way a person experiences himself as himself" (Kohut, 1977, p. xv), a mental structure encompassing thoughts, feelings, and actions that are subjectively experienced as "me." In his formulation, the core self or "nuclear self" serves as the basis for "our sense of being an independent center of initiative and perception, integrated with our most central ambitions and ideals and with our experience that our body and mind form a unit in space and a continuum in time. This cohesive and enduring psychic configuration . . . forms the central sector of the personality" (pp. 178–179).

Kohut placed subjective experience at the center of his theoretical project, bridging structural and phenomenological perspectives in his renderings of the person. Classical Freudian thought had focused on the vicissitudes of sexual and aggressive drives, emphasizing analysis of neurotic conflict. Kohut (1977) saw Freud as having "illuminated and explained a vast area of human psychic life that had heretofore been covered by darkness," but his drive psychology "left a significant and important layer of human experience essentially untouched" (p. 238). Classical theory, he wrote, "cannot illuminate the essence of fractured, enfeebled, discontinuous human existence" (p. 238). Kohut's "Tragic Man" struggles to fulfill the aims of the core self—to realize values, ideals, ambitions, and goals that transcend the pleasure principle of Freud's drive psychology.

Kohut discussed a range of phenomena that the drive model failed to explain, focusing on fundamental concerns in the realm of personal subjectivity: cohesion, coherence, and continuity in states of being; embodiment and the sense of vitality and aliveness; capacities for agency and initiative; and the ways in which one brings self to bear and generates experience felt as real, meaningful, and distinctly one's own.

In the years since his death in 1981, self psychology has emerged as an influential school of thought, shaping theoretical developments and clinical practice in relational psychoanalysis, contemporary psychotherapy, and social work. More broadly, Kohut's work has informed thinking in theology, philosophy, religion, ethics, and the humanities, and scholars have recognized him as an important figure in the transition from modern to postmodern conceptions of the self and social life.

Life and Work

Kohut was born in Vienna on May 3, 1913, and died in Chicago on October 8, 1981. He was raised in an upper-middle-class assimilated Jewish family in Vienna. His father, Felix Kohut, had been trained as a classical pianist; after serving in World War I, however, he left his musical career and entered the paper business, depleted, depressed, and embittered, having been traumatized by his experience as a prisoner of war. His mother, Else Lampl, was devoted to her only child. From an early age, Strozier (2001) writes in his biography, she refused to allow separations between herself and her adored son: "His mother was everywhere in his life" (p. 19). Kohut, experiencing his mother as intrusive and controlling, would recall his early years as unhappy and lonely.

Early in his adolescence, his mother hired a tutor, Ernst Morawetz, to provide companionship and accompany her son to the opera, the theater, and art museums. Kohut formed a strong bond with his tutor and describes their relationship in his autobiographical case study, "The Two Analyses of Mr. Z." He entered the Doblinger Gymnasium at age eleven, after four years of private tutoring at home, and began to immerse himself in the classical and humanistic traditions of Europe. He read *The Iliad* and *The Odyssey* in their original Greek, discovered the writings of Goethe and Thomas Mann, and began to explore music, the arts, and cultural life.

He enrolled in medical school at the University of Vienna at the age of nineteen. In the course of his studies, following the death of his father, he initiated psychoanalysis with August Aichhorn, a close friend of Freud, who was widely regarded as a master clinician. He established a strong bond with Aichhorn, who brought integrity and "human freedom" to the therapeutic process; the treatment was ended prematurely, however, by the Nazi annexation of Austria in spring of 1938 (Strozier, 2001). Kohut graduated from medical school that year and in 1939 left Vienna for England, where he remained for a year before coming to the United States in 1940. He joined his childhood friend Siegmund Levarie in Chicago.

Kohut completed residencies in neurology and psychiatry at the University of Chicago in the early 1940s and began to train at the Chicago Institute for Psychoanalysis in 1946, undergoing psychoanalysis with Ruth Eissler. He married Elizabeth Meyers in 1948; she trained as a social worker. Their only child, Thomas August, was named after Aichhorn. He joined the faculty of the institute following his graduation in 1950 and served as clinical lecturer in the Department of Psychiatry at the University of Chicago. He would work as an independent practitioner over the course of his career.

Kohut began to publish articles on psychoanalysis and the arts in the 1950s; his first publication, "On the Enjoyment of Listening to Music," was coauthored with his close friend Levarie, who had become a professor of music at the University of Chicago. His first major paper, however, focused on empathy. In "Introspection, Empathy, and Psychoanalysis," published in 1959, he argued that empathy—"vicarious introspection"—constituted the fundamental mode of knowing in psychoanalysis.

He viewed himself as a classical Freudian psychoanalyst, placing his work in the ego psychological tradition, and served as president of the American Psychoanalytic Association in 1964. In his first book, *The Analysis of the Self: A Systematic Analysis of the Treatment of Narcissistic Personality Disorders*, Kohut saw himself as extending Freud's theory of narcissism. In his account of personality development, Freud (1914/1957b) had described the transition from a state of primary narcissism to the capacity for object love as a defining feature of normal maturation. Classical views implied that narcissistic concerns diminish as development proceeds; the individual renounces infantile wishes and engages in relational life. In elaborating his views, however, Kohut (1984) theorized that fundamental narcissistic needs operate across the course of life in healthy functioning, and capacities for object love develop in a parallel manner. He described the "narcissistic personality disorder" as a diagnostic category and linked problems in functioning to disruptions in the development of the self.

In his second work, *The Restoration of the Self*, appearing in 1977, he engaged "the psychology of the self in the broader sense," where the self is seen as "the center of the psychological universe" (p. xv). He departed from classical Freudian theory in this work, viewing the emergence of the self as the fundamental organizing force in personality development. He emphasized the crucial role of relational life—attuned, responsive "selfobject" environments—in the maturation of the self. A year later, his papers, edited by Paul Ornstein, were published in two volumes entitled *Search for the Self*. Although Kohut struggled with life-threatening illnesses in later life, he continued to write, teach, and practice. His last book, *How Does Analysis Cure?* was nearly finished at the time of his death.

As he developed his ideas, Kohut created a close circle of collaborators in Chicago, including Arnold Goldberg, Ernest Wolf, Michael Franz Basch, Marian and Paul Tolpin, Anna and Paul Ornstein, and David Terman, all of whom would continue to develop and extend his formulations. In the field of social work, Miriam Elson, who served as lecturer at the University of Chicago's School of Social Service Administration, began to apply the concepts of self psychology to psychosocial intervention (Elson, 1986). Joseph Palombo, Constance Goldberg, and Jill Gardner have elaborated self psychological perspectives over the course of their teaching, supervision, and practice in Chicago. Strozier provides a scholarly and compelling account of Kohut's life and work in his biography, *Heinz Kohut: The Making of a Psychoanalyst* (2001).

Theoretical Perspectives

Kohut (1977, 1982) understood psychoanalysis as the science of complex mental states—he characterized it as "the science of the human soul"—and defined its methods of investigation as empathy and introspection. In his conception of the discipline, knowledge is generated through empathic immersion in the subjective states of experience, not through observation of behavior. "We designate phenomena as mental, psychic or psychological if our mode of observation includes introspection and empathy as an essential constituent" (Kohut, 1959, p. 462).

He made distinctions between "experience-near" and "experience-distant" theory in his writings on psychoanalytic research and clinical practice. Theoretical formulations generated by empathic processing of the individual's experiential world are experience-near; theoretical formulations based on external frames of reference are experience-distant.

Kohut came to see classical psychoanalytic theory—based on an outdated nineteenth-century philosophy of science, and predicated on notions of "objective" truth—as mechanistic, reductive, and experience-distant, removed from the lived experience of actual people, and he believed that theoreticians should return to the subjective experience of individuals in continued revision and elaboration of ideas. In the context of the therapeutic situation, he urged clinicians to remain close to the experience-near as participant-observers, seeking to understand the meaning and functions of behavior from the patient's point of view, and forming provisional hypotheses about what is the matter, rather than imposing predetermined categories of meaning from grand theoretical systems.

Although Kohut began to develop his formulations within the framework of Freudian drive psychology, he departed from classical thought and introduced what he would come to see as an alternative depth psychology. His theoretical perspective emerged out of his clinical practice with narcissistically vulnerable patients, many of whom were unable to make use of traditional psychoanalytic methods of treatment that had been developed for neurotic problems in functioning.

In his view, the structural model of ego psychology failed to account for the vulnerabilities that he encountered in his practice. The individuals he was working with experienced a range of problems in functioning, including periods of fragmentation following loss of cohesion in sense of self; difficulties in generating experience felt as real and meaningful; states of depletion, emptiness, and deadness; fluctuations in morale and self-esteem; lapses in empathy; feelings of entitlement and envy; incessant longings for admiration and reassurance; and ongoing disappointment in relational life. Something was the matter, Kohut realized, in the way his patients experienced themselves as people (see Greenberg & Mitchell, 1983; Mitchell & Black, 1995).

Using his method of vicarious introspection and empathic attunement, Kohut attempted to listen anew to his patients and immerse himself in their worlds, seeking to understand experience from their subjective perspective. In the course of his clinical work, he found that narcissistically vulnerable patients generated particular patterns of interacting that he eventually conceptualized as forms of selfobject transference. He traced the needs for mirroring and idealization that emerged in the therapeutic relationship to earlier lapses and failings in care that had arrested the development of the self. He came to see his patients' behavior in the therapeutic situation as efforts to reengage developmental processes that had been compromised and generate experience that would help them negotiate defects or deficits in their sense of self, which had predisposed them to vulnerability, fragmentation, and maladaptive patterns of functioning.

On the basis of his clinical experience, Kohut understood selfobject transferences and relational provisions as crucial elements in efforts to reinstate arrested developmental processes and strengthen the cohesion of the self. In contrast to Freudian concepts of therapeutic action that had emphasized neutrality, abstinence, and interpretation of neurotic conflict, Kohut saw patients as having aborted developmental needs that clinicians must recognize, understand, and meet in the course of the therapeutic process.

Personality Development

The core of personality development, as Kohut (1977) came to understand it, is the maturation of a cohesive sense of self, generated and sustained through the attunement, empathy, and responsiveness of caretaking figures who meet ongoing needs for validation, support, and a sense of belonging. Like Bowlby, Kohut sees the infant as "pre-adapted" or "hardwired" to form connections and elicit crucial responses from caretaking figures in the social surround, whose ongoing responsiveness brings a sense of coherence and continuity to the emerging self. In his account of development, the self emerges in the interplay between innate potential and the empathic provisions of caretaking figures.

Although one cannot yet speak of a self at the start of life, Kohut theorized, caregivers relate to the infant *as if* it has a self, an empathic provision that Kohut regards as essential in the development of the rudimentary self. The attunement and responsiveness of the caretaking environment fosters the child's healthy sense of omnipotence. Parental figures mirror the infant's grandiosity and provide opportunities for idealization, fostering the development of the self. These narcissistic states of being—crucial in the formation of the core or "nuclear" self—are slowly transformed through exposure to reality. As maturation proceeds, the child is increasingly able to manage frustration of narcissistic needs following incremental lapses in the caretaking experience. Like Winnicott, Kohut views "optimal frustration" as a critical provision in later stages of development. Over time, the child comes to realize the illusory nature of his or her experience of self and others, consolidating capacities to preserve cohesive and continuous states of being as he or she negotiates the vicissitudes of ordinary everyday life.

Caregivers serve crucial functions as selfobjects in his formulations of personality development, providing coherence and continuity to the nascent self. As Kohut came to define the term, selfobjects are neither "self" nor "objects" as such; rather, the concept refers to the subjective experience of psychologically sustaining functions provided by individuals or objects. The selfobject relationship, then, is an intrapsychic experience, not an interpersonal relationship per se (Kohut, 1971). Kohut (1977) writes: "The child's rudimentary psyche participates in the selfobject's highly developed psychic organization; the child experiences the feeling states of the selfobject—they are transmitted to the child via touch and tone of voice and perhaps by still other means—as if they were his own" (p. 86). What matters is our experience of others, who, as Strozier (2001) explains, are used "to form the fabric of our beings" (p. 195).

As Kohut continued to develop his theory, he conceptualized three forms of selfobject experience that he came to see as fundamental in the development of the self, which he categorized as mirroring, idealizing, and twinship.

Mirroring selfobjects confirm the child's "innate sense of vigor, greatness, and perfection" (Kohut & Wolf, 1978, p. 414), providing experiences of recognition, acceptance, and admiration, and affirming the wholeness, essential goodness, and grandeur of the self. Validation and mirroring processes foster the development of self-esteem, assertiveness, and ambition and are closely linked to capacities for fulfillment in one's achievements and pleasure in the pursuit of interests and activities. In the context of his developmental schema, the "grandiose self" of infancy is slowly transformed through the affirming and admiring responses of mirroring selfobjects, leading to capacities for healthy self-assertiveness.

Idealizing selfobjects serve as sources of strength, providing opportunities for the child to merge with omnipotent figures who generate experiences of power, infallibility, and calm. The experience of idealization fosters the development of capacities for self-regulation and self-soothing; it is also closely linked with the establishment of ideals and values, essential concerns and goals, and capacities for respect and admiration in relational life.

Alter-ego selfobjects strengthen the self by evoking the experience of twinship, a presence of essential likeness with others, and fostering a sense of connection, belonging, and kinship. Kohut related twinship or alter-ego experiences to the establishment of capacities to make optimal use of talents and skills. In subsequent writings, Ernest Wolf (1988), one of Kohut's collaborators, introduced the concept of the adversarial selfobject, which sustains the self by providing experiences of difference that foster the development of personal agency and self-assertiveness.

Kohut describes selfobjects as providing "nutrients" to the self, and he compares the empathic responsiveness of caretaking figures to "psychological oxygen." The selfobject functions provided by others are gradually internalized as self-functions, or inner psychic structure, through the process of transmuting internalization. In Kohut's developmental schema, "optimal frustration" compels the infant to internalize the selfobject in the form of particular functions; over time, the child withdraws the magical, narcissistic expectations of the selfobject and comes to carry out the function that the object previously provided. Selfobject functions foster development of capacities for self-cohesion, self-regulation, self-soothing, and self-righting (Kohut, 1971; Tolpin, 1983).

The fundamental task of early development, in Kohut's schema, is to establish cohesion and vitality in sense of self and to form an "inner program" or "blueprint for life" that will foster realization of innate skills and talents. The nuclear self "contains the individual's most enduring values and ideals but also his most deeply anchored goals, purposes and ambitions" (Strozier, 2001, p. 179). The need for selfobjects continues across the course of life,

Kohut believes, arguing that we need affirming, empathic support from others for health, well-being, and fulfillment, just as we need oxygen for physical survival (Kohut, 1984). "In the view of self psychology," he writes,

> man lives in a matrix of selfobjects from birth to death. He needs selfobjects for his psychological survival, just as he needs oxygen in his environment throughout life for physiological survival. Certainly the individual is exposed to the anxiety and guilt of unsolvable conflict and to the miseries of lowered self-esteem following the realization that he has failed to reach his aims or live up to his ideals. But as long as he feels that he is surrounded by selfobjects and feels reassured by their presence—either by their direct responses to him, or on the basis of past experiences, via his confidence in their lasting concern—even conflict, failure, and defeat will not destroy his self, however great his suffering may be. (Kohut, 1980, p. 478)

Kohut's relational perspective challenged the notions of autonomy, independence, and self-reliance that had shaped fundamental views of personality development, health, and normality in ego psychology. He is explicit on this point: "Self psychology does not see the essence of man's development as a move from dependence to independence, from merger to autonomy" (Kohut, 1980, p. 478). For Kohut, the person is a social being, embedded in relational life, and the self is inseparable from selfobjects.

Vulnerability and Psychopathology

Kohut traced the origins of psychopathology to disruptions in self-selfobject relations during infancy and childhood. If caretakers fail to meet the child's needs for empathic responsiveness, he theorized, development is undermined, leading to structural deficits and pathological defenses, and predisposing the individual to vulnerability, states of fragmentation, and problems in living. The inadequacies of early mirroring, the unavailability of idealizable parental figures, and the absence of sustaining twinship experiences can undermine the development of the core self or nuclear self. While Kohut initially focused on vulnerabilities associated with narcissistic personality organization, he came to link a range of problems in functioning to arrests in the development of the self.

In his last book, Kohut (1984) writes: "Self psychology is now attempting to demonstrate . . . that all forms of psychopathology are based either on deficits in the structure of the self, on distortions of the self, or on weakness of the self. It is trying to show, furthermore, that all these flaws in the self are due to disturbances of self-selfobject relationships in childhood" (p. 53). From the perspective of self psychology, symptomatic behavior reflects efforts to preserve or restore internal cohesion. Fragmentations of self occur along a continuum that ranges from worry to the panic resulting from fears of falling apart (Wolf, 1988).

Disorders of the self are characterized by inabilities to regulate emotion, self-esteem, and morale; to pursue meaningful goals; or to negotiate need and desire in age-appropriate forms. Kohut and Wolf (1978) described primary disturbances of the self, encompassing borderline and narcissistic personality organization, and secondary disturbances of the self, where cohesive self-organization is compromised by stressful circumstances. In the context of self psychology, borderline states are characterized by an enfeeblement of the self; rigid defensive operations deflect selfobject attachments, protecting the self from further fragmentation and emergence of psychotic states (Wolf, 1988). Narcissistic personality organization is associated with a range of problems in functioning, including depression, depletion, limited capacities for empathy, hypersensitivity, entitlement, maladaptive patterns of interpersonal interaction, and disappointment in relational life.

Kohut described two modes of splitting in his conceptions of self-organization and psychopathology. Following traditional formulations, he characterized repression as a "horizontal split" between conscious and unconscious domains of experience. By way of example, grandiose fantasies about the self may be repressed via the horizontal split, allowing the individual to avoid painful exposure to reality (see Wolf, 1988). A "vertical split" describes the side-by-side existence of incompatible psychic attitudes in the psyche (Kohut, 1971). Here, the individual does not repress intrapsychic content but rather ignores the implications of its meaning. Such disavowal leads to the coexistence of unrelated intrapsychic contents. In Kohut's metaphor, the psyche's "right hand" does not know what the "left hand" is doing; there exist, side by side, "cohesive personality attitudes with different goal structures, different pleasure aims, different moral and aesthetic values" (Kohut, 1971, p. 183). Lionel Corbett (1989) has pointed out the ways in which Jung's conceptions of intrapsychic splitting and complexes, which emphasize the plurality of the self, prefigure Kohut's thinking.

Beyond the foregoing diagnostic classifications, Kohut and Wolf also described a series of "self states" that perpetuate problems in functioning. The understimulated self, lacking a sense of vitality, is characterized by boredom and apathy; one may attempt to generate excitement through maladaptive behavior, including addictions and inappropriate sexual behavior. The fragmented self is characterized by loss of cohesion and continuity. The overstimulated self is subject to grandiose fantasies and anxiety following recognition and success. The overburdened self is characterized by deficits in capacities to self-soothe that precipitate fear and anxiety states.

Broadly understood, disorders of the self are "environmental deficiency diseases" (Greenberg & Mitchell, 1983). In the context of Kohut's developmental model, caretakers have failed "to allow the child to establish and slowly dissolve the requisite narcissistic selfobject configurations which, through transmuting internalization, generate healthy structures within the self. No further psychic growth is possible without these experiences; disorders of the self reflect desperate and necessarily futile attempts to shore up the defective self" (Greenberg & Mitchell, 1983, p. 356).

Clinical Perspectives

The fundamental aim of the therapeutic endeavor, from the perspective of self psychology, is to reinstate developmental processes that have been compromised by earlier lapses in caretaking through the provision of selfobject experiences. The clinician's empathic attunement and responsiveness strengthen the cohesion of the self and foster the development of capacities to enrich and make use of relational elements. "The essence of the psychoanalytic cure," Kohut (1984) writes, "resides in the patient's newly acquired ability to identify and seek out appropriate selfobjects as they present themselves in his realistic surroundings and to be sustained by them" (p. 77).

Drawing on his seminal formulations of empathy, Kohut (1971) emphasized the importance of "vicarious introspection" in the therapeutic process, defining the essence of psychoanalysis as "protracted empathic immersion" in the patient's experience (p. 300). The clinician seeks to process experience from the subject's point of view, communicating empathic understanding and acceptance of the underlying needs and longings reflected in the patient's ways of being and relating. Empathic modes of responding affirm the validity of the individual's experience, allowing the clinician to be used as a selfobject. Interpretive observations are crucial, Kohut believes, not because they provide missing information or bridge gaps in understanding, as classical conceptions would hold, but because they communicate the clinician's empathic attunement with the patient's experiential world.

The clinician, functioning as a new source of selfobject experience, and responding to emerging needs expressed in transference states, reengages development at the point where earlier attempts to generate crucial forms of selfobject experience had failed (Elson, 1986). The reactivation of arrested needs inevitably generates resistance, which Kohut understood as fears of retraumatization. "The patient always reaches out," as Paul Ornstein (1998) observes, "but this reaching out is often covered over with often difficult to penetrate defensive layers" (p. 225). Acceptance, understanding, and explanation, conveyed through empathic processing of experience, mediate defensive reactions.

The basic forms of selfobject transference—mirroring, idealizing, and twinship—emerge in the psychotherapy of patients with disorders of the self. In Kohut's view, the formation of narcissistic illusions in the therapeutic situation—assuming the form of grandiosity or idealization—reflects the patient's efforts to establish crucial developmental opportunities—a selfobject relationship that was not available in childhood. As Stephen Mitchell (1988) emphasizes, such narcissistic phenomena do not represent a defensive retreat from reality, as Freud and Sullivan would argue, but constitute "the growing edge of an aborted developmental process which was stalled because of parental failure to allow the child sustained experiences of illusions of grandeur and idealization" (p. 190). Accordingly, the emergence of self-object transferences provides opportunities for the restoration of the self. The "optimal frustration" that inevitably emerges in the give-and-take of the therapeutic process fosters development of self-structures through "transmuting internalization."

Incrementally, the patient consolidates psychic structure as the clinician empathizes with his or her experience of unfulfilled need. Paul Ornstein (1998) explains: "Belated structure building accomplishes the 'cure.' Kohut then went beyond structure building as the ultimate expression of cure by claiming that it is the capacity to find an empathically responsive selfobject milieu post-analytically that characterizes the essence of a psychoanalytic cure" (p. 225).

To summarize, since psychopathology is arrested development, the aim of psychotherapy is to reengage the compromised self through empathic responsiveness and the reinstatement of development through transmuting internalization. Like Winnicott, Kohut believes that the clinician must allow him- or herself to be used according to the patient's developmental needs and capacities. The establishment of the selfobject transference supports the vulnerable self. Processing of transference phenomena facilitates transmuting internalization and establishment of selfobject functions. The task is not to deepen insight and understanding through interpretive interventions, as in classical psychoanalysis, but to foster the clinician's development as a selfobject. The clinician functions in a manner analogous to the ways in which parental selfobjects should have functioned. The aim of intervention is "structure building" and the establishment of an empathically responsive selfobject surround that will sustain functioning following completion of psychotherapy.

Clinical Applications

The following case illustration shows how the clinician integrated core concepts from self psychology with cognitive and behavioral procedures in the psychotherapy of a young adult following development of post-traumatic stress disorder.

William A., age twenty-nine, initiated psychotherapy after he developed insomnia, diffuse anxiety, signs of depression, and dissociative states five months following his return from military service in Afghanistan. He reported feelings of demoralization, hopelessness, and helplessness and described fluctuating periods of numbing detachment and intrusive recollections of traumatic events during his tour of duty, when he had witnessed the deaths of civilians and soldiers. His growing sense of isolation and alienation intensified longings for closeness and connection with others, but he found himself avoiding contact with family and friends, fearful that they would expect him to talk about what he had witnessed in Afghanistan. The patient met diagnostic criteria for post-traumatic stress disorder.

Following evidence-based practice guidelines, the clinician drew on a range of cognitive and behavioral procedures in addressing the symptoms and problems in functioning associated with post-traumatic stress disorder. The perspective of self psychology enlarged the focus of intervention, emphasizing the client's loss of cohesion in sense of self and disruptions in relational life that perpetuated his experience of isolation, alienation, and fragmentation. The therapist considered the ways in which earlier patterns of care and relational life had shaped the development of the self, defensive functioning, patterns of coping, and particular ways of being and relating and explored the meaning of traumatic experience in light of earlier developmental events, relationships, disappointments, and losses.

From the perspective of self psychology, the clinician can serve a range of selfobject functions. In this course of intervention, the patient looked to the clinician for validation of his experience. He developed a mirror transference, and the practitioner's acceptance and confirmation of his experience appeared to strengthen the patient's sense of self. The clinician's ongoing attunement, responsiveness, and empathic processing of experience facilitated his efforts to negotiate problems in functioning associated with post-traumatic stress disorder and restore sustaining relationships with family members and friends.

Kohut in Context: Contemporary Perspectives

More than any other thinker, Kohut challenged the Freudian hegemony in the United States, introducing what many regard as a new paradigm. Over the last quarter century, his core formulations have generated the development of theory within the domains of self psychology and the broader field of relational psychoanalysis. They have informed empirical research in developmental psychology as well. In the context of clinical practice, his contributions have deepened our understanding of relational experience and curative factors in psychosocial intervention. Although a systematic review of these developments is beyond the scope of this chapter, it is important to identify key contributions and major lines of inquiry that continue to influence theory, research, and practice.

In the field of developmental psychology, Daniel Stern (1985) has carried out pioneering studies of mother-infant interaction that provide empirical support for Kohut's core conceptions of self-experience. He describes four phases of self-development, or "domains of relatedness," that are shaped by constitution and temperament, innate maturational capacities, and the relative attunement and responsiveness of the caretaking surround.

The sense of emergent self, extending from birth through two months, centers on the infant's growing capacities to process information about relational life and form attachments with caretaking figures. The sense of core self and the domain of core relatedness, extending from two to six months, are based on the infant's consolidation of an organizing subjective perception and experience of a coherent physical self. Conceptions of the core self encompass four elements: self-agency, self-coherence, self-affectivity, and self-history. The sense of subjective self and the domain of intersubjective relatedness, extending from seven to fifteen months, follow from the infant's growing capacities to experience subjective mental states. The sense of verbal self, which forms after fifteen months, is reflected in emerging capacities for language and symbolization. This verbal domain of relatedness brings new complexity to the child's experience of self and others, strengthening capacities for empathy and engagement in symbolic play (Stern, 1985).

Allan Schore (2003a, 2003b), drawing on core concepts of self psychology, has constructed a neurobiological conception of the development and structuralization of the self, focusing on the experience-dependent maturation of the right brain. He applies this developmental neuropsychoanalytic perspective to the development of deficits in the self-system. He introduces a model of the neurobiology and self psychology of trauma, post-traumatic stress disorders, and borderline organization and considers the ways in which psychotherapy addresses the neurobiology of regulatory structures.

Robert Stolorow has challenged the concepts of "one-person psychology" and the "isolated self" that shaped traditional models of psychoanalytic psychotherapy through the twentieth century. He embraces a two-person psychology, seeing behavior as mediated by two interacting and mutually influencing domains of experience, which he calls the intersubjective field. In his theory of intersubjectivity, patterns of interaction in the infant-caregiver relationship are internalized, shaping subjective experience and subsequent patterns of relating. He views such structures—"organizing principles"—as core constituents of personality development.

The concept of the intersubjective field captures the embeddedness of the individual within a relational matrix. From this perspective, the development of the self, transference, and therapeutic action originate in relational fields and are shaped by ongoing interactive experience (see Fosshage, 2003; E. Goldstein, 2001).

In the domain of psychosocial intervention, clinical theorists have continued to emphasize the crucial functions of empathic attunement and responsiveness. As Mitchell and Black (1995) observe, contemporary self psychologists view the most fundamental features of Kohut's contributions as his methodological approach of sustained empathic immersion in the patient's subjective reality and his concepts of the selfobject and selfobject transferences.

Chapter 12

Emergence of the Relational Paradigm

They are not all exploring elephants. Some may be grappling with giraffes.
To try to contain the same reports within one framework may lead to strange
hybrids: four stout legs; a long, graceful neck; four thin legs; a long trunk; and
so on.

—Stephen Mitchell, *Relational Concepts in Psychoanalysis*

As we have seen, the work of Adler, Jung, Rank, and Ferenczi constituted the
earliest attempts to broaden the field of psychodynamic understanding. Although this first generation of theorists introduced independent points of
view, they shared overlapping concerns, emphasizing the roles of relationship and social life in their conceptions of personality development, health,
problems in living, and therapeutic action. Drawing on their work, as the
preceding accounts show, a series of creative thinkers in Great Britain and
America continued to enlarge and elaborate relational perspectives. Over
time, the contributions of Klein, Fairbairn, Winnicott, Sullivan, and Kohut
shaped the development of three schools of thought in contemporary psychoanalytic understanding, broadly characterized as object relations psychology, interpersonal psychoanalysis, and self psychology.

The foregoing lines of inquiry have brought about a relational turn in
contemporary psychoanalytic understanding. As Paul Wachtel (2008) observes, we have increasingly come to realize that "human beings exist in relationships, whether those relationships be to other people with whom they
have ongoing interactions, to imagoes of past important figures, to cultural
traditions, values, and identifications, or to images and experiences of their
own past, present, and future selves" (p. 1). This defining feature of human
experience has shaped conceptions of therapeutic practice across the major
schools of thought. Clinicians have increasingly recognized the crucial role of
the helping relationship in psychosocial intervention and the functions of
empathic attunement, interpersonal interaction, and experiential learning in
efforts to facilitate change and growth. Converging lines of study document
the fundamental importance of the therapeutic alliance and interactive experience in the outcomes of treatment (see Norcross, 2002; Wampold, 2007).

In the first part of this chapter, I review the domains of concern that
distinguish the foundational schools of thought. In the second section, I

describe the defining features of the larger relational paradigm, outlining conceptions of personality and self; health, well-being, and the common good; and vulnerability, psychopathology, and problems in living. I consider the strengths and limits of the relational paradigm and identify concerns in the continuing development of theory, research, and practice. In the following chapter I describe core elements of psychosocial intervention in light of relational understanding and show how conceptions of pluralism and pragmatism strengthen integrative approaches in clinical practice.

Foundational Schools of Thought

Object Relations Psychology

More than any other thinker, Fairbairn's developmental psychology serves as the foundation for contemporary object relations thought. Object relations perspectives focus on intrapsychic representations of self and others. Theorists emphasize concepts of internalization and representation in formulations of development, personality structure, and self-organization. Although various thinkers differ in their conceptions of the cognitive and emotional processes believed to mediate the development of personality, they all assume that the internalization of interpersonal experience shapes inner representations of self, others (objects), and modes of relating (self in relation to others). Concepts of representation serve as the basis for Bowlby's formulation of internalized working models of self and relational life; they also inform Joseph Sandler's influential rendering of the representational world (Sandler & Rosenblatt, 1962) and Otto Kernberg's (1976) focus on self and object representations. More broadly, we find overlap in cognitive formulations of personal constructs, schemas, and the assumptive world (Berlin, 2002; Fonagy & Target, 2007; Wachtel, 1993, 2008).

While theorists believe that core representations originate in ongoing interactions in the social environment, they assume that such schemas are also influenced by individual differences in constitution and temperament, unconscious fantasy process, early developmental experience, and life-shaping events; accordingly, they do not see working models as veridical representations of actual experience. What is central in understanding object relations perspectives is the realization that we experience others as we *perceive* them, not necessarily as they actually are (Wachtel, 1993).

Concepts of motivation center on the fundamental need for attachment and connection through life. Developmental lines of study focus on the nature of early caretaking experience and emerging capacities for relatedness. Basic prototypes of connection established in infancy and childhood, preserved in the form of internalized representations of self and others, are believed to shape subjective states of self, perceptions of others, and modes of interaction.

Formulations of psychopathology focus on the nature of inner representations and the ways in which working models of self and others limit perceptions of experience, precipitate dysfunctional behaviors, and perpetuate representative problems in functioning. From this perspective, the tendency to repeat maladaptive patterns of interaction reflects ongoing efforts to preserve continuity and cohesion in sense of self and to maintain connections with important figures from the past.

Concepts of therapeutic action emphasize the role of relational provisions and experiential learning in the context of the treatment process. From this perspective, the therapeutic relationship and ongoing interaction in the clinical situation facilitate efforts to revise inner representations and develop more effective ways of processing information and negotiating relational experience.

Object relations theories have increasingly informed empirical research on personality development, psychopathology, and therapeutic intervention. Independent lines of research provide considerable support for views that infants are pre-adapted to establish relationships and engage in complex forms of interaction with caretaking figures (see, e.g., Beebe & Lachmann, 1988; Demos, 1992; Fonagy, 2001; Fonagy & Target, 2007; Schore, 2003a, 2003b; Stern, 1985). Longitudinal studies point to the critical role of attachment styles and early dyadic caregiving systems in personality organization, interpersonal functioning, and patterns of coping and adaptation (Fonagy, 2001; Fonagy & Target, 2007; Schore, 2003a, 2003b; Sroufe, Egelund, Carlson, & Collins, 2005; Sroufe, Egelund, & Kreutzer, 1990). Object relations formulations of unconscious mental processing and concepts of self-representation have informed cognitive study of perception, memory, and learning (for reviews, see Bornstein & Masling, 1998; Fonagy, 2001; Fonagy & Target, 2007; Westen, 1998). Social psychologists have employed object relations constructs in investigation of social perception, causal attribution, and interpersonal influence (see, e.g., Aronson, 1992; Bornstein & Pitmann, 1992; Fonagy, 2001; Roth & Fonagy, 2005). Clinical researchers have explored ways in which inner models of relational experience and patterns of social cognition precipitate problems in functioning associated with depression, personality disorders, and other forms of psychopathology (for reviews, see Blatt & Homann, 1992; Blatt & Zuroff, 1992; Fonagy & Target, 2007; Luborsky & Barrett, 2006; Masling & Bornstein, 1994; Roth & Fonagy, 2005; Schore 2003a, 2003b; Westen, 1998).

Interpersonal Perspectives

While object relations perspectives emphasize the role of internalization processes and cognitive representations of self and others, interpersonal lines of inquiry focus on the *interactive determinants* of personality and the social contexts of relationship. As such, they complement the emphasis on intrapsychic phenomena in object relations approaches. Sullivan provides the most comprehensive theory of personality and psychopathology, and his thinking continues to influence conceptual foundations and therapeutic practice in this tradition.

As we have seen, Sullivan locates personality or self in the social field. In departing from structural models of the individual, he defines personality as "the relatively enduring pattern of recurrent interpersonal situations which characterize a human life" (Sullivan, 1953, pp. 110–111). He conceives of self as process shaped by interactive experience in relational fields. Personality, he argues, can "never be isolated from the complex of interpersonal relations in which the person lives and has his being" (p. 10).

According to his developmental theory, vulnerability and conditions of care in early relational experience inevitably generate anxiety and restrict ways of negotiating need. Over time, the individual elaborates repetitive patterns of interaction in ongoing efforts to adapt to the requirements of particular interpersonal environments, maximize satisfaction and security, and preserve connections with others. His formulations of psychopathology, or "dynamisms of difficulty," emphasize defensive operations and self-defeating, maladaptive ways of relating.

Concepts of therapeutic action center on the interactive nature of psychosocial intervention. By way of review, Sullivan views the clinician as a "participant-observer" in the interactive field of the therapeutic situation. The clinician not only is an observer focusing on representative patterns of interaction but is engaged in the interpersonal process as "subject" and "object" (see Wolitzky & Eagle, 1997, p. 63).

Therapeutic intervention explores problematic aspects of interactions with others, including the clinician, and provides opportunities for experiential learning that enlarge ways of being and relating. A growing body of research has documented the effectiveness of interpersonal approaches in treatment of a variety of problems in functioning (see reviews by Luborsky & Barrett, 2006; Messer & Warren, 1995; Roth & Fonagy, 2005).

Self Psychology

As the preceding chapter shows, clinical scholars have continued to elaborate Kohut's original models of personality development, psychopathology, and psychotherapy. By way of review, conceptions of motivation encompass the primary need for connection and relationship in human experience but emphasize a fundamental thrust to establish and maintain a unitary, integrated sense of self. Following Kohut's formulations, conceptions of personality development emphasize the ways in which the empathic provisions of primary caretaking figures or "selfobjects," attuned to the child's subjective states, facilitate the emergence of a cohesive, vital sense of self. Caretakers with mature psychological organizations perform crucial regulatory functions for the developing child that foster the vitalization and structural cohesion of the self.

From this perspective, caretaking functions are gradually internalized as psychic structure, strengthening capacities to regulate inner states and maintain continuity and stability in sense of self. The individual is increasingly able to carry out the regulating, integrating, and adaptive functions that had previously been provided through selfobject experience. Lapses and failings in the relational surround undermine development, leading to structural deficits and defensive strategies limiting further disorganization of self and disruption of functioning. Disorders of the self are characterized by difficulties in negotiating need, regulating emotion, maintaining self-esteem, and pursuing meaningful goals (see Gardner, 1999; Schore, 2003a, 2003b).

Concepts of therapeutic action stress the role of relational experience in efforts to strengthen the self. The clinician provides empathic, attuned selfobject experiences that facilitate development of psychic structure and enhanced functioning. Self psychological perspectives recognize ongoing needs for dependency, connection, and affirmation through the life course. For Kohut (1984), health, well-being, and the good life depend upon the "responsive selfobject milieu" (p. 21). Self psychology has emerged as an influential perspective in contemporary psychoanalysis and clinical social work, as we have seen, and a growing number of researchers are linking core concepts with empirical lines of inquiry in neuroscience and developmental psychology (Schore, 2003a, 2003b).

The Relational Paradigm

The foregoing schools of thought were established as independent perspectives within the broader psychodynamic tradition, and there was surprisingly little communication among representatives of the groups in the development of their formulations (Borden, 2000). In the early 1980s, however, psychoanalytic scholars began to carry out comparative studies of theoretical systems in efforts to identify the defining features and common elements of different points of view.

In their classic work *Object Relations in Psychoanalytic Theory,* published in 1983, Jay Greenberg and Stephen Mitchell explored representative lines of study set forth in the interpersonal, object relations, and self psychological traditions, clarifying shared assumptions, concepts, and themes that would serve as the basis for subsequent formulations of the relational perspective. They distinguished two competing paradigms in psychodynamic understanding: Freud's drive model and the relational model, which encompassed the views of a variety of thinkers associated with object relations, interpersonal, and self psychological traditions. In their formulation of the relational paradigm, the basic focus of attention is not the individual but the interactive fields in which we work to establish connection, preserve ties, and differentiate ourselves. Relations with others, actual and internalized, rather than instinctual drives, are the core constituents of human experience.

In their comparative study, Greenberg and Mitchell (1983) observed that the interpersonal perspectives of Sullivan, Horney, and Fromm emphasized actual behavior in the social field and the realities of the outer world but lacked a fully developed theory of intrapsychic processes. By contrast, Klein's theoretical system, the object relations theories of Fairbairn and Winnicott, and the self psychology of Kohut centered on intrapsychic domains of experience but failed to adequately consider the role of actual behavior in the social field. Each perspective thereby provided correctives for the other and offered the possibility of enlarging the focus of clinical practice.

Mitchell (1988, 1993, 1997, 2000) continued to explore overlapping themes and issues in relational thought, fashioning an integrative perspective that would encompass the major traditions and the views of the major theorists. In the course of his writings he explored fundamental domains of concern in psychoanalytic understanding from a relational perspective, enlarging conceptions of self, constitutionality, infantilism, sexuality, and narcissism. He established a journal devoted to relational thought, *Psychoanalytic Dialogues*, in 1993 and founded the International Association of Relational Psychoanalysis and Psychotherapy. In the years since his death in 2000, thinkers have elaborated theoretical and clinical perspectives, broadening the scope of the field. The contributions of Emmanuel Ghent, Irwin Hoffman, Lewis Aron, Jessica Benjamin, Jody Davies, Nancy Chodorow, and Neil Altman have been particularly influential in the development of relational psychoanalysis (see Mitchell & Aron, 1999, for a review of seminal papers).

Although the paradigm encompasses a variety of perspectives, we can distinguish overlapping conceptions of personality development; health, well-being, and the common good; psychopathology; and concepts of therapeutic action. I review core concepts in the following section, enlarging earlier accounts of the relational perspective (Borden, 2000, 2008b).

Personality Development

Theorists emphasize fundamental needs for contact, connection, and relationship through the life course in their conceptions of motivation. As we have seen, Bowlby regards attachment as a function of instinctual, reflexive behaviors that preserve self and facilitate development. Other thinkers, notably Fairbairn, Sullivan, and Winnicott, emphasize what they see as an innate need and desire for relatedness in its own right (for further discussion of these points, see Mitchell, 1988, pp. 17–40). Kohut stresses the role of others in efforts to establish and maintain a cohesive sense of self and identity.

Relational experience and social surrounds shape the development of mind, personality, and self. From this perspective, the core constituents of human experience are relations with others. While drive psychology explains psychic structure as the outcome of instinctual process, relational lines of understanding see personality as the developmental sequelae of ongoing interpersonal experience; personality is structured through ongoing interactions with others in the social environment. The self, the core of the person, is constructed in a relational matrix. Empirical research in developmental psychology and neuroscience has increasingly informed relational conceptions of development (see Doidge, 2007; Kandel, 2005, 2006; Schore, 2003a, 2003b).

From the perspective of object relations psychology, as we have seen, structures of mind encompass representations of self, others, and interactive experience. According to interpersonal lines of understanding, personality or self is realized in social contexts and continually mediated by interactions with others. Thinkers conceive of social relations as biologically rooted, genetically encoded fundamental motivational processes; biological and relational experience constitute ongoing cycles of mutual influence in the development of personality and the social surround through the life course (see Borden, 2000; Ghent, 1992; Mitchell, 1988, 1993, 2000).

Health, Well-Being, and the Common Good

Conceptions of health, well-being, and the common good emphasize the role of others in the development of the person and the generative functions of relationship, social interaction, and community through the life course. As Greenberg and Mitchell (1983) show in their presentation of the paradigm, overlapping traditions of social and political thought elaborated by Jean-Jacques Rousseau, G. W. F. Hegel, and Karl Marx provide philosophical contexts for relational views of human life and fulfillment. For Rousseau, social participation leads to higher forms of existence; the "social contract" allows the individual to transcend private, isolated experience and become part of a "larger whole" from which he or she "draws life and being" (Rousseau, 1762/1954, p. 58). For Marx (1845/1959), "human essence is no abstraction in each individual. In its reality it is the ensemble of social relations" (p. 244). By virtue of being human, people form relationships and seek social interaction. From this perspective, as Greenberg and Mitchell (1983) observe, "human satisfactions and goals are realizable only within a community" (p. 401). As we have seen, Adler emphasizes the crucial functions of social life and community in his views of health, well-being, and the common good.

Conceptions of health and maturity center on the development of basic structures of personality, self, and mind and corresponding capacities for relatedness that influence levels of functioning. Subjective states, inner representations of self and others, and modes of relating in the interpersonal field are fundamental domains of concern (Borden, 2000).

Mature identity is characterized by relative cohesion and continuity in sense of self, affirming but realistic views and expectations of self and others that reflect self and object representations, and stable and enduring relationships. Flexible ways of being and relating are signs of health; one is able to transcend the identifications and constraints of earlier relational life, engage in give-and-take with others in the outer world, and assimilate new experiences.

Theorists hold that conflict is inherent in the human situation, however, and they describe fundamental dilemmas in ongoing efforts to negotiate vulnerability, need, and desire through the life course; a number of thinkers describe "central polarities" and "opposing motivational thrusts" in formulations of conflict and compromise (see, e.g., Aron, 1996; Ghent, 1992).

Thinkers view sexuality as a central domain of human experience, regarding sexual behavior as a crucial medium for elaboration of fundamental dynamics in relational life (see Mitchell, 1988, for a critique of Freudian conceptions of sexuality and alternate relational views). Sexuality plays a central role in most intimate relationships, Mitchell (1988) observes, explaining: "This is not because pleasure regulation itself is the fundamental human aim . . . as Freud understood it. . . . Rather, it is the establishment and maintenance of relatedness that is fundamental, and the mutual exchange of intense pleasure and emotional responsiveness is perhaps the most powerful medium in which emotional connection and intimacy is sought, established, lost, and regained" (p. 107). He theorizes that the fundamental meanings of sexuality often originate in basic relational patterns of search, surrender, and escape, providing powerful transformative experiences.

Relational thinkers are increasingly challenging the pathologizing of difference and recognizing the diversity of human experience, enlarging conceptions of gender and identity. Theorists view homosexuality and bisexuality as normal variants in human development and generally do not pathologize other forms of sexual behavior that historically have been characterized as "perversions" (see Curtis & Hirsch, 2003, p. 74). Mitchell was a leading figure in efforts to depathologize conceptions of homosexuality in the field of mental health.

Winnicott and Horney link relational experience to qualities of personhood in their developmental perspectives, emphasizing notions of vitality, authenticity, creativity, and personal meaning in their conceptions of health, well-being, and fulfillment. For Kohut, maturity, health, and well-being depend upon evolving capacities to make use of relational experience in efforts to maintain inner cohesion, morale, and self-esteem.

From relational points of view, we generate meaning in the give-and-take of interpersonal life, and a number of thinkers draw on narrative perspectives and stress ways in which social surrounds influence efforts to process experience, construct meaning, and elaborate life stories (see, e.g., Borden, 1992,

2000; H. Goldstein, 1990; Howard, 1991; Schafer, 1983, 1992). Most theorists integrate concepts of mastery, coping, adaptation, and self-actualization in formulations of health and well-being (Greenberg & Cheselka, 1995).

Vulnerability, Psychopathology, and Problems in Living

The relational perspective encompasses divergent conceptions of vulnerability, psychopathology, and social dysfunction. Some thinkers, notably Winnicott, Horney, and Kohut, emphasize "arrests" or "deficits" in the development of the self. Winnicott distinguishes "true self" and "false self" states of experience in his formulations of neurosis, defensive processes, and maladaptive behavior. Following Winnicott, Christopher Bollas (1989) introduced the term "normatic personality" to characterize people who sacrifice their individuality or personal idiom in conforming to values of society. Horney parallels Winnicott's thinking in her relational conceptions of self and neurosis. Kohut traces structural deficits in the organization of the self to earlier lapses and failings in care that compromise capacities to regulate emotion, integrate experience, and engage in relational life. Drawing on Jung's formulations, some thinkers emphasize concepts of dissociation in formulations of neurosis.

Other thinkers trace the origins of maladaptive behavior to rigid, anachronistic models of relational experience. In Fairbairn's theoretical system, for example, internalized representations of interpersonal experience limit ways of being and relating in the outer world. Bowlby focuses on the ways in which working models of self, other, and modes of interactive experience skew perceptions of interactive experience and constrict relational life (see Fonagy, 2001).

Yet another group of theorists working in the interpersonal tradition emphasize outer domains of experience, identifying patterns of behavior in the social field that perpetuate problems in living. Sullivan, for example, speaks of "dynamisms of difficulty"; Horney and Wachtel speak of "vicious circles" of behavior.

Sullivan preferred the phrase "problems in living" over diagnostic classifications of mental disorders, as we have seen, and many relational thinkers influenced by the interpersonal tradition are critical of the disease model inherited from medicine (see Curtis & Hirsch, 2003). They see patterns of behavior as having been learned in the give-and-take of relational life; as such, they are understood as adaptive, reasonable ways of negotiating experience in view of particular circumstances and requirements for conditions of care. If problematic ways of being are learned, presumably, new ways of relating can be developed as well.

Adler and the core thinkers who formed the interpersonal tradition—Sullivan, Horney, and Fromm—explored the ways in which social, cultural, political, and economic conditions perpetuate vulnerability, problems in living, sexism, and racism. Fromm criticized the conformist personality he saw in American culture. More recently, Paul Wachtel (1989, 1997, 2000, 2008) has applied psychodynamic perspectives in his writings on racism, oppression, and disenfranchised groups, and his compelling critiques of individualism and consumerism in American culture are informed by his integrative psychodynamic perspective.

Domains of concern in assessment of vulnerability and problems in living include subjective states; inner representations of self, others, and relational experience; and modes of interaction in the interpersonal field. According to contemporary object relations and interpersonal perspectives, dysfunction is a dynamic cyclical process "in which feared and anticipated relational events tend to be elicited and enacted by the individual" in interactions with others, who, in turn, respond in complementary ways (see Messer & Warren, 1995, pp. 119–120). Ironically, patterns of interaction tend to confirm maladaptive views and reinforce problematic behaviors. Wachtel (1993, 1997, 2008), drawing on Sullivan's theory, emphasizes the role of fear and defensive operations that lead to avoidance of experience and compromise crucial skills in living.

Psychopathology is self-perpetuating because it is embedded in more general ways of being and relating established over the course of development. As Mitchell (1988) emphasizes in his integrative relational model, there is a "pervasive tendency to preserve the continuity, connections, and familiarity of one's personal, interactional world" (p. 33). From the perspective of self-organization, Mitchell explains, problematic ways of being and relating are perpetuated because they preserve ongoing experiences of self. What is new is threatening because it lies beyond the bounds of experience in which one recognizes oneself as a cohesive, continuous being. From the perspective of object relations views, dysfunction is repeated because it serves to preserve connections to significant others. "What is new is frightening because it requires what one experiences as the abandonment of old loyalties, through which one feels connected and devoted" (Mitchell, 1988, p. 291). From the interpersonal point of view, dysfunction is repeated because it regulates fear and anxiety. Following Sullivan, Mitchell (1988) explains: "Security operations steer [the individual] into familiar channels and away from the anxiety-shrouded unknown" (p. 291).

Accordingly, however dysfunctional certain behaviors may be, they serve to preserve continuity and coherence in sense of self, maintain connections with internalized representations of others, and provide safety and security in negotiation of interpersonal experience.

The Relational Paradigm in Context: Inner Experience and Outer Realities

The larger relational paradigm centers our attention on fundamental concerns in human experience, as we have seen, and it provides orienting perspectives for continued development of theory, research, and practice methods. In this section, I expand earlier discussions of the relational paradigm in light of essential concerns in contemporary thought and clinical practice (Borden, 1999, 2000, 2008b).

In the broadest sense, relational perspectives encompass biological, psychological, and social domains of experience and bridge concepts of person and environment in process-oriented models of human functioning. Contemporary thinkers take a dialectical approach to human experience, connecting theoretical systems and empirical research through critical inquiry and comparative analysis. "Perhaps the most important aspect of the term relational," Aron (1996) wrote in his early formulation of the paradigm, "is precisely that it includes the relation between the individual and the social" (p. 63).

Similarly, Emmanuel Ghent (1992) was careful to explain that the term "relational" emphasizes "process as against reified entities and the relations among processes all the way along the continuum from the physical and physiological, through the neurobiological, ultimately the psychological, and for some, even the spiritual" (p. xx). Neil Altman (1995) drew on systems concepts and ecological models in his elaboration of relational perspectives, emphasizing the need to consider institutional, community, and social contexts of human difficulty in development of theory and research.

As a general frame of reference, the relational paradigm continues to provide contexts of understanding for practitioners in ongoing efforts to connect biological, psychological, and social domains of concern; to enlarge conceptions of person and environment; and to deepen appreciation of interactive processes at multiple systems levels.

In conceiving of self as fundamentally social, contemporary thinkers locate individuality in the interpersonal field and emphasize concepts of relationship, centering on the motivational force of attachment and the interactive nature of human experience through the life course. Core constructs provide ways of conceptualizing relational processes that shape personality development, coping, adaptation, health, and well-being.

In contrast to the deterministic character of classical Freudian thought, relational views of the individual stress notions of personal agency, intention, and will, elaborating the humanistic concerns that shaped the theoretical systems of Adler and Rank. As reviews of resilience research show, the course of life is not determined exclusively by past events or current environments; individuals process experience, create meaning, and shape their lives. Contemporary thinkers affirm the potential for self-determination, change, and growth, embracing humanistic perspectives that have informed social work practice from the start of the profession.

Relational lines of inquiry have deepened interest in notions of subjectivity, personal meaning, and the self. Drawing on the contributions of Sullivan, Horney, Fairbairn, Winnicott, and Kohut, contemporary theorists continue to consider ways in which relational processes and social environments mediate the establishment of subjectivity and qualities of personhood, reflected in capacities to create meaning and generate experience that feels authentic, vital, sustaining, and empowering (see, e.g., Bollas, 1987, 1989; Chodorow, 1999; Wachtel, 2008; Winnicott, 1971a). As Jonathan Lear (1990) emphasizes, human reality is constituted by subjectivity: *"what it is* to be a person is shaped by *what it is like* for that person to be. The meanings, emotions and desires alive in a person's soul play a crucial role in determining who that person is" (p. 4).

The individual's subjective experience and personal meaning—what Oliver Sacks (1984) has characterized as the "human being first and last . . . the experiencing, acting, living 'I'" (p. 177)—has become a central focus in contemporary psychotherapy. Psychodynamic perspectives continue to center on phenomenological experience and the individuality of the person as well as the social surrounds that shape ways of being, relating, and living. Some relational thinkers have embraced postmodern and constructivist perspectives that emphasize the ways in which meaning and understanding emerge from intersubjective experience in social life, challenging the fundamental assumptions of positivist science (see Mills, 2005, for a discussion of epistemological views in relational psychoanalysis).

Despite ongoing revision of theoretical formulations, relational conceptions of personality development and psychopathology remain problematic in certain respects. Here I briefly review concerns that have shaped critical discussion of theoretical formulations in recent years (for extended critiques, see Mills, 2005; Wachtel, 2008).

As we have seen, Winnicott, Fairbairn, and Kohut focused largely on the mother-child relationship and viewed caretaking systems as crucial determinants of health. They linked problems in functioning to lapses in early care and corresponding arrests in the development of the self, assuming that deprivations in maternal care and traumatic events during critical periods in infancy and early childhood inevitably place people at risk for subsequent psychopathology (Borden, 2000). Although empirical findings point to the importance of early caretaking systems in personality development and subsequent patterns of behavior (Sroufe et al., 2005), researchers emphasize the need to consider ways in which self-righting tendencies, use of relational experience, and social environments influence functioning across the course of life (see, e.g., Anthony & Cohler, 1987; Galatzer-Levy & Cohler, 1993; Stern, 1985; Walsh, in press; Westen, 1998). The findings of empirical research on risk and resilience challenge developmental arrest models of development and psychopathology (see Anthony & Cohler, 1987; Fonagy, 2001).

Mitchell (1988) argues that the developmental arrest theorists overemphasize the importance of the early mother-child relationship and reduce "lifelong relational issues to early, circumscribed phases" of childhood (p. 140). In doing so, he shows, they distort "the very nature of those issues and the ways in which they manifest themselves at different points throughout the life cycle." Theorists and researchers have proposed alternative perspectives that emphasize "domains of relatedness" and "forms of social experience" rather than "critical periods" or distinct phases in conceptions of development through the life course (Stern, 1985, p. 34; see also Fonagy & Target, 2007; Schore, 2003a, 2003b; Westen, 1998).

Feminist thinkers have challenged core assumptions of psychoanalytic understanding in trenchant critiques over the last quarter century, arguing that theorists conflate formulations of female identity and motherhood; represent mothers as causal agents of psychopathology; fail to consider the cultural meanings of motherhood, gender inequalities, and differences in material resources; and privilege notions of separation and individuation in views of maturity and health (see Burack, 1998). Thinkers have drawn on the full range of relational theories in enlarging conceptions of gender, identity, and subjectivity, and a growing number of clinical scholars have applied feminist perspectives in the field of relational psychoanalysis, broadening the scope of theory and practice (see Benjamin, 1988, 1995, 1998; Chodorow, 1988, 1998; Dimen, 2003; Flax, 1990, 1993; Harris, 2005).

Critics from a variety of perspectives have argued that the foundational theorists emphasize intrapsychic phenomena over actual experience in the outer world, failing to recognize the influence of cultural, political, and economic forces in human life. Practitioners have attempted to broaden the scope of psychoanalytic understanding in recent years, emphasizing social concerns in their conceptions of vulnerability and need, focusing on disenfranchised, economically deprived groups whose problems in living challenge traditional conceptions of psychoanalytic psychotherapy (see Altman, 1995; Borden, 2006; Bucci, 2002; Javier & Moskowitz, 2002; Wachtel, 2008).

Relational perspectives have informed Wachtel's writings (1989, 1997, 1999, 2002, 2003, 2008) on social justice and racism and his compelling critiques of individualism and consumerism in American culture. He bridges psychological and social domains of concern in his conceptions of the therapeutic endeavor, linking the health and well-being of the individual with patterns of life and values in community and culture.

Eric Ornstein and Carol Ganzer (1997, 2000, 2003, 2005) emphasize conceptions of vulnerability, diversity, and social justice in their applications of relational theory in social work practice in mental health, homeless, child welfare, and substance abuse settings. As they show in their accounts, relational approaches privilege the individuality of the client, offering ways of understanding the complexities of self and interpersonal life, and strengthening the individual's sense of personal agency, narrative competence, and potential for change and growth.

As we will see in the last chapter, the orienting perspectives of self psychology, object relations thought, and interpersonal theory deepen our appreciation of the tenacity of problems in living and broaden our understanding of facilitating processes in psychosocial intervention.

Chapter 13

Relational Theory and Integrative Perspectives in Clinical Practice

You must bring out of each word its practical cash-value, set it at work within the stream of our experience. . . . Theories thus become instruments. . . . Pragmatism unstiffens our theories, limbers them up.

—William James, *Pragmatism*

The broader psychodynamic tradition encompasses a range of theoretical models and therapeutic languages, as we have seen, and practitioners continue to make pragmatic use of concepts and methods from a variety of sources. In the first part of this chapter, I review concepts of therapeutic action set forth in the contemporary relational schools of thought and show how comparative perspectives enlarge ways of working over the course of intervention. In doing so, I focus on Stephen Mitchell's formulations of therapeutic action in his framing of the relational paradigm and review earlier case reports in order to illustrate orienting perspectives and approaches to treatment. In the second section, I return to the pluralist point of view introduced at the start of the book and review the ways in which comparative perspectives strengthen integrative practice in psychosocial intervention.

Relational Perspectives and Psychosocial Intervention

Concepts of therapeutic action set forth in the relational schools of thought outlined in the preceding chapter center on the crucial role of the helping relationship and the functions of interpersonal interaction and experiential learning in efforts to help clients deepen understandings of self, others, and life experience; strengthen coping capacities; and negotiate problems in living. Theorists recognize the influence of common elements believed to foster change and growth across the foundational schools of thought, including the sustaining functions of the helping relationship, the setting of the intervention, conceptual schemes that provide explanations of what is the matter and what carries the potential to help, and the core activities of the therapeutic process (Frank & Frank, 1991; Wampold, 2007; see Borden, 2008a, in press, for a review of common factors in psychosocial intervention).

From the perspective of relational psychoanalysis, however, formulations of curative factors emphasize the constancy of care in the therapeutic holding environment (Winnicott, 1963/1965b); attunement, empathic responsiveness, and selfobject transference experience (Kohut, 1977, 1984); experiential learning through interpersonal interactions (Sullivan, 1940, 1954; Wachtel, 1993, 2008); interpretive procedures that deepen understandings of self, others, interpersonal behavior, and life experience (Wachtel, 1993, 2008); reinforcement, modeling, and identification (Strupp & Binder, 1984; Wachtel, 1997, 2008); and use of tasks to generate action and strengthen development of crucial skills in living (Borden, 2008b; Wachtel, 1997, 2008). Relational thinkers challenge classical conceptions of transference, resistance, and the analytic frame, rejecting the principles of neutrality, abstinence, and anonymity. They emphasize the importance of "corrective emotional experience" (Alexander & French, 1946), "new relational experience" (Frank, 1999), and Fairbairn's (1958) conception of "an actual relationship with a reliable and beneficent parental figure" (p. 377).

The therapeutic relationship itself serves as a facilitating medium for change and provides crucial sources of experiencing and learning in efforts to reinstate arrested developmental processes, modify internalized representations of self and others, develop interpersonal skills, and improve social functioning (Borden 1998, 1999, 2008b). Enactments of maladaptive behavior over the course of intervention deepen understandings of dysfunctional modes of interaction and guide efforts to develop more effective ways of negotiating interpersonal life. Emerging lines of inquiry in neuroscience and cognitive psychology explore the ways in which the interactive experience of intervention alters associational networks and fosters the development of new linkages and patterns of behavior (Kandel, 2005, 2006; Schore, 2003a, 2003b; Westen & Gabbard, 2002a, 2002b).

Although practitioners emphasize the importance of establishing a clear, circumscribed focus in their formulations of intervention, they assume that the core activities of the therapeutic process carry the potential to foster change and growth across domains of functioning, helping individuals (1) strengthen their ability to process subjective experience; (2) deepen awareness of their own and others' behavior; (3) develop problem-solving skills and coping capacities; and (4) enlarge their understandings of self, others, and life experience. As reviews of outcome studies show, the process of intervention generally helps clients develop more positive views of their world, communicate more effectively, strengthen interpersonal skills, and expand their social networks (Wampold, 2007). Clinical researchers assume that improved interpersonal functioning increases morale and reduces the difficulties associated with all forms of psychopathology (see Binder, Strupp, & Henry 1995, p. 44; Frank & Frank, 1991; Luborsky & Barrett, 2006; Roth & Fonagy, 2005).

As we have seen, relational formulations of transference and countertransference emphasize the dyadic, reciprocal nature of therapeutic interactions (Aron, 1996; Gill, 1982, 1994, 1995; I. Z. Hoffman, 1998; Mitchell, 1997; Wachtel, 2008). Generally speaking, theorists conceptualize transference reactions as patterns of expectations established over the course of development and life experience. Cognitive representations of self and others and expectations shape interpretations of events, constructions of meaning, and corresponding behaviors in interpersonal situations that have the potential to perpetuate maladaptive patterns.

The clinician's countertransference states constitute sources of experience that deepen understandings of dynamic processes that perpetuate the client's problems in functioning. Contemporary lines of understanding in interpersonal psychoanalysis conceptualize countertransference reactions as role-responsive complements or counterparts to transferential phenomena. The clinician functions as a participant-observer and provides opportunities for recognition, clarification, and revision of maladaptive perceptions and patterns of relating.

In their efforts to extend concepts of mutuality, relational theorists stress that the client and the practitioner both participate in the helping process; as such, each party influences the other in conscious and unconscious ways. Concepts of intervention increasingly take into consideration the personal characteristics and immediate emotional experience of the clinician (see Aron, 1996, p. 125; I. Z. Hoffman, 1998; Mitchell, 1997, 2000; Wachtel, 2008; Wampold, 2007). As Jon Mills (2005) observes, relational thinkers emphasize a "natural, humane, and authentic" manner of engagement in the therapeutic situation; he characterizes practitioners as "more revelatory, interactive, and inclined to disclose accounts of their own experience . . . , enlist and solicit perceptions from the patient about their own subjective comportment, and generally acknowledge how a patient's responsiveness and demeanor is triggered by the purported attitudes, sensibility, and behavior" of the clinician (p. 155). The practitioner's ongoing processing of countertransference states, therapeutic impasses, and the client's experience of the clinician is a radical shift in clinical practice that has increasingly focused attention on the *process* of intervention (see Mills, 2005; Mitchell, 2000; Wachtel, 2008). Relational thinkers who conceptualize treatment from narrative perspectives view the practitioner as a co-participant in the client's efforts to process experience, construct meaning, and elaborate adaptive life stories (see, e.g., Borden, 1992; Howard, 1991; Schafer, 1983, 1992; Spence, 1982). Social constructivist conceptions of therapeutic interaction emphasize the mutual influence of client and practitioner in the interactive field over the course of intervention (I. Z. Hoffman, 1998).

Clinicians are increasingly emphasizing the importance of the therapeutic relationship and interpersonal expertise in conceptions of evidence-based practice. As noted in the preface, converging lines of study in psychotherapy research document the ways in which the client *and* the practitioner influence the process and outcome of treatment, and relational perspectives strengthen conceptualizations of interpersonal experience in evidence-based practice (see APA Presidential Task Force on Evidence-Based Practice, 2006; Borden, 2008b; Wampold, 2007).

The theoretical perspectives encompassed in the broader relational paradigm deepen understandings of vulnerabilities and patterns of behavior that have the potential to compromise the establishment of the therapeutic alliance and precipitate strain or rupture over the course of treatment. Relational models of intervention emphasize flexible use of interactive experience in light of the individual, social, and cultural contexts of the client; interpersonal capacities and skills; and the nature of problems in functioning. Reviews of research show that the efficacy of varying treatment approaches appears to lie more in shared features and qualities of relatedness than in technical procedures associated with various schools of thought (Frank & Frank, 1991; Wampold, 2007). Relational perspectives promise to strengthen approaches to assessment, case formulation, treatment planning, and methods of intervention in evidence-based practice (Borden, 2008b).

Social, cultural, political, and economic forces continue to restrict contexts of practice and modes of service delivery across the range of settings. The influence of managed care has challenged clinicians to broaden their conceptions of the therapeutic endeavor and to develop pragmatic, focused modes of intervention in their efforts to address a wider range of vulnerable groups and problems in living. Drawing on relational concepts, practitioners have introduced flexible models of brief treatment that extend the range of client populations and problems in functioning addressed in traditional formulations of short-term intervention (see Binder, 2004; Borden, 1999, 2000, 2008b; Brandell, 2004; E. Goldstein & Noonan, 1999; Messer & Warren, 1995).

Practitioners assume that time-limited approaches carry the potential to strengthen coping strategies, enhance capacities for relationship, and improve social functioning. From the perspective of most relational theories, even very brief periods of intervention may reinstate developmental processes and facilitate personality reorganization (Borden, 1999; Gardner, 1999; Schmidt, 1999; Winnicott, 1971b).

In the broader context of psychosocial intervention, relational formulations strengthen conceptualizations of brief intervention, case management, family and group treatment, environmental intervention, organizational development, advocacy, and social action.

Comparative Perspectives in Relational Understanding

Mitchell (1988) links core concepts from self psychology, object relations theories, and interpersonal psychoanalysis in his integrative approach and describes overlapping conceptions of therapeutic action, change, and growth in his relational model. He focuses our attention on the core domains of the relational matrix: self-organization, internal object representations, and transactional patterns.

Self and Subjectivity

From the perspective of self-organization, the therapeutic situation allows the individual to recover and experience aspects of self that have been hidden, disclaimed, or disavowed. The relationship with the practitioner is inevitably structured along the lines of earlier ways of being and relating. "Anxiety and disappointment are anticipated where they were previously experienced, and various areas of self-experience are hidden" (Mitchell, 1988, p. 289).

The clinician's exploration of problematic areas of experience and participation in new forms of interaction facilitate efforts to encounter, name, and appreciate previously unknown states of self. The individual can be a different kind of person in his or her experience of the clinician and others than he or she could previously allow him- or herself to be.

It will be useful to consider this domain of experience in light of earlier clinical illustrations. Mary, whose case was presented in chapter 8, told the clinician in the assessment interview that she *never* experienced feelings, viewing emotion as "disgusting" and "dangerous." Over the course of her psychotherapy, however, she came to identify and accept a range of feelings, recognizing her experience of emotion as a source of aliveness and a mode of knowing. Robert, discussed in chapters 6 and 10, developed capacities to process his experience of vulnerability, fear, and uncertainty, which he had previously managed through splitting, projective identification, and aggressive behavior. Martha, presented in chapter 8, came to recognize core experiences of need and desire that she had repudiated in her adaptive, reactive ways of being and relating.

The Inner World of Others

From the perspective of object relations thought, early relationships are internalized, structured, and preserved as powerful presences. Contemporary experience is processed through working models of self and others and modes of interactive experience. "Areas of deprivation, constriction, and intrusion result in attachments to these qualities in [other people] as the form through which contact is made, as vehicles for maintaining a sense of connectedness and relation," explains Mitchell (1988, p. 290).

In this domain of experience, change entails reorganization of core internal structures. The clinician is inevitably experienced as a familiar other in the transference. Over time, through empathic attunement and responsiveness, interpretive efforts, and experiential learning in the give-and-take of the therapeutic process, the practitioner becomes a different, responsive other. The gradual internalization of this experience facilitates efforts to release reflexive ties to past forms of relation. The intrapsychic domain of the relational matrix is thereby transformed. The individual experiences him- or herself as "a different sort of person, . . . residing in a profoundly different human environment" (Mitchell, 1988, p. 290).

Anne viewed expressions of her most fundamental needs and desires as betrayals of her parents. As we saw in discussion of her case in chapter 7, she experienced extended periods of fear, anxiety, and dissociation as she challenged the constraints of her inner world of others through new forms of behavior. Robert, too, identified with the internalized presences of his parents, and he felt a deep sense of loss as he suspended aggressive modes of behavior that he associated with his father and learned how to process his experience of vulnerability in interaction with others. Loren, presented in chapter 7, had developed strong ties to internalized representations of abusive figures from her past, and she would experience diffuse periods of anxiety and loss as she worked through the effects of earlier trauma and neglect.

The Interpersonal Field

From the perspective of interpersonal theory, "anxiety about anxiety" has forced the individual into constricted, repetitive patterns of interaction. "It is the ritualized action that delimits the experience of both self and other" (Mitchell, 1988, p. 290). The clinician facilitates efforts to identify and process these patterns of interaction, encouraging the individual to "try something different," to explore different interpersonal situations where richer experiences of self and other are possible (Mitchell, 1988, p. 290). Such shifts in transactional patterns occur in the give-and-take of the therapeutic process as well as in relational life in the outer world.

In spite of her fears, Martha came to learn how to assert her needs and bring her core self to bear in ways of relating and acting that reflected her deepest concerns. Robert, too, strengthened his ability to communicate more effectively in interactions with coworkers, expand patterns of activity in day-to-day functioning, and engage opportunities for friendship.

Mitchell (1988) reflects: "Operating with old illusions and stereotyped patterns reduces anxiety and provides security not simply because the illusions and patterns are *familiar*, but because they are *familial* and preserve a sense of loyalty and connection. Bad-object ties are adhesive and repetitive not simply because they are familial but also because they are familiar and minimize anxiety. . . . The maintenance of a coherent sense of self and the preservation of secure patterns of interaction are inextricably linked to securing connections with others" (p. 291).

The Process of Intervention

The pluralist perspective described in the first chapter enlarges conceptions of therapeutic action in psychosocial intervention. By way of illustration, I return to the case of Robert and explore the ways in which comparative approaches enrich ways of working in the clinical situation. To review, the client had been suspended from his job and initiated psychotherapy in efforts to address ongoing patterns of strain, rupture, and loss in relational life. As we will see, the relational schools of thought provide different understandings of essential concerns, core activities, and change processes in therapeutic intervention.

Self Psychology.   The perspective of self psychology focuses our attention on Robert's loss of cohesion in his sense of self and disruptions in relational life that perpetuate his experience of vulnerability, demoralization, and fragmentation. We recognize the crucial functions of attunement and responsiveness in therapeutic interactions and the importance of processing experience from his point of view, and communicating empathic understanding and acceptance of subjective states. We consider emerging patterns of transference (mirroring, idealization, twinship) that carry the potential to reinstate development and foster growth.

Object Relations Perspectives.   Object relations perspectives focus our attention on the ways in which Robert's internal models of self and others and modes of interactive experience influence his perceptions of relationships in contemporary life and shape patterns of behavior in the therapeutic situation. We center on defensive operations that perpetuate problems in functioning (splitting, projective identification) and view patterns of strain and rupture in therapeutic interactions as sources of experiential learning in efforts to identify maladaptive behavior and help Robert develop more adaptive ways of being and relating. The core conditions of the helping relationship, internalization of positive experience, and identification with the clinician carry the potential to help him renegotiates ties to internalized presences of caretaking figures and strengthen capacities to establish constructive relationships and modes of interaction.

Interpersonal Perspectives.   Interpersonal perspectives focus our attention on the domains of internal and external experience which Robert avoids as a result of his experience of fear; defensive operations; and vicious circles of thought, feeling, and action that perpetuate his problems in functioning. In working from an interpersonal approach, we press for concrete detail in efforts to understand what actually happens between Robert and others in the context of particular circumstances and settings, exploring the ways in which earlier conditions of care in family life have shaped ways of being and relating. In the role of participant-observer, we expect to process patterns of interaction in the sessions, exploring his experience of the helping relationship, defensive strategies, and potential enactments in therapeutic interaction. The task of treatment, from this perspective, is to help Robert disrupt vicious circles of thought, feeling, and behavior and strengthen capacities for constructive ways of being, relating, and living.

The orienting perspectives of self psychology, object relations theory, and interpersonal thought provide different conceptions of therapeutic action, change, and growth. As Mitchell frames the therapeutic situation, the client attempts to preserve old and familiar ways of being, relating, and living while searching for something new and different. The client re-creates earlier relational worlds in the interactive experience of the therapeutic process, engaging the clinician through long-standing patterns of behavior. His conceptions of the therapeutic action emphasize the dialectical nature of stability and change as the client attempts to perpetuate comfortable ways of being *and* establish new ways of living.

Critical Pluralism and the Therapeutic Endeavor

According to the conceptions of critical pluralism introduced in the opening chapter of the book, the clinician's understanding of the major therapeutic systems in the broader psychoanalytic tradition provides conceptual foundations for the use of different ideas and strategies in integrative practice. Pluralist perspectives preserve the integrity of the core theoretical systems and make the multiplicity of different approaches a defining feature of clinical practice. The assumption is that all theories have inherent strengths and limits, and thinkers emphasize the crucial role of ongoing dialogue across different schools of thought in efforts to identify common elements, clarify differences, and consider the relative merits of various perspectives. The clinician draws on multiple theoretical models, therapeutic languages, and modes of intervention in efforts to address the particular needs of the clinical situation.

While pluralist perspectives enlarge the scope of understanding and strengthen critical thinking over the course of intervention, they place considerable demands on the clinician in the give-and-take of day-to-day practice. The clinician must consider multiple therapeutic models and negotiate ongoing tensions between a particular approach and alternate modes of intervention. In doing so, the practitioner must consider higher-level theoretical constructs *and* remain focused on the practical application of ideas and procedures in the concrete particularity of the clinical situation, tacking back and forth between ideas and experience.

Movement from one orientation to another is guided by the nature of the client's problems in functioning; vulnerabilities, capacities, and strengths; the immediate focal concerns of intervention; and the ways in which the individual makes use of different approaches over the course of treatment. Following the pragmatic orientation of pluralist perspectives, the clinician judges the validity of concepts and methods on the basis of their *effectiveness* in the context of the individual case (for an expanded account of pluralist perspectives, see Borden, in press).

In following pluralist lines of understanding, we realize that we cannot reduce the complexity of the clinical situation to any single rendering of human difficulty or particular form of therapeutic practice. We realize that no theory mirrors reality and that no single perspective, however encompassing, can possibility meet all our needs over the course of intervention. Different perspectives allow practitioners to approach problems from a range of positions and to shift points of entry in light of particular vulnerabilities, tasks, and circumstances.

The critical root of theory, *theoria*, means "to behold from changing points of view." At its best, theory enlarges the field of observation, offering ways of seeing and understanding, and helping us expand the range of options and consider courses of action that carry the potential to help. As James would remind us, we cannot make the big claim from a fixed point of view. In his pragmatic stance, the question is not "Is it true?" but rather "How would our work be better if we were to believe it?" What is the use of a truth?

Concluding Comments

We have explored conceptions of self, relational life, growth, and therapeutic action across the range of theoretical perspectives in contemporary psychoanalytic thought. Pluralism has been a defining feature of the broader psychodynamic tradition from the very beginning, as we have seen, and psychoanalysis remains an evolving field of understanding and experience, engaging work in a wide range of disciplines. Psychodynamic perspectives continue to shape conceptions of self, relationship, and social life, enlarging notions of health, well-being, and the common good, and they provide orienting perspectives in divergent modes of psychosocial intervention.

In the course of our clinical training and practice, as I observed in the opening chapter, we must come to terms with fundamental tensions between purer conceptions of the therapeutic endeavor and more pragmatic versions of what we do as we carry out our work. From the pluralist perspective I have described, we master multiple theoretical models, therapeutic languages, and methods of intervention, sorting out the strengths and limits of various perspectives. In doing so, we locate ourselves in the broader therapeutic landscape and establish a clinical sensibility and therapeutic style that is distinctly our own.

References

Abram, J. (1997). *The language of Winnicott*. Northvale, NJ: Jason Aronson.

Adler, A. (1930). Individual psychology. In C. Murchison (Ed.), *Psychologies of 1930* (pp. 395–405). Worcester, MA: Clark University Press.

Adler, A. (1956). *The individual psychology of Alfred Adler* (H. Ansbacher & R. Ansbacher, Eds. & Trans.). New York: Basic Books.

Adler, A. (1980). *Co-operation between the sexes: Writings on women, love and marriage, sexuality, and its disorders* (H. Ansbacher & R. Ansbacher, Eds. & Trans.). New York: Jason Aronson.

Adler, A. (1992). *Understanding human nature* (C. Brett, Trans.). Oxford: Oneworld Publications. (Originally published 1927)

Ainsworth, M. (1974). *Citation for the G. Stanley Hall Award to John Bowlby*. Unpublished manuscript.

Alexander, F., & French, T. (1946). *Psychoanalytic therapy: Principles and application*. New York: Ronald Press.

Alford, C. F. (1989). *Melanie Klein and critical social theory*. New Haven, CT: Yale University Press.

Alford, C. F. (1998). Melanie Klein and the nature of good and evil. In P. Marcus & A. Rosenberg (Eds.), *Psychoanalytic versions of the human condition* (pp. 117–139). New York: New York University Press.

Altman, N. (1995). *The analyst in the inner city*. Hillsdale, NJ: Analytic Press.

Anthony, E. J., & Cohler, B. J. (1987). *The invulnerable child*. New York: Guilford Press.

APA Presidential Task Force on Evidence-Based Practice. (2006). Evidence-based practice in psychology. *American Psychologist, 61*(4), 271–285.

Applegate, J., & Bonovitz, J. (1995). *The facilitating partnership: A Winnicottian approach for social workers and other helping professionals*. Northvale, NJ: Jason Aronson.

Aron, L. (1996). *A meeting of minds: Mutuality in psychoanalysis*. Hillsdale, NJ: Analytic Press.

Aron, L., & Harris, A. (1993). Sándor Ferenczi: Discovery and rediscovery. In L. Aron & A. Harris (Eds.), *The legacy of Sándor Ferenczi* (pp. 1–36). Hillsdale, NJ: Analytic Press.

Aronson, E. (1992). *The social animal*. New York: W. H. Freeman.

Auden, W. H. (1945). In memory of Sigmund Freud. *The collected poetry of W. H. Auden*. New York: Random House. (Originally published 1940)

Bacal, H., & Newman, K. (1990). *Theories of object relations: Bridges to self psychology*. New York: Columbia University Press.

Bair, D. (2005). *Jung: A biography*. New York: Little, Brown.

Balint, M., Ornstein, P. H., & Balint, E. (1972). *Focal psychotherapy: An example of applied psychoanalysis*. London: Tavistock.

Beebe, B., & Lachmann, M. (1988). The contribution of mother-infant mutual influence to the origins of self and object representations. *Psychoanalytic Psychology, 5*, 305–337.

Benjamin, J. (1988). *The bonds of love: Psychoanalysis, feminism, and the problem of domination*. New York: Pantheon.

Benjamin, J. (1995). *Like subjects, love objects: Essays on recognition and sexual difference*. New Haven, CT: Yale University Press.

Benjamin, J. (1998). *The shadow of the other: Intersubjectivity and gender in psychoanalysis*. New York: Routledge.

Berlin, S. (2002). *Social work practice: A cognitive-integrative perspective*. New York: Oxford University Press.

Binder, J. (2004). *Brief dynamic psychotherapy*. New York: Guilford Press.

Binder, J., Strupp, H., & Henry, W. (1995). Psychodynamic therapies in practice: Time-limited dynamic psychotherapy. In B. Bonger & L. E. Beutler (Eds.), *Comprehensive textbook of psychotherapy* (pp. 48–63). New York: Oxford University Press.

Bion, W. (1988). *Learning from experience*. London: Heinemann. (Originally published 1962)

Blank, G., & Blank, R. (1974). *Ego psychology: Theory and practice*. New York: Columbia University Press.

Blatt, S. J., & Homann, E. (1992). Parent-child interactions in the etiology of dependent and self-critical depression. *Clinical Psychology Review, 12*, 47–91.

Blatt, S. J., & Zuroff, D. C. (1992). Interpersonal relatedness and self definition: Two prototypes for depression. *Clinical Psychology Review, 12*, 527–562.

Bollas, C. (1987). *The shadow of the object*. New York: Columbia University Press.

Bollas, C. (1989). *Forces of destiny*. London: Free Association Books.

Borden, W. (1992). Narrative perspectives in psychosocial intervention following adverse events. *Social Work, 37*(2), 135–143.

Borden, W. (1994). *Making use of theory in practice: Legacies of the Independent Tradition.* Paper presented at the annual conference of the Illinois Society for Clinical Social Work, Chicago.

Borden, W. (1997). Essay review: An object relations approach to psychotherapy. *Journal of Analytic Social Work, 4*(3), 83–90.

Borden, W. (1998). The place and play of theory in practice: A Winnicottian perspective. *Journal of Analytic Social Work, 5*(1), 25–40.

Borden, W. (1999). Pluralism, pragmatism, and the therapeutic endeavor in brief dynamic treatment. In W. Borden (Ed.), *Comparative approaches in brief dynamic psychotherapy* (pp. 7–42). Binghamton, NY: Haworth Press.

Borden, W. (2000). The relational paradigm in contemporary psychoanalysis: Toward a psychodynamically-informed social work perspective. *Social Service Review, 74*(3), 352–379.

Borden, W. (2001). Donald Winnicott. In L. Balter (Ed.), *Parenthood in America: An encyclopedia*. Santa Barbara, CA: ABC-CLIO.

Borden, W. (2006). Psychoanalysis, social justice, and the therapeutic endeavor. *Psychoanalytic Social Work, 13*(2), 67–76.

Borden, W. (2008a). Comparative theory and integrative perspectives in psychosocial intervention. In A. R. Roberts (Ed.), *Social workers' desk reference*. New York: Oxford University Press.

Borden, W. (2008b). Contemporary object relations psychology and psychosocial intervention. In A. R. Roberts (Ed.), *Social workers' desk reference*. New York: Oxford University Press.

Borden, W. (in press). Taking multiplicity seriously: Pluralism, pragmatism, and integrative perspectives in social work practice. In W. Borden (Ed.), *The play and place of theory in social work*. New York: Columbia University Press.

Bornstein, R. F., & Masling, J. (1998). Introduction: The psychoanalytic unconscious. In R. F. Bornstein & J. Masling (Eds.), *Empirical perspectives on the psychoanalytic unconscious* (pp. xiii–xxviii). Washington, DC: American Psychological Association.

Bornstein, R. F., & Pitmann, T. S. (1992). *Perception without awareness: Cognitive, clinical and social perspectives*. New York: Guilford Press.

Bottome, P. (1939). *Alfred Adler, apostle of freedom*. London: Faber and Faber.

Bowlby, J. (1940). The influence of early environment in the development of neurosis and neurotic character. *International Journal of Psychoanalysis, 21*, 154–178.

Bowlby, J. (1958). The nature of the child's tie to his mother. *International Journal of Psychoanalysis, 39*, 350–373.

Bowlby, J. (1960). Grief and mourning in infancy and early childhood. *The Psychoanalytic Study of the Child, 15*, 9–52.

Bowlby, J. (1969). *Attachment and loss: Vol. 1. Attachment.* New York: Basic Books.

Bowlby, J. (1973). *Attachment and loss: Vol. 2. Separation: Anxiety and anger.* New York: Basic Books.

Bowlby, J. (1979). *The making and breaking of affectional bonds.* London: Tavistock.

Bowlby, J. (1980). *Attachment and loss: Vol. 3. Loss, sadness and depression.* New York: Basic Books.

Bowlby, J. (1986). An interview with John Bowlby on the origins and reception of his work. *Free Associations, 6,* 36–64.

Bowlby, J. (1988). *A secure base.* New York: Basic Books.

Bowlby, J. (1994). Interview. In V. Hunter, *Psychoanalysts talk* (pp. 111–139). New York: Guilford Press.

Brabant, E., Falzeder, E., & Giampieri-Deutsch, P. (Eds.). (1994). *The correspondence of Sigmund Freud and Sándor Ferenczi: Vol. 1. 1908–1914* (P. Hoffer, Trans.). Cambridge, MA: Belknap Press of Harvard University Press.

Brandell, J. R. (2002). The marginalization of psychoanalysis in academic social work. *Psychoanalytic Social Work, 9*(2), 41–50.

Brandell, J. R. (2004). *Psychodynamic social work.* New York: Columbia University Press.

Bretherton, I. (1992). The origins of attachment theory: John Bowlby and Mary Ainsworth. *Developmental Psychology, 28,* 759–775.

Breuer, J., & Freud, S. (1955). Studies in hysteria. In J. Strachey (Ed. & Trans.), *The standard edition of the complete psychological works of Sigmund Freud* (Vol. 2, pp. 1–305). London: Hogarth Press. (Originally published 1893–1895)

Brome, V. (1982). *Ernest Jones: Freud's alter ego.* London: Caliban Books.

Bucci, W. (2002). The challenge of diversity in modern psychoanalysis. *Psychoanalytic Psychology, 19*(1), 216–226.

Burack, C. (1998). Feminist psychoanalysis: The uneasy intimacy of feminism and psychoanalysis. In P. Marcus & A. Rosenberg (Eds.), *Psychoanalytic versions of the human condition* (pp. 392–411). New York: New York University Press.

Celani, D. P. (1993). *The treatment of the borderline patient.* Madison, CT: International Universities Press.

Chodorow, N. (1989). *Feminism and psychoanalytic theory.* New Haven, CT: Yale University Press.

Chodorow, N. (1998). Toward a relational individualism: The mediation of self through psychoanalysis. In S. Mitchell & L. Aron (Eds.), *Relational psychoanalysis: The emergence of a tradition* (pp. 109–130). Hillsdale, NJ: Analytic Press. (Originally published 1986)

Chodorow, N. (1999). *The power of feelings.* New Haven, CT: Yale University Press.

Corbett, L. (1989). Kohut and Jung: A comparison of theory and therapy. In D. Detrick & S. Detrick (Eds.), *Self psychology: Comparisons and contrasts* (pp. 223–247). Hillsdale, NJ: Analytic Press.

Crews, F. (1996). The verdict on Freud. *Psychological Science, 7,* 63–67.

Curtis, R., & Hirsch, I. (2003). Relational approaches to psychoanalytic psychotherapy. In A. Gurman & S. Messer (Eds.), *Essential psychotherapies* (pp. 69–106). New York: Guilford Press.

Cushman, P. (1995). *Constructing the self, constructing America.* Reading, MA: Addison Wesley.

Danto, E. (2005). *Freud's free clinics: Psychoanalysis and social justice, 1918–1938.* New York: Columbia University Press.

Davanloo, H. (1988). The technique of unlocking the unconscious. *International Journal of Short-Term Psychotherapy, 3,* 99–121.

Davis, M., & Wallbridge, D. (1981). *Boundary and space: An introduction to the work of D. W. Winnicott.* New York: Brunner/Mazel.

Davies, J. (1998). Repression and dissociation—Freud and Janet: Fairbairn's new model of unconscious process. In N. J. Skolnick & D. E. Scharff (Eds.), *Fairbairn, then and now* (pp. 53–70). Hillsdale, NJ: Analytic Press.

Demos, E. V. (1992). The early organization of the psyche. In J. W. Baron, M. N. Eagle, & D. L. Wolitzky (Eds.), *Interface of psychoanalysis and psychology* (pp. 200–232). Washington, DC: American Psychological Association.

Dicks, H. V. (1970). *Fifty years of the Tavistock Clinic*. London: Routledge.

Dimen, M. (2003). *Sexuality, intimacy, power.* Hillsdale, NJ: Analytic Press.

Doidge, N. (2007). *The brain that changes itself.* New York: Viking.

Dore, M. (1990). Functional theory: Its history and influence on contemporary social work practice. *Social Service Review, 64*(3), 358–374.

Edelman, G. (1992). *Bright air, brilliant fire: On the matter of the mind*. New York: Basic Books.

Edelman, G. (2004). *Wider than the sky: The phenomenal gift of consciousness*. New Haven, CT: Yale University Press.

Eigen, M. (1993). The area of faith in Winnicott, Lacan and Bion. In A. Phillips (Ed.), *The electrified tightrope* (pp. 109–138). Northvale, NJ: Jason Aronson. (Originally published 1981)

Ellenberger, H. (1970). *The discovery of the unconscious*. New York: Basic Books.

Elliott, A. (1994). *Psychoanalytic theory*. Oxford: Blackwell.

Elson, M. (1986). *Self psychology in clinical social work*. New York: Norton

Erikson, E. H. (1950). *Childhood and society*. New York: Norton.

Etchegoyen, R. (1991). *The fundamentals of psychoanalytic technique*. London: Karnac Books.

Fairbairn, W. R. D. (1946). Object-relationships and dynamic structure. *International Journal of Psychoanalysis, 27,* 30–37.

Fairbairn, W. R. D. (1952a). Endopsychic structure considered in terms of object-relationships [and 1951 addendum]. In *Psychoanalytic studies of the personality* (pp. 82–136). London: Tavistock. (Originally published 1944)

Fairbairn, W. R. D. (1952b). Repression and the return of bad objects (with special reference to the "war neuroses"). In *Psychoanalytic studies of the personality* (pp. 59–81). London: Tavistock. (Originally published 1943)

Fairbairn, W. R. D. (1952c). A revised psychopathology of the psychoses and psychoneuroses. In *Psychoanalytic studies of the personality* (pp. 25–58). London: Tavistock. (Originally published 1941)

Fairbairn, W. R. D. (1952d). Schizoid factors in the personality. In *Psychoanalytic studies of the personality* (pp. 3–28). London: Tavistock. (Originally published 1940)

Fairbairn, W. R. D. (1952e). A synopsis of the development of the author's views regarding the structure of the personality. In *Psychoanalytic studies of the personality* (pp. 162–182). London: Tavistock. (Originally published 1951)

Fairbairn, W. R. D. (1994). On the nature and aims of psycho-analytical treatment. In D. E. Scharff & E. F. Birtles (Eds.), *From instinct to self* (pp. 74–92). Northvale, NJ: Jason Aronson. (Originally published 1958)

Fairbairn Birtles, E. (1998). Developing connections: Fairbairn's philosophic contribution. In N. J. Skolnick & D. E. Scharff (Eds.), *Fairbairn, then and now* (pp. 33–52). Hillsdale, NJ: Analytic Press.

Ferenczi, S. (1980). The confusion of tongues between adults and the child: The language of tenderness and passion. In M. Balint (Ed.) & E. Mosbacher et al. (Trans.), *Final contributions to the problems and methods of psycho-analysis* (pp. 156–167). London: Karnac Books. (Originally published 1933)

Ferenczi, S. (1988). *The clinical diary of Sándor Ferenczi* (J. Dupont, Ed.; M. Balint & N. Z. Jackson, Trans.). Cambridge, MA: Harvard University Press.

Ferenczi, S., & Rank, O. (1986). *The development of psychoanalysis*. Madison, CT: International Universities Press. (Originally published 1924)

Fiscalini, J. (2004). *Co-participant psychoanalysis: Toward a new theory of clinical inquiry*. New York: Columbia University Press.

Flax, J. (1990). *Thinking fragments: Psychoanalysis, feminism, and postmodernism in the contemporary West*. Berkeley and Los Angeles: University of California Press.

Flax, J. (1993). *Disputed subjects: Essays on psychoanalysis, politics, and philosophy*. New York: Routledge.

Fonagy, P. (2000). *Grasping the nettle: Or why psychoanalytic research is such an irritant.* Paper presented at the annual research lecture of the British Psychoanalytical Society, London.

Fonagy, P. (2001). *Attachment theory and psychoanalysis*. New York: Other Press.

Fonagy, P., & Target, M. (2007). The rooting of the mind in the body: New links between attachment theory and psychoanalytic thought. *Journal of the American Psychoanalytic Association, 55*(2), 411–456.

Ford, D., & Urban, H. (1963). *Systems of psychotherapy*. New York: Wiley.

Ford, D., & Urban, H. (1998). *Contemporary models of psychotherapy*. New York: Wiley.

Fosshage, J. L. (2003). Contextualizing self psychology and relational psychoanalysis. *Contemporary Psychoanalysis, 39,* 411–448.

Foucault, M. (1984). What is an author? In P. Rabinow (Ed.), *The Foucault reader* (pp. 101–120). New York: Pantheon.

Frank, J., & Frank, J. (1991). *Persuasion and healing*. Baltimore, MD: Johns Hopkins University Press.

Frank, K. (1999). *Psychoanalytic participation*. Hillsdale, NJ: Analytic Press.

Freud, S. (1952). *An autobiographical study* (J. Strachey, Trans.). New York: Norton. (Originally published 1935)

Freud, S. (1953). On psychotherapy. In J. Strachey (Ed. & Trans.), *The standard edition of the complete psychological works of Sigmund Freud* (Vol. 7, pp. 257–268). London: Hogarth Press. (Originally published 1905)

Freud, S. (1954). Project for a scientific psychology. In M. Bonaparte, A. Freud, & E. Kris (Eds.), *The origins of psychoanalysis: Letters to Wilhelm Fliess, drafts, and notes, 1887–1902* (pp. 355–445). New York: Basic Books. (Originally published 1895)

Freud, S. (1955). Lines of advance in psychoanalytic psychotherapy. In J. Strachey (Ed. & Trans.), *The standard edition of the complete psychological works of Sigmund Freud* (Vol. 17, pp. 167–168). London: Hogarth Press. (Originally published 1919)

Freud, S. (1957a). From the history of an infantile neurosis. In J. Strachey (Ed. & Trans.), *The standard edition of the complete psychological works of Sigmund Freud* (Vol. 14, pp. 3–122). London: Hogarth Press. (Originally published 1918)

Freud, S. (1957b). On narcissism: An introduction. In J. Strachey (Ed. & Trans.), *The standard edition of the complete psychological works of Sigmund Freud* (Vol. 14, pp. 67–102). London: Hogarth Press. (Originally published 1914)

Freud, S. (1958a). The dynamics of transference. In J. Strachey (Ed. & Trans.), *The standard edition of the complete psychological works of Sigmund Freud* (Vol. 12, pp. 99–108). London: Hogarth Press. (Originally published 1912)

Freud, S. (1958b). On beginning treatment. In J. Strachey (Ed. & Trans.), *The standard edition of the complete psychological works of Sigmund Freud* (Vol. 12, pp. 121–144). London: Hogarth Press. (Originally published 1913)

Freud, S. (1958c). Recommendations to physicians practicing psycho-analysis. In J. Strachey (Ed. & Trans.), *The standard edition of the complete psychological works of Sigmund Freud* (Vol. 12, pp. 109–120). London: Hogarth Press. (Originally published 1912)

Freud, S. (1959a). The question of lay analysis. In J. Strachey (Ed. & Trans.), *The standard edition of the complete psychological works of Sigmund Freud* (Vol. 20, pp. 183–258). London: Hogarth Press. (Originally published 1926)

Freud, S. (1959b). Some points in a comparative study of organic and hysterical paralyses. In E. Jones (Ed.), *Collected papers* (Vol. 1, pp. 42–58). New York: Basic Books. (Originally published 1893)

Freud, S. (1961). The ego and the id. In J. Strachey (Ed. & Trans.), *The standard edition of the complete psychological works of Sigmund Freud* (Vol. 19, pp. 2–66). London: Hogarth Press. (Originally published 1923)

Freud, S. (1964a). Analysis terminable and interminable. In J. Strachey (Ed. & Trans.), *The standard edition of the complete psychological works of Sigmund Freud* (Vol. 23, pp. 209–253). (Originally published 1937)

Freud, S. (1964b). New introductory lectures on psycho-analysis. In J. Strachey (Ed. & Trans.), *The standard edition of the complete psychological works of Sigmund Freud* (Vol. 22, pp. 1–182). London: Hogarth Press. (Originally published 1933)

Freud, S. (1964c). An outline of psychoanalysis. In J. Strachey (Ed. & Trans.), *The standard edition of the complete psychological works of Sigmund Freud* (Vol. 23, pp. 139–207). London: Hogarth Press. (Originally published 1940)

Fromm, E. (1965). *Escape from freedom*. New York: Avon Books. (Originally published 1941)

Frosh, S. (1999). *The politics of psychoanalysis: An introduction to Freudian and post-Freudian theory* (2nd ed.). New Haven, CT: Yale University Press.

Galatzer-Levy, R., & Cohler, B. J. (1993). *The essential other*. New York: Basic Books.

Gardner, J. (1999). Using self psychology in brief treatment. In W. Borden (Ed.), *Comparative approaches in brief dynamic psychotherapy* (pp. 43–86). Binghamton, NY: Haworth Press.

Gay, P. (1988). *Freud: A life for our time*. New York: Norton.

Ghent, E. (1992). Foreword. In N. J. Skolnick & S. C. Warshaw (Eds.), *Relational perspectives in psychoanalysis* (pp. xiii–xxii). Hillsdale, NJ: Analytic Press.

Gill, M. (1982). *The analysis of transference: Vol. 1. Theory and technique*. New York: International Universities Press.

Gill, M. (1994). *Psychoanalysis in transition*. Hillsdale, NJ: Analytic Press.

Gill, M. (1995). Classical and relational psychoanalysis. *Psychoanalytic Psychology, 12,* 89–108.

Goldstein, E. (1995). *Ego psychology and social work practice* (2nd ed.). New York: Free Press.

Goldstein, E. (2001). *Object relations theory and self psychology in social work practice*. New York: Free Press.

Goldstein, E., & Noonan, M. E. (1999). *Short-term treatment and social work practice: An integrative perspective*. New York: Free Press.

Goldstein, H. (1990). The knowledge base of social work practice: Theory, wisdom, analogue, or art? *Families in Society, 73,* 32–43.

Gomez, L. (1997). *An introduction to object relations*. New York: New York University Press.

Green, A. (1978). Potential space in psychoanalysis: The object in the setting. In S. Grolnick & L. Barkin (Eds.), *Between fantasy and reality: Transitional objects and phenomena* (pp. 166–189). New York: Jason Aronson.

Greenberg, J., & Cheselka, O. (1995). Relational approaches to psychoanalytic psychotherapy. In A. Gurman & S. Messer (Eds.), *Essential psychotherapies* (pp. 55–84). New York: Guilford Press.

Greenberg, J., & Mitchell, S. (1983). *Object relations in psychoanalytic theory*. Cambridge, MA: Harvard University Press.

Grosskurth, P. (1986). *Melanie Klein: Her world and her work*. Cambridge, MA: Harvard University Press.

Grosskurth, P. (1991). *The secret ring: Freud's inner circle and the politics of psychoanalysis*. Reading, MA: Addison-Wesley.

Grotstein, J. S. (1998). A comparison of Fairbairn's endopsychic structure and Klein's internal world. In N. J. Skolnick & D. E. Scharff (Eds.), *Fairbairn, then and now* (pp. 71–98). Hillsdale, NJ: Analytic Press.

Grotstein, J. S., & Rinsley, D. B. (Eds.). (1994). *Fairbairn and the origins of object relations*. London: Free Association Books.

Guisinger, S., & Blatt, S. J. (1994). Individuality and relatedness: Evolution of a fundamental dialectic. *American Psychologist, 19,* 104–111.

Guntrip, H. (1971). *Psychoanalytic theory, therapy, and the self*. New York: Basic Books.

Hall, C., Lindzey, G., & Campbell, J. (1998). *Theories of personality*. New York: Wiley.

Harris, A. (2005). *Gender as soft assembly*. Hillsdale, NJ: Analytic Press.

Havens, L., & Frank, J. (1971). Review of *Psychoanalysis and Interpersonal Psychiatry* by P. Mullahy. *American Journal of Psychiatry, 127,* 1704–1705.

Heard, D. (1988). Introduction. In I. Suttie, *The origins of love and hate* (pp. xv–xl). London: Free Association Books.

Hinshelwood, R. (1989). *A dictionary of Kleinian thought*. London: Free Association Books.

Hoffman, E. (1994). *The drive for self*. New York: Addison-Wesley.

Hoffman, I. Z. (1998). *Ritual and spontaneity in the psychoanalytic process*. Hillsdale, NJ: Analytic Press.

Hogenson, G. (1994). *Jung's struggle with Freud*. Wilmette, IL: Chiron.

Homans, P. (1989). *The ability to mourn: Disillusionment and the social origins of psychoanalysis*. Chicago: University of Chicago Press.

Homans, P. (1995). *Jung in context* (2nd ed.). Chicago: University of Chicago Press.

Horney, K. (1937). *The neurotic personality of our time*. New York: Norton.

Horney, K. (1939). *New ways in psychoanalysis*. New York: Norton.

Horney, K. (1942). *Self analysis*. New York: Norton.

Horney, K. (1945). *Our inner conflicts*. New York: Norton.

Horney, K. (1950). *Neurosis and human growth*. New York: Norton.

Horney, K. (1980). *The adolescent diaries of Karen Horney*. New York: Basic Books.

Howard, G. (1991). Culture tales: A narrative approach to thinking, cross cultural psychology, and psychotherapy. *American Psychologist, 46*(3), 187–197.

Hughes, J. (1989). *Reshaping the psychoanalytic domain: The work of Melanie Klein, W. R. D. Fairbairn, and D. W. Winnicott*. Berkeley and Los Angeles: University of California Press.

Humbert, E. (1984). *Jung*. Wilmette, IL: Chiron.

Huopainen, H. (2002). Freud's view of hysteria in light of modern trauma research. *Scandinavian Psychoanalytic Review, 25,* 92–107.

Jaffé, A. (1971). *From the life and work of C. G. Jung* (R. F. C. Hulle, Trans.). New York: Harper & Row.

James, W. (1911). The one and the many. In *Some problems of philosophy: A beginning of an introduction to philosophy* (pp. 113–146). New York: Longmans, Green.

James, W. (1946). *Pragmatism*. New York: Longmans, Green. (Originally published 1907)

Javier, R., & Moskowitz, M. (2002). Notes from the trenches. *Psychoanalytic Psychology, 19*(1), 144–148.

Jones, E. (1953–1957). *The life and work of Sigmund Freud*. 3 vols. New York: Basic Books.

Joseph, B. (1989). *Psychic equilibrium and psychic change*. London: Routledge.

Jung, C. G. (1953–1978). *The collected works of C. G. Jung* (H. Read, M. Fordham, & G. Adler, Eds.). 21 vols. Princeton, NJ: Princeton University Press. (Cited in the text as *CW*)

Jung, C. G. (1961). *Memories, dreams, reflections*. New York: Random House.

Kandel, E. (2005). *Psychiatry, psychoanalysis, and the new biology of mind*. Arlington, VA: American Psychiatric Publishing.

Kandel, E. (2006). *In search of memory*. New York: Norton.

Kanter, J. (1990). Community-based treatment of the psychotic client: The contributions of D. W. and Clare Winnicott. *Clinical Social Work Journal, 18*(1), 23–41.

Kanter, J. (2004). *Face to face with children: The life and work of Clare Winnicott*. London: Karnac Books.

Karen, R. (1994). *Becoming attached*. New York: Warner Books.

Kernberg, O. (1976). *Object relations theory and clinical psychoanalysis*. New York: Jason Aronson.

Kerr, J. (1993). *A most dangerous method*. New York: Knopf.

King, P., & Steiner, R. (1991). *The Freud-Klein controversies, 1941–45*. London: Routledge.

Klein, M. (1942). *Draft statement*. January 1, 1942. London, British Psychoanalytical Society Archives.

Klein, M. (1975). *Envy and gratitude and other works, 1946–1963*. New York: Delacorte. (Originally published 1957)

Klein, M., & Riviere, J. (1964). *Love, hate, and reparation*. New York: Norton.

Kohut, H. (1959). Introspection, empathy, and psychoanalysis. *Journal of the American Psychoanalytic Association, 8,* 567–583.

Kohut, H. (1971). *The analysis of the self*. New York: International Universities Press.

Kohut, H. (1977). *The restoration of the self*. Madison, CT: International Universities Press.

Kohut, H. (1980). Reflections on advances in self psychology. In A. Goldberg (Ed.), *Advances in self psychology* (pp. 473–554). New York: International Universities Press.

Kohut, H. (1982). Introspection, empathy, and the semi-circle of mental health. *International Journal of Psychoanalysis, 63*, 395–407.

Kohut, H. (1984). *How does analysis cure?* Chicago: University of Chicago Press.

Kohut, H. (1987). *The Kohut seminars on self psychology and psychotherapy with adolescents and young adults* (M. Elson, Ed.). New York: Norton.

Kohut, H., & Wolf, E. (1978). The disorders of the self and their treatment: An outline. *International Journal of Psychoanalysis, 59*, 413–424.

Kramer, H. (1942). The first child guidance clinic and its first patient. *Individual Psychology Bulletin, 2*, 35–37.

Lear, J. (1990). *Love and its place in nature: A philosophical interpretation of Freudian psychoanalysis*. New Haven, CT: Yale University Press.

Levenson, E. (1972). *The fallacy of understanding: An inquiry into the changing structure of psychoanalysis*. New York: Basic Books.

Levenson, E. (1983). *The ambiguity of change*. New York: Basic Books.

Lieberman, E. J. (1985). *Acts of will*. New York: Free Press.

Lieberman, E. J. (Ed.). (1998). *Otto Rank: Psychology and the soul*. Baltimore, MD: Johns Hopkins University Press.

Loevinger, J. (1976). *Ego development*. San Francisco: Jossey-Bass.

Luborsky, L., & Barrett, M. (2006). The history and empirical status of key psychoanalytic concepts. *Annual Review of Clinical Psychology, 2*(1), 1–19.

Main, M. (Ed.). (1995). *Behavior and the development of representational models of attachment: Five methods of assessment*. Cambridge: Cambridge University Press.

Malan, D. (1979). *Individual psychotherapy and the science of psychodynamics*. London: Butterworth.

Mann, J., & Goldmann, R. (1982). *A casebook of time-limited psychotherapy*. New York: McGraw-Hill.

Marcus, P., & Rosenberg, A. (1998). Introduction. In P. Marcus & A. Rosenberg (Eds.), *Psychoanalytic versions of the human condition* (pp. 1–11). New York: New York University Press.

Marx, K. (1959). Theses on Feuerbach. In L. Feuer (Ed.), *Basic writings on politics and philosophy: Karl Marx and Friedrich Engels*. Garden City, NY: Anchor. (Originally published 1845)

Masling, J. M., & Bornstein, R. (1994). *Empirical perspectives on object relations theory*. Washington, DC: American Psychological Association.

Menaker, E. (1982). *Otto Rank: A rediscovered legacy*. New York: Columbia University Press.

McCaughan, D. (1999). On learning to learn again. In W. Borden (Ed.), *Comparative perspectives in brief dynamic psychotherapy* (pp. 203–218). Binghamton, NY: Haworth Press.

Messer, S., & Warren, S. (1995). *Models of brief psychodynamic therapy*. New York: Guilford Press.

Mills, J. (2005). A critique of relational psychoanalysis. *Psychoanalytic Psychology, 22*(2), 155–188.

Mitchell, S. (1988). *Relational concepts in psychoanalysis*. Cambridge, MA: Harvard University Press.

Mitchell, S. (1993). *Hope and dread in psychoanalysis*. New York: Basic Books.

Mitchell, S. (1997). *Influence and autonomy in psychoanalysis*. Hillsdale, NJ: Analytic Press.

Mitchell, S. (2000). *Relationality: From attachment to intersubjectivity*. Hillsdale, NJ: Analytic Press.

Mitchell, S., & Aron, L. (1999). Preface. In S. Mitchell & L. Aron (Eds.), *Relational psychoanalysis: The emergence of a tradition* (pp. ix–xx). Hillsdale, NJ: Analytic Press.

Mitchell, S., & Black, M. (1995). *Freud and beyond*. New York: Basic Books.

Modell, A. (2003). *Imagination and the meaningful brain*. Cambridge, MA: MIT Press.

Mosak, H. (1987). *Haha and aha: The role of humor in psychotherapy*. Chicago: Accelerated Development.

Mudd, P. (1990). The dark self: Death as a transferential factor. *Journal of Analytical Psychology, 35*, 125–141.

Newcombe, N., & Lerner, J. (1981). Britain between the wars: The historical context of Bowlby's theory of attachment. *Psychiatry, 45*, 1–12.

Norcross, J. (2002). *Psychotherapy relationships that work: Therapist contributions and responsiveness to patients*. New York: Oxford University Press.

O'Dowd, W. T. (1986). Otto Rank and time-limited psychotherapy. *Psychotherapy, 23*, 140–149.

Ogden, T. (1986). *Matrix of the mind*. Northvale, NJ: Jason Aronson.

Ornstein, E., & Ganzer, C. (1997). Mitchell's relational conflict model: An analysis of its usefulness in clinical social work. *Clinical Social Work Journal, 25*, 391–405.

Ornstein, E., & Ganzer, C. (2000). Strengthening the strengths perspective: An integrative relational approach. *Psychoanalytic Social Work, 7*(3), 57–78.

Ornstein, E., & Ganzer, C. (2003). Dialectical constructivism in clinical social work: An exploration of Irwin Hoffman's approach to treatment. *Clinical Social Work Journal, 31*, 355–369.

Ornstein, E., & Ganzer, C. (2005). Relational social work: A model for the future. *Journal of Contemporary Social Services, 86*(4), 565–572.

Ornstein, P. (1998). Heinz Kohut's vision of the essence of humanness. In P. Marcus & A. Rosenberg (Eds.), *Psychoanalytic versions of the human condition* (pp. 206–232). New York: New York University Press.

Paris, B. (1994). *Karen Horney: A psychoanalyst's search for self-understanding*. New Haven, CT: Yale University Press.

Paris, B. (Ed.). (1999). *The therapeutic process: Essays and lectures*. New York: Columbia University Press.

Perry, H. S. (1982). *Psychiatrist of America: The life of Harry Stack Sullivan*. Cambridge, MA: Harvard University Press.

Phillips, A. (1988). *Winnicott*. Cambridge, MA: Harvard University Press.

Quinn, S. (1987). *A mind of her own: The life of Karen Horney*. New York: Summit Books.

Rachman, A. (2007). Sándor Ferenczi's contributions to the evolution of psychoanalysis. *Psychoanalytic Psychology, 24*, 74–96.

Rank, O. (1936). *Will therapy* (J. Taft, Trans.). New York: Knopf.

Rank, O. (1945). *Will therapy and truth and reality* (J. Taft, Trans.). New York: Knopf.

Racker, H. (1968). *Transference and countertransference*. New York: International Universities Press.

Reid, W. (1997). Long-term trends in clinical social work. *Social Service Review, 71*(2), 200–213.

Ricœur, P. (1970). *Freud and philosophy*. New Haven, CT: Yale University Press.

Rodman, F. R. (2003). *Winnicott: Life and work*. Cambridge, MA: Perseus Books.

Roth, A., & Fonagy, P. (2005). *What works for whom? A critical review of psychotherapy research*. New York: Guilford Press.

Rousseau, J.-J. (1954). *The social contract* (W. Kendall, Trans.). South Bend, IN: Gateway. (Originally published 1762)

Rudnytsky, P. (1991). *The psychoanalytic vocation: Rank, Winnicott, and the legacy of Freud*. New Haven, CT: Yale University Press.

Rudnytsky, P. (2002). *Reading psychoanalysis*. Ithaca, NY: Cornell University Press.

Sacks, O. (1984). *A leg to stand on*. New York: Touchstone Books.

Sacks, O. (1985). *The man who mistook his wife for a hat*. New York: Touchstone Books.

Sacks, O. (1992). *Awakenings* (Rev. ed.). New York: Touchstone Books.

Sacks, O. (1995). *An anthropologist on Mars*. New York: Vintage Books.

Sacks, O. (1998). The other road: Freud as neurologist. In M. Roth (Ed.), *Freud: Conflict and culture* (pp. 231–234). New York: Knopf.

Sacks, O. (2004). In the river of consciousness. *New York Review of Books, 51*(1), 41–44.

Samuels, A. (1985). *Jung and the post-Jungians*. London: Routledge.

Samuels, A. (2000). Post-Jungian dialogues. *Psychoanalytic Dialogues, 10*, 403–426.

Samuels, A., Shorter, B., & Plaut, F. (1986). *A critical dictionary of Jungian analysis*. London: Routledge.

Sandler, J., & Rosenblatt, B. (1962). The concept of the representational world. *The Psychoanalytic Study of the Child, 17*, 128–145.

Sayers, J. (1991). *Mothers of psychoanalysis: Helene Deutsch, Karen Horney, Anna Freud, and Melanie Klein*. New York: Norton.

Schafer, R. (1983). *The analytic attitude*. New York: Basic Books.

Schafer, R. (1992). *Retelling a life*. New York: Basic Books.

Scharff, D., & Fairbairn Birtles, E. (Eds.). (1994). *From instinct to self: Selected papers of W. R. D. Fairbairn*. Northvale, NJ: Jason Aronson.

Schmidt, E. (1999). Development, psychopathology, and brief psychotherapy. In W. Borden (Ed.), *Comparative approaches in brief psychodynamic psychotherapy* (pp. 131–144). New York: Haworth Press.

Schore, A. (2003a). *Affect dysregulation and disorders of the self*. New York: Norton.

Schore, A. (2003b). *Affect regulation and the repair of the self*. New York: Norton.

Schwartz, J. (1999). *Cassandra's daughters: A history of psychoanalysis*. New York: Viking.

Segal, H. (1964). *Introduction to the work of Melanie Klein*. London: Basic Books.

Seinfeld, J. (1990). *The bad object*. Northvale, NJ: Jason Aronson.

Seinfeld, J. (1996). *Containing rage, terror, and despair: An object relations approach to psychotherapy*. Northvale, NJ: Jason Aronson.

Sifneos, P. (1987). *Short-term dynamic psychotherapy: Evaluation and technique* (2nd ed.). New York: Plenum Press.

Skolnick, N. J., & Scharff, D. E. (Eds.). (1998). *Fairbairn, then and now*. Hillsdale, NJ: Analytic Press.

Slade, A. (1998). Attachment theory and research: Implications for the theory and practice of individual psychotherapy with adults. In J. Cassidy & P. Shaver (Eds.), *The handbook of attachment theory and research* (pp. 575–594). New York: Guilford Press.

Spence, D. P. (1982). *Narrative truth and historical truth: Meaning and interpretation in psychoanalysis*. New York: Norton.

Sroufe, L. A., Egeland, B., Carlson, E., & Collins, A. (2005). *The development of the person*. New York: Guilford Press.

Sroufe, L. A, Egelund, B., & Kreutzer, T. (1990). The fate of early experience following developmental change: Longitudinal approaches to individual adaptation in childhood. *Child Development, 61*, 1363–1373.

Stein, H., & Edwards, M. (1998). Alfred Adler: Classical theory and practice. In P. Marcus & A. Rosenberg (Eds.), *Psychoanalytic versions of the human condition* (pp. 64–93). New York: New York University Press.

Stein, M. (Ed.). (1995). *Jungian analysis* (2nd ed.). Chicago: Open Court.

Stein, M. (1996). *Practicing wholeness*. New York: Continuum.

Stein, M. (1998). Jung's vision of the human psyche. In P. Marcus & A. Rosenberg (Eds.), *Psychoanalytic versions of the human condition* (pp. 37–63). New York: New York University Press.

Sterba, R. (1951). A case of brief psychotherapy by Sigmund Freud. *Psychoanalytic Review, 38*, 75–80.

Stern, D. (1985). *The interpersonal world of the infant*. New York: Basic Books.

Stevens, A. (1990). *On Jung*. London: Routledge.

Strenger, C. (1997). Hedgehogs, foxes, and critical pluralism: The clinician's yearning for unified conceptions. *Psychoanalysis and Contemporary Thought, 20*(1), 111–145.

Strozier, C. (2001). *Heinz Kohut: The making of a psychoanalyst*. New York: Other Press.

Strupp, H., & Binder, J. (1984). *Psychotherapy in a new key*. New York: Basic Books.

Sullivan, H. S. (1940). *Conceptions of modern psychiatry.* New York: Norton.

Sullivan, H. S. (1964). The illusion of personality individuality. In *The fusion of psychiatry and the social sciences* (pp. 198–226). New York: Norton. (Originally published 1950)

Sullivan, H. S. (1953). *The interpersonal theory of psychiatry.* New York: Norton.

Sullivan, H. S. (1954). *The psychiatric interview.* New York: Norton.

Sullivan, H. S. (1956). *Clinical studies in psychiatry.* New York: Norton.

Sulloway, F. (1979). *Freud, biologist of the mind: Beyond the psychoanalytic legend.* New York: Basic Books.

Summers, F. (1994). *Object relations theories and psychopathology.* Hillsdale, NJ: Analytic Press.

Sutherland, J. (1989). *Fairbairn's journey into the interior.* London: Free Association Books.

Sutherland, J. (1994). *The autonomous self: The work of John D. Sutherland.* Northvale, NJ: Jason Aronson.

Suttie, I. (1935). *The origins of love and hate.* London: Kegan Paul.

Symington, N. (1986). *The analytic experience.* London: Free Association Books.

Tolpin, P. (1983). A change in the self: The development and transformation of an idealizing transference. *International Journal of Psychoanalysis, 64,* 461–485.

Tosone, C. (1997). Sándor Ferenczi: Forerunner of modern short-term psychotherapy. *Journal of Analytic Social Work, 4,* 23–41.

Ulanov, A. (1995). Spiritual aspects of clinical work. In M. Stein (Ed.), *Jungian analysis* (2nd ed., pp. 50–78). Chicago: Open Court.

Vaillant, G. (1993). *The wisdom of the ego.* Cambridge, MA: Harvard University Press.

Wachtel, P. (1989). *The poverty of affluence: A psychological portrait of the American way of life.* Philadelphia: New Society Publishers.

Wachtel, P. (1993). *Therapeutic communication: Principles and effective practice.* New York: Guilford Press.

Wachtel, P. (1997). *Psychoanalysis, behavior therapy, and the outside world.* Washington, DC: American Psychological Association.

Wachtel, P. (1999). *Race in the mind of America: Breaking the vicious circles between blacks and whites.* New York: Routledge.

Wachtel, P. (2000). Psychotherapy in the twenty-first century. *American Journal of Psychotherapy, 54,* 441–450.

Wachtel, P. (2002). Psychoanalysis and the disenfranchised: From therapy to justice. *Psychoanalytic Psychology, 19*(1), 199–215.

Wachtel, P. (2003). Full pockets, empty lives: A psychoanalytic exploration of the contemporary culture of greed. *American Journal of Psychoanalysis, 39,* 5–26.

Wachtel, P. (2008). *Relational theory and the practice of psychotherapy.* New York: Guilford Press.

Walsh, F. (in press). Integrating developmental and systemic theory: A family resilience framework for clinical practice. In W. Borden (Ed.), *The play and place of theory in social work practice.* New York: Columbia University Press.

Wampold, B. E. (2001). *The great psychotherapy debate: Models, methods, and findings.* Mahwah, NJ: Lawrence Erlbaum.

Wampold, B. E. (2007). Psychotherapy: The humanistic (and effective) treatment. *American Psychologist, 2*(8), 857–873.

Westen, D. (1998). The scientific legacy of Sigmund Freud: Toward a psychodynamically informed psychological science. *Psychological Bulletin, 124*(3), 333–371.

Westen, D., & Gabbard, G. (2002a). Developments in cognitive neuroscience: Conflict, compromise, and connectionism. *Journal of the American Psychoanalytic Association, 50,* 53–90.

Westen, D., & Gabbard, G. (2002b). Developments in cognitive neuroscience: Implications for theories of transference. *Journal of the American Psychoanalytic Association, 50,* 99–134.

Westkott, M. (1986). *The feminist legacy of Karen Horney.* New Haven, CT: Yale University Press.

Winnicott, D. W. (1965a). Classification: Is there a psycho-analytic contribution to psychiatric classification? In *The maturational processes and the facilitating environment* (pp. 124–139). New York: International Universities Press. (Originally published 1959)

Winnicott, D. W. (1965b). Dependence in infant-care, in child-care, and in the psycho-analytic setting. In *The maturational processes and the facilitating environment* (pp. 249–259). New York: International Universities Press. (Originally published 1963)

Winnicott, D. W. (1965c). Ego distortion in terms of true and false self. In *The maturational processes and the facilitating environment* (pp. 140–152). New York: International Universities Press. (Originally published 1960)

Winnicott, D. W. (1965d). Ego integration in child development. In *The maturational processes and the facilitating environment* (pp. 56–63). New York: International Universities Press. (Originally published 1962)

Winnicott, D. W. (1965e). The psychotherapy of character disorders. In *The maturational processes and the facilitating environment* (pp. 203–216). New York: International Universities Press. (Originally published 1963)

Winnicott, D. W. (1965f). The theory of the parent-infant relationship. In *The maturational processes and the facilitating environment* (pp. 37–55). New York: International Universities Press. (Originally published 1960)

Winnicott, D. W. (1971a). *Playing and reality*. London: Tavistock.

Winnicott, D. W. (1971b). *Therapeutic consultations in child psychiatry*. New York: Basic Books.

Winnicott, D. W. (1975a). Anxiety associated with insecurity. In *Through paediatrics to psycho-analysis* (pp. 97–100). New York: Basic Books. (Originally read before the British Psycho-analytical Society in 1952)

Winnicott, D. W. (1975b). Metapsychological and clinical aspects of regression within the psychoanalytical set-up. In *Through paediatrics to psycho-analysis* (pp. 278–294). New York: Basic Books. (Originally published 1954)

Winnicott, D. W. (1975c). Mind and its relation to the psyche-soma. In *Through paediatrics to psycho-analysis* (pp. 243–254). New York: Basic Books. (Originally published 1954)

Winnicott, D. W. (1975d). Primitive emotional development. In *Through paediatrics to psycho-analysis* (pp. 145–156). New York: Basic Books. (Originally published 1945)

Winnicott, D. W. (1975e). Psychoses and child care. In *Through paediatrics to psycho-analysis* (pp. 219–228). New York: Basic Books. (Originally published 1952)

Winnicott, D. W. (1987). *The spontaneous gesture: Selected letters of D. W. Winnicott* (F. R. Rodman, Ed.). Cambridge, MA: Harvard University Press.

Winnicott, D. W. (1988). *Human nature*. New York: Schocken Books.

Wolf, E. (1988). *Treating the self*. New York: Norton.

Wolitzky, D. (2003). The theory and practice of traditional psychoanalytic treatment. In A. Gurman & S. Messer (Eds.), *Essential psychotherapies* (pp. 24–68). New York: Guilford Press.

Wolitzky, D., & Eagle, M. N. (1997). Psychoanalytic theories of psychotherapy. In P. Wachtel & S. Messer (Eds.), *Theories of psychotherapy: Origins and evolution* (pp. 39–96). Washington, DC: American Psychological Association.

Wolstein, B. (1987). Experience, interpretation, and self-knowledge. *Contemporary Psychoanalysis, 23*, 329–349.

Young-Eisendrath, P., & Dawson, T. (Eds.). (1997). *Cambridge companion to Jung*. New York: Cambridge University Press.

Zaretsky, E. (2004). *Secrets of the soul: A social and cultural history of psychoanalysis*. New York: Knopf.

Index